LAW OF EVIDENCE

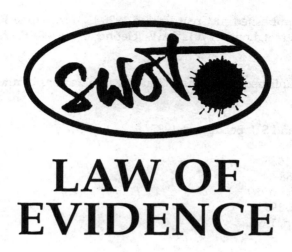

LAW OF EVIDENCE

Fourth Edition

Chris Carr, MA, BCL

University of Central Lancashire

John Beaumont, LLM

Head of the School of Law, Leeds Metropolitan University

Series Editor: C.J. Carr, MA, BCL

BLACKSTONE
PRESS LIMITED

This edition published in Great Britain 1996 by Blackstone Press Limited, 9-15 Aldine Street, London W12 8AW. Telephone: 0181-740 1173

Previously published by Financial Training Publications Limited

© C. J. Carr and S. J. Beaumont, 1985

First edition, 1985
Reprinted 1988
Second edition, 1989
Third edition, 1991
Fourth edition, 1996

ISBN: 1 85431 486 6

British Cataloguing in Publication Data
A CIP catalogue record for this book is available from the British Library

Typeset by Montage Studios Limited, Tonbridge, Kent
Printed by Bell & Bain Limited, Glasgow

CONTENTS

judgments — Planning your revision — Examination questions — Conclusion — Further reading

Introduction — Examination in chief — Cross-examination — Re-examination — Planning your revision — Conclusion — Further reading the latest evidence continues to de...p quickly and since the third edit

PREFACE

The law of evidence continues to develop quickly and since the third edition of this book development has proceeded apace. The provisions of the Criminal Justice and Public Order Act 1994 have made significant changes in some important areas and we have covered these matters at appropriate points in the text. The Civil Evidence Act 1995 is not in force at the time of writing, but we have sought to explain its impact on the law of hearsay in Chapter 8.

We continue to be grateful to those students and lecturers who have written to us and our publishers with their views on previous editions of this book. Their comments continue to be encouraging and we have taken note, wherever possible, of points of criticism.

Our objective in this new edition remains the same as for the previous three. The book is directed at the needs of students preparing for assessments and examinations in the law of evidence.

Once again we wish to record our sincere thanks to all the staff at Blackstone Press for their unfailing enthusiasm, support and efficiency. We continue to be proud of our association with Blackstone Press and we are grateful for the firm, but tolerant way in which they manage their relationship with us, as authors.

John Beaumont
Chris Carr
Feast of St Joseph, 19 March 1996

PREFACE TO THE FIRST EDITION

Writing a preface is the apotheosis of the draftsman's art. Relatives are thanked, publishers are flattered and the world is told that an important work of scholarship has hit the bookshops. We rejoice in doing the first; we are prepared to do the second. We draw the line at the third.

It is one of the sadder facts of life that many law teachers proceed on the basis that their subject is the only subject and that their students have little else of value on which to spend their time than in probing the mysteries of Wigmore's 10, 11 or 12 volumes (or was it thirty seven?) on Evidence. We have written a book which is designed to help you plot your course through the pitted terrain of the subject.

We have not tried to write a law textbook. In truth, such books are frequently written by academics with more than a weather eye for other academics. This book is written only for students. Our purpose is not to provide you with a comprehensive exposition of the law of evidence. We want to answer other questions, no less important, and so often put to us by students: Is this topic important? Do I need to know that? What does this vast topic all mean? How do I tackle this for an examination?

We have sought to indicate strategies which can be followed to help you maximise your success in this subject. Some of what we say may be controversial. Some of it may be obvious. We feel that whatever the differences in individual courses, and even teaching approaches, there are important common techniques which apply if you are to perform to the limit of your ability.

We have not covered every topic which might be dealt with on your particular evidence course. There was no need. We hope we have said enough on the areas we have covered to give you a clear idea of the tactical approach you should take in relation to any evidence topic you may come across.

We have written the book on the assumption that the Police and Criminal Evidence Act 1984 is in force, although we have sought to comment on the pre-Act law where we have felt this to be helpful.

Finally, we promised a mention to our respective children, which is, of course, a pleasure. So, hello and love to Andrew, Helen, William, Amy and Olivia.

John Beaumont
Chris Carr
Feast of St Anicetus, 17 April 1985

TABLE OF CASES

1 STUDY TECHNIQUES IN EVIDENCE

INTRODUCTION

The last 10 years have seen some fundamental and far-reaching changes in the ways in which law is taught, and in the structures under which it is taught, in our universities. If it were ever true that the main objective of a law programme was to ensure that students acquired large amounts of legal knowledge, that is certainly not true today. The recognition that the acquisition of legal skills is a significant part of what good legal education is about, coupled with radical changes in traditional degree course structures, has led to major developments in the ways in which the undergraduate legal curriculum is both taught and assessed.

In 1985, when the first edition of this book was published, it was possible to state with a reasonable degree of confidence that 'the majority of law degree programmes offered in this country are assessed mainly or exclusively by conventional three-hour examinations papers'. This had certainly been the case for the preceding half-century, and was undoubtedly the dominant model for assessment. Whatever the reason behind this was, it meant that the major objective of undergraduate law students was to acquire as much legal knowledge as they could on the subjects that they studied, and to demonstrate in the examination how much of that knowledge they had remembered. This was done in the context of degree programmes which followed a more leisurely path than they do today. Courses were studied over a full academic year. Adequate time was available for revision and the pace of legislative activity seemed less frenetic. Law students themselves were subject to less pressure, whether externally or self-imposed. The compelling need which many of today's undergraduates feel to obtain at least an upper second class honours degree did not exist to anything like the same extent, and the requirement of many modern LLB programmes that students study, even if only to a very limited extent, a subject other than law, was not really as prevalent.

The environment in which students of all disciplines are now studying has become much more pressurised. Modularisation and semesterisation of academic programmes have become commonplace. While there are un-doubted benefits to be had from educational developments of this kind, they leave students with less space than hitherto to cope with an increasingly crowded curriculum. If one adds to this the new imperatives in legal education, and, in particular, the impact of the newly perceived importance of skills acquisition as a central feature of the academic and vocational training of any lawyer, it is clear that law students need to devote even more attention than hitherto to the questions around maximising their perform-ance in all the forms of assessment to which they are exposed.

Legal education is not static and both the content of, and mechanisms by which, legal subjects are assessed will continue to develop. Typical features of the assessment regime for most undergraduate law programmes in the United Kingdom are that it will involve an unseen examination, usually of between two and three hours' duration, together with some kind of in-course assessment. This may be by a relatively conventional assessed essay or comparable piece of work, or, in more adventurous institutions, may involve oral presentations, assessed mooting or even participation in mock trials. The proportion which each element of the assessment regime will have in the final grade for a particular legal subject will vary from university to university — it is clearly in your own interests to find out the exact position in your own institution.

In terms of the final determination of your degree classification, the final honours classification which is awarded to a student is based on his or her performance in the second and/or third years of the course. The first year is invariably regarded as a qualifying year where the primary objective for a student is to pass, rather than obtain any particular standard of marks, but the level of performance in the subsequent years of the course is crucial in terms of the final honours classification. An increasingly common feature of degree programmes is that the final performance of students will be based on a grade point average, determined after taking into account the marks of a student on the range of courses, course units or modules which the student will have built up into his or her own degree programme.

The precise formula which will apply to the determination of the final result will vary across universities, but a relevant factor will often be the *level* of the unit which has been studied and the stage of the course when the unit has been taken.

Despite what has been said above, an unseen written examination of some kind is a common, and even dominant, feature of most law degree programmes. That given, it is surprising that more time and effort are not devoted to mastering those skills which are necessary to enable a candidate to do full justice to him or herself in an examination room. It is always a depressing business to be sitting in an assessment board meeting discussing and assessing the performance of candidates in the sure and certain knowledge that a good number of those who are being considered have simply not performed to the limit of their abilities. Often it is very clear to those charged with the responsibility of marking that where the candidate has gone wrong is in his or her detailed preparation for an examination and the way that the material has been handled, rather than because of any inherent difficulty which the student may have with the subject. In the law of evidence candidates very often do not display the abilities they have shown in class during the year, simply because they have not fully mastered the approach they should take in handling an unseen examination.

The overall purpose of this book is to help you to maximise your performance in the law of evidence. Even in the modern environment in which law degree programmes are being taught, unseen examinations are likely to form a major component of your overall assessment, and, consequently, the major focus of the book, and of chapters 1 and 2, is on that method of assessment. The purpose of the remainder of this chapter is to look at some of the steps you can take during your course and in the run-up to any examination to enable you to perform as well as possible. Chapter 2 explores some of the general issues concerned with the preparation for, and sitting of, unseen examinations.

HEALTHY STUDY TECHNIQUES AND THE LAW OF EVIDENCE

The pressure of time upon the workload of law students is greater than it has ever been. It follows that to perform to the best of your ability in any form of assessment you will need to be as efficient and effective as you can in the ways in which you work. Students who are following an evidence course within a semester-based system, and who are assessed within and at the end of that semester, will be particularly aware of the need to stay on top of the required workload at all stages. Even where the course you are studying is taught over a full academic year, time pressures will still be very acute, and you will need to ensure that you do not waste valuable revision time by having to make up gaping holes in your notes.

It is obviously true that, all else being equal, a person who studies in a conscientious and thoughtful manner throughout his evidence course will be in a much better position come the day of the examination than the idle layabout who has not troubled to open a book all year. If you are going to do well in the examination you need to make sure that your initial coverage of any topic is more or less complete at the time that you deal with that particular issue as part of your course. One of the things you will discover about the law of evidence, if you have not come across this already, is that the subject is closely integrated. What we mean by this is that material you will cover at one point in the course will relate to and overlap with material covered at other points. This will often necessitate a lecturer introducing a topic in an introductory form, leaving the detailed content of that topic to be covered at a later stage. What this means in practice is that you will spend quite a lot of your time in revising this subject in trying to understand how all the different parts of the material you have covered fit together. You ought not to be in the position where your revision time is taken up in reading basic material which should have been dealt with months before. The rest of this chapter sets out the kind of strategy which you can adopt during the course of your study of evidence in order to ensure that you squeeze the most out of the programme as part of your longer-term objective of doing as well as you possibly can in the examination.

LECTURES

On most undergraduate law degree programmes lectures are regarded by the staff teaching the course and by the students taking the course as fundamental. This is so even where it is quite clear that different lecturers in different institutions will have greatly differing ideas about what lectures are supposed to achieve. Some will want to make sure that their students get a good set of notes during the course and they will tailor the style and content of their lectures accordingly. Others may be relatively indifferent to the quality (or the quantity) of the notes which a student can take in a one-hour lecture and may see the allotted time as an opportunity to explore and illuminate in a discursive fashion those aspects of the subject which are of particular academic or controversial significance. Perhaps the ideal lecturer is the one who sees his or her role as a mixture of the two possible functions outlined above. He is conscious as a sensitive and humane lecturer (as most evidence teachers surely are) of the need of his students to be given some kind of guiding hand through the pathways of the subject, while recognising that the formal lecture is an important opportunity to develop academic arguments on areas of the subject which are of particular interest. With a bit of luck this is the kind of lecturer you have.

Students often get through the whole of their undergraduate programme without ever fully sorting out just what they should be writing down in lectures. From the lecturer's point of view, students often seem to be overly concerned to write down as much as they possibly can, whether or not they properly understand it, and without any assessment being made by the student of the overall significance of what is being written down. You will need to make some judgment for yourself as to whether you are more interested in trying to write down a verbatim account of what a lecturer says, or whether you are looking for the lecturer's insights into the subject. In the long run the latter are of more use to you, although you cannot do without the former. The amount of factual information which may be covered in a one-hour lecture may be enormous. If you are going to get the most out of your lectures you need to be discriminating in your attitude.

One of the most important things you should grasp is that it should not be any part of your objective to write down as much as you can in the time which the lecture lasts. You will inevitably find in evidence that at the end of the course you have far more material in your notes than you can possibly master, so there is not much point in adding to it unnecessarily by compiling over-long and over-detailed lecture notes. What you should try to do is compile just sufficient notes to cover clearly and concisely the essential points covered in the lecture, but in so doing you should concentrate as much as you can on listening and thinking about what the lecturer is saying. One of the points we shall cover in more detail later is that in order to do well in an examination you will often need to go further than actually stating what the law is and say something *about* the law. You will find that any reasonable evidence lecturer will convey a variety of views on the law on a particular topic and set out arguments of academic interest as he progresses through the course. You should use these ideas and arguments as a stimulus for your own thoughts and ideas on the subject.

Finally, some dos and don'ts about lectures:

(a)   Abbreviate your notes as much as you can. There is no point in their being longer than necessary. One of the things you will find about evidence is that by the time you have reached the end of the year you will have dealt with a vast number of cases, and there is no realistic way in which you will be able to learn masses of information about each and every one. Accordingly, there is no point in trying to record every factual detail about every case which might be mentioned in the lecture. However, one thing you must get right is the name of the case. One of the more obvious indications that a candidate in an examination has not read a case is when he gets the name more or less right, but misspells it. If *Woolmington* v *DPP* [1935] AC 462 appears as *Bloomingdale* ... it leaves an examiner with an overwhelming impression that you have not read the case! Ironically, if you had introduced the case by saying something along the lines of, 'In one case of crucial significance a trial judge directed the jury that once the prosecution had proved that the accused had killed his wife, that killing was presumed to be murder unless he could prove that the killing was an accident ...', the examiner will probably be more charitable and assume that you have read the case, but have simply forgotten its name!

(b)   It is worth trying to keep your handwriting tolerably legible. If your notes end up looking like Shredded Wheat it may be possible for you to decipher them, but you will hardly be able to read them comfortably. If you make a little effort at the time you write your notes it will save a lot of effort subsequently when you come to read them back.

(c)   Do not waste your time by rewriting your notes after the lecture in a 'fair copy' form. No one else is going to read your lecture notes. All that matters is that they mean something to you. Your time will be much better spent in reading and re-reading your original notes.

SEMINARS AND TUTORIALS

Most of the time you spend in studying evidence will be spent in preparing material for discussion in seminars or tutorials. We have used the terms 'seminars' and 'tutorials' interchangeably in the text, although conventionally tutorials refer to smaller groups than seminars. On practically every law degree course in this country tutorial discussion has a central role in the programme of study. Tutorials are seen as providing a focus for the study of a particular topic or group of topics and they give an invaluable opportunity, for those students prepared to take it, to sort out any problems they may have in a particular area and to explore some of the ramifications of the rules that they have been studying. At least, that is the theory. In practice the situation might be a little less rosy. Students often have to work to a tight schedule of lectures, tutorials and essays and, with the best will in the world, it is not always possible to have mastered a particular topic completely for the weekly or fortnightly class. Even if you have managed to read all the cases and articles it is quite likely that you have not managed to assimilate (or even understand) all aspects of that topic. Tutorials often seem to proceed on the basis that the student has had nothing to do in the previous fortnight than to read evidence cases and articles, and it is one of nature's immutable laws that a tutor's expectations of what is realistically achieveable in terms of reading is vastly different from that of the perception of the student.

To get the most out of tutorials and the preparation you do for them, there are a number of basic guidelines we can set out which will help you to become more efficient and effective in your studies. These guidelines should be treated as such — they do not amount to a universal formula which will guarantee success; rather they show you (in study terms) how to squeeze a quart into a pint pot.

TEXTBOOKS

As an academic subject to be studied at undergraduate level, evidence is now an important optional (or compulsory) course on most law degree programmes. There are a number of reasons for this: in the last 30 years it has been put into a systematic format in a number of good textbooks devoted to the subject; it has become an increasingly important subject in terms of subsequent professional qualification; finally, it can be an extremely interesting subject and it is always topical.

There are now a number of major textbooks and casebooks which are directed at the undergraduate market and at the time of writing there are several good textbooks which you can use with confidence. Your own lecturers will refer you to the textbook which they regard as most suitable for your course, but, whatever book has been recommended to you it is worth making some general observations about a few of the more popular texts.

For a long time *Cross on Evidence* (now *Cross and Tapper on Evidence*) has been regarded as the classic textbook on evidence. There is no doubt that if you are unsure on a point of law or are looking for the most analytical and academic of the textbook treatments, *Cross and Tapper* is the place to find it. The problem with *Cross and Tapper*, however, lies in its very completeness. It becomes very difficult on some of the more complex areas, such as character or hearsay, to fathom a way through the vast amount of material contained in the book and understand what a particular topic is about. However, certain chapters, although very demanding, do treat topics in a manner altogether more profound than the general run of evidence textbooks.

A text which is different in its treatment of the subject is *Murphy on Evidence*. This has a refreshing, if rather unusual approach (in that the subject is tackled through the medium of a case study) and is pitched at a level much more comprehensible to the average undergraduate than *Cross and Tapper*. Admittedly it does not contain quite the same depth of academic argument and it does not provide the same kind of detailed footnote references, but it does give the student a clear and straightforward statement of the law.

A recently established addition to the range of available texts is Keene, *The Modern Law of Evidence*, which provides a comprehensive and readable account of the subject. This book benefits from a well-structured treatment of the areas covered and a not inconsiderable advantage of the book is its very clear presentation — a large typeface, clearly set out on each page, makes this book less burdensome than some of the other texts when trying to make notes from it.

Casebooks in evidence have gone through something of a revival in the past few years and there are now a number of acceptable books on the market — Carter, *Cases and Statutes on Evidence*, Heydon, *Evidence Cases and Materials*, and Cooper, Murphy and Beaumont, *Cases and Materials on Evidence*. All of these books are useful, but the book by Heydon in particular contains some fascinating material, although its content is biased towards Commonwealth legal systems. Other useful texts include Elliott and Phipson, *Manual of the Law of Evidence*, which provides a clear and concise account of the main principles of the law, and May, *Criminal Evidence*, which, as the title implies, is limited in its coverage. Those seeking a detailed exploration of the underlying theoretical principles of the subject will enjoy reading Zuckerman's, *The Principles of Criminal Evidence*.

With a subject as difficult as the law of evidence, it may be useful to read about a specific topic in a less detailed work before moving to the larger texts. This is where Professor Smith's recent book, *Criminal Evidence* comes in useful. The book is aimed at students studying evidence for the first time. Of course, it is confined to criminal cases, but then most of the topics and controversial areas of the modern law come from this field. You will profit from a close examination of this text.

Whatever textbook you are using, to get your money's worth out of it you should use it properly. The basic evidence textbooks provide you with a general, and more or less detailed, overview of the subject taken as a whole and of each of the separate topics comprising the subject. They also provide you with an orderly and comprehensive account of particular evidential rules. Finally, they give you valuable basic information about cases and statutes.

How should you treat a textbook? Is reading it enough? Should you take notes? If so, how extensive should the notes be?

There are different views as to how textbooks should be used. Some argue that, as the material is already there in written form and is readily available to you, there is really no point in writing parts of it out again. Others take the view that the whole process of distilling the content of the textbook is both sensible and important. We take the latter view for the following reasons:

(a) The taking of notes helps you to understand the law. Because good-quality note-taking is a slow business, you are compelled by the exercise to take time in dealing with the subject-matter. This gives you more time to think. The relative slowness of the operation also allows more time for the information to sink in.

(b) A textbook is an important source of basic information. If you do not reduce this information to a manageable amount, you will be faced with an impossible task when the examination looms. This is because it is beyond the abilities of most people to assimilate and learn the contents of several hundred pages of detailed text without reducing them first.

There is no single perfect method of note-taking. Some students will write out most of a chapter verbatim (which is foolish); others will be satisfied with a page of sparse jottings (which may not be of much use subsequently). Somewhere in the middle of these two possibilities is the ideal solution.

One of the most difficult things to do when you come to a new chapter in a textbook for the first time is to distinguish the important from the unimportant. If you dive head first into taking notes then you must not be too surprised if you end up with a thick wad of paper full of over-detailed information at the end of the session. This is because on a first reading of anything complex, and much of evidence is complex, you will not be able to discriminate fully between more relevant and less relevant information. Accordingly, before you write any notes at all you should read through the chapter generally. It might be useful (if you do not mind mutilating your book) to highlight, e.g., by underlining, those parts of the chapter which seem to be most important, but your main concern on the first reading is to understand what is going on. Until you understand what you are reading you cannot hope to make any decent notes of it.

When you have a clear idea of the basic structure of a chapter you are in a position to make some notes. Go through the chapter again. You will find that because you have already made an effort to become familiar with the content of the chapter you will have sorted out which are the most important points. Because you know what is important you ought not to be too tempted to write out large amounts of material of lesser significance. Remember, when you come to revising for the examination you will find that you will spend a lot of time in reducing even further the notes that you have already made. The lesson is clear — keep your notes brief in the first place. Above all, do not be tempted to write out lists of footnote cases which you are never going to read. You might feel a powerful urge to do this when compiling your notes, but these will be the first things to be jettisoned when your revision starts.

READING CASES

You will be aware by this stage of your studies that part of the traditional discipline of an undergraduate law degree consists of reading cases in the law reports. The extent to which case law is important for the study of a particular subject depends on the subject itself. The law of evidence is a substantial case-law subject. Our view is that a student can only properly understand evidence through a thorough reading of the important cases. There are not really any shorter ways. Only relatively confined areas of the subject have been codified by statute and even in those areas the amount of case law which overlays the statutory framework is usually quite considerable.

Undergraduates are subjected to various and sometimes conflicting advice on how to tackle the matter of reading cases. The advice we incorporate here is based on our own experience of learning the subject as students and in teaching and examining the law of evidence subsequently.

On the assumption that the case to which you have been referred resides somewhere in the law reports (rather than in, say, the *Criminal Law Review*) the first thing that you can assume is that it is *not* adequate simply to read the headnote. Headnotes, almost by definition, are brief and edited accounts of the facts and decision in a case. Although the statement of law contained in a headnote will usually be accurate it will not always convey the flavour of the reasoning of the court nor will it explore the reasons which underpin a particular decision. By all means cull your note of the *facts* of a case from the headnote and use the headnote to guide you to the part of the judgment concerned with the point of law on evidence that you are looking for, but you need to look at the judgment(s) to appreciate fully the interplay of issues of law and policy which may be relevant. You will also find that if you rely solely on headnote treatments of cases you will form a thoroughly distorted view of a particular area of law. For example, it would be possible to read all the important decisions on similar fact evidence in headnote form and reach the conclusion that the area has been one of steady and unbroken judicial development from the time of *Makin* v *Attorney-General for New South Wales* [1894] AC 57 up to the present day. Such a conclusion ignores the conceptual upheaval in the topic following *DPP* v *Boardman* [1975] AC 421 and the subsequent consideration of the subject in the Court of Appeal, and more recently in the House of Lords.

Finally it is very difficult to make some kind of informed and intelligent criticism of a rule (and these are the kinds of things which help you to do well in assessments and examinations) without a good understanding of why the courts apply the rules of evidence in a particular way. Headnotes simply do not tell you enough about the kinds of things you need to know.

However, we are not suggesting that you should read the full report of each and every case you look at. Where all the members of the House of Lords or Court of Appeal deliver parallel judgments it may often be quite sufficient to read only one or perhaps two out of the judgments handed down. In any event, given the formidable nature of many tutorial reading lists, it may be impossible to read the whole of every case to which you are referred. If a particular case is pin-pointed as being of crucial significance then a full reading of all, or most, of the judgments may be needed. For example, if you are looking at the question of the admissibility of statements contained in documents for the purposes of criminal proceedings you may well begin your analysis of the modern law by looking at the House of Lords' decision in *Myers* v *DPP* [1965] AC 1001. This is still a very useful case because, although it has been superseded by statute it contains a very full discussion of the complexity and rigidity of the rule against hearsay. A knowledge of the reasoning of at least one of the majority judges, together with a similar knowledge of why the two dissenting judges dissented, casts considerable light on the shape and form of the modern hearsay rule.

How should a case be noted? Just as when noting textbooks, there is a strong temptation to pick up a pen before opening the law report and start writing as soon as you reach the prescribed page. Sometimes this can work in evidence cases, particularly when you have been referred to references in the *Criminal Law Review*, where the reports of cases are very short. But generally you should read the case first, before you write down anything at all. You may find the following strategy a useful one:

(a)   First, read the headnote. This will give you a quick perspective on the case as a whole and, where the evidence point is one only of the grounds of an appeal, will direct you to the relevant part of the judgment(s).

(b)   Often, when reading the judgment, you will be able to skip over the first page or two, because judgments often begin with a recitation of the facts. You will already know the facts from reading the headnote.

(c)   You need to read the relevant part of the judgment slowly and carefully, making sure that you understand the basic issues and the general nature of the legal reasoning and policy considerations which the judge employs.

(d)   Only when you have read and understood the case should you attempt to make a note of it. As with noting textbooks, be as brief as you reasonably can, and in particular be careful not to go overboard in your account of the facts of the case. When you come to revise for the examination you do not want to have to spend a large amount of time cutting your notes of cases down to manageable proportions.

You may occasionally find it useful to write down a quotation from a judgment, but as a general practice you should be careful not to write down quotations which are too extensive — it takes too long and is not a very efficient way of noting the main points.

(e)   If you are studying evidence as one of your final-year options, as most students do, then you should by now have well-developed habits as to the manner in which you note a case. Nevertheless, it may be helpful to remind you of the kinds of things you should be looking for when studying a case. First, you must attempt to extract the *ratio decidendi* of the case always assuming, of course, that it is discoverable. Secondly, you need to identify the essential reasons justifying the adoption of the particular rule under consideration in that case. These reasons may simply turn on the binding nature of earlier authorities or may revolve around considerations of policy. Whatever the reasons are, you need to find them. Thirdly, it is often useful to know what the principal arguments for adopting a *different* rule are, and these are sometimes reviewed in the course of a judgment. A brief note of what these arguments were and why they were rejected can be helpful. Fourthly, where there are a number of judgments each saying more or less the same thing, then it is not usually necessary to be completely familiar with all of them. For example, in the House of Lords in *DPP* v *Boardman* [1975] AC 421 all the judgments followed the same lines. Different members of the House used different examples and placed a slightly different emphasis on the test of admissibility for similar fact evidence which they were individually applying, but the overall tenor of each of the judgments was the same. This is simply illustrated by the way in which the various judgments in *DPP* v *Boardman* were used by the House of Lords in *R* v *P* [1991] 2 AC 447. However, it is often important to be familiar with dissenting judgments. Appellate judges do not dissent lightly, and where there is a dissent there will invariably be a good reason for it. Dissents often give a valuable insight into the competing directions in which the law may be pulling and inevitably, because of the way the doctrine of *stare decisis* works, dissents will only appear where there is some uncertainty in the law, or where very strong considerations of policy pull one judge away from the line being taken by his colleagues. Of course, it is precisely these areas of uncertainty or controversy which are food and drink to the evidence examiner. A good historical example of a powerful dissent which played a full part in the eventual development of the law is that of Lord Edmund-Davies in *Hoskyn* v *Metropolitan Police Commissioner* [1979] AC 474 where he argued that where a wife was a competent witness against her husband in a case of personal violence, she should also be compellable. This finally became the law in s. 80 of the Police and Criminal Evidence Act 1984.

Perhaps fortunately for evidence students there are not many dissenting judgments of great significance — but where they do exist they are perhaps even more valuable, simply because of their rarity.

JOURNAL ARTICLES

Usually a tutorial reading list will refer a student to any particularly relevant or useful articles on a topic. The law of evidence is increasingly well-served by the various journals in terms of the space devoted to articles on the subject and the *Criminal Law Review* in particular has, in recent years, devoted much of its space to mainstream evidence issues.

Any student who hopes to do well in the subject needs to be aware of the main journal literature. Just as in other subjects, topical issues tend to be covered fully in the journals, whereas textbooks, by their very nature, may only be able to devote a small amount of space to a matter which can receive a full-blown treatment in a journal. For example, in recent years there have been a number of articles dealing in depth with such issues as confessions and similar fact evidence. It is impossible for any textbook of reasonable length to reflect fully the arguments set out in these articles, and in any event no textbook can hope to be as up to date or as fresh in its discussion of an issue as can an article.

In addition to the full-length article in an academic journal you will find casenotes in the *Law Quarterly Review*, the *Modern Law Review* and the notes on cases in the *Criminal Law Review* to be of considerable value. Such notes highlight in a brisk manner a point of particular interest and usually contain some observations from the author of the note about the quality, validity or desirability of the decision which has been reached.

The same ground rules apply to noting articles as apply to noting textbooks and cases.

First, you should always read through the whole of the casenote or article before you actually commit pen to paper. Until you have read the article you do not know what the author is trying to say.

Second, try to keep your notes brief. It will often be the case that the author will be trying to convey just one central point in the 2, 10 or 20 pages at his disposal. Much of what he writes will be background argument and information. You may need sufficient detail of this to remind yourself at a future date of the logic of his argument, but you will never need the full detail of such background material.

A third useful guideline you can follow with confidence is that there is no short cut to reading an article. Authors often summarise the principal elements of their argument at the end, but such conclusions are generally too terse to be of much use to you on their own and in any event will not normally review the essential reasoning which underlies the conclusion.

Finally, it is sometimes a good idea to spend a moment or two, after you have read an article, considering its merits. You can incorporate into your notes some kind of commentary indicating whether you agree with the conclusions of the writer (whether as a matter of law, logic or common sense) and whether you think there are any flaws in the argument, or issues which have not been considered. This kind of critical analysis will be useful to you when revising, in that it will help you to formulate views and ideas about a particular topic which will lend some individuality to your assessed essay or examination script at the end of the course.

CONCLUSION

Much of what we have set out above is simply a matter of common sense. The basic message with which we should like you to leave this chapter is that one of the keys to a worthwhile performance in an examination is to be found in efficient and intelligent study during the course. The law of evidence can be a fearsome subject if tackled haphazardly and the only sure way to come to grips with its complexities is to approach your study of the subject in an organised and forthright manner. If you can do that you will not go far wrong.

2   REVISION AND EXAMINATION TECHNIQUES

Law examinations have many of the characteristics of a primitive tribal ritual. They are public, painful and sometimes leave lasting scars. Of course, there is always the odd masochist who actually appears to enjoy examinations and who seems to relish the dreadful process of revision, although such unwholesome characters are relatively few. Nevertheless, examinations have to be endured and, because so much hangs on their outcome, they have to be taken seriously.

Many law students do not perform as well as they should in examinations. This may be because they have taken things too easily during the course or because they have not allowed enough time to prepare properly for the examination. But very often it is because the student does not display to the full the knowledge and ideas he has about a subject in his exam script. The purpose of this chapter is to highlight those things you should think about when preparing for your evidence examination and give some general guidance about how you should handle yourself in the examination room. Subsequent chapters deal with specific strategies which you can adopt when dealing with particular topics.

A STRATEGY FOR REVISING EVIDENCE

As a breed, evidence examiners are generally human. Their concern in the examination paper is to find out what you do know rather than what you do not. Their jobs (and salaries) depend on students passing their examinations.

It would really be quite easy for any examiner in evidence to set impossibly difficult questions. Many areas of the subject contain all sorts of obscure issues, but very few examiners will fill an exam paper with such matters, unless they are sadists or madmen. Generally speaking, your examiner will be concerned to find out whether you have grasped fundamental principles and whether you can make intelligent assessments about the law. It is important to fix this point firmly in your thinking, because it will help to condition the correct approach towards the whole question of revision.

How should one go about revision? There is no absolute answer, because different people approach this task in different ways. Also, much will depend on the nature of the course you have followed. It may be that one of the consequences of the modulisation or semesterisation of your course is that you are assessed on the semester's work only 14 or 15 weeks after you commenced learning the subject. Such a programme will put a premium on your remaining right on top of your work as the semester progresses, with only a short period for intensive revision at the end. For other students (and they are still a substantial majority) the examination will come at the end of the academic year, whether or not the course has been followed on a semesterised basis. This may give you a little more leeway in planning your revision.

Being realistic there is little real hope for most students that they will reach the end of their evidence course having remembered everything they have done through its progress. However, although you may not be able to learn everything as you go along, it is vitally important that you keep on top of your work during the course, because you cannot hope to do justice to the subject or to yourself during the revision period if you have gaping holes in your notes. Any student who keeps up with the work during the course will probably have a much better overall grasp of the subject than the candidate who has been dilatory. More importantly, he will not need to spend time when he should be revising in actually creating notes for the first time. Of course, staying on top of the work during the course is no guarantee of success. You are bound to know of students who read everything but who cannot put it together for an examination. However, it is important to realise that although conscientious study during the course is not a guarantee of success, it is usually a precondition.

You should aim to complete your programme of study, and begin the revision period, with a comprehensive set of notes drawn from lectures, textbooks, law reports and the academic journals. One point worth remembering is that a good stock of references to articles will look glossy if you can mention them in an examination script, but beware of throwing down a list of scholarly writings if your answer demonstrates a complete failure to grasp the basic issues being examined.

Length of Revision Period

However efficient you are in your studies, it is inevitable that you will not be able to devote as much time as you would ideally like to revision. Nevertheless, you must begin thinking about revision for examinations in general, and evidence in particular, in good time. You will find that there are some particular problems, which you might not have foreseen, in revising for evidence and it is important that you allow yourself enough time to overcome them. For example, you will probably find that the sheer number of cases (in an overwhelmingly case-law subject) causes some difficulty. Similarly, you may find that the theoretical complexities of topics such as the character of the accused and the detail of hearsay take considerable effort to master, while the changes in the law introduced by the Police and Criminal Evidence Act 1984, the Criminal Justice Act 1988, the Criminal Justice Act 1991 and the Criminal Justice and Public Order Act 1994 will make considerable demands for a number of years in terms of grasping both the position under the Acts and the situations which led to their enactment.

To meet the above points you should draw up as realistic a revision programme as possible, spreading over the four or five weeks before the examination. Even if your teaching programme continues until just before the examination, as is sometimes the case, you must begin revision in good time. In giving this advice we are not preaching some kind of unrealistic gospel. You are bound to have noticed in preparing for examinations in earlier years of the course that, however much you knew of a subject come the day of the examination, there were other, perhaps important, issues which you would have preferred to have been more comfortable with.

Designing your Revision Programme

You can take one of two broad approaches towards learning your subjects. First, and the approach we would not recommend, is to learn your subjects one at a time, so that if your revision period lasts four weeks and you have four subjects to learn, you can spend one week on each. The disadvantage with this approach is that you will become thoroughly bored if you are looking at nothing but evidence for a stretch of a week, and after a time your revision will become counter-productive. Second, and in our view much more satisfactory, is to intermingle to some extent the subjects you are studying. This does not mean that you have to pursue a contemporaneous revision programme in all of your subjects at the same time, but if you spend a morning and afternoon looking at evidence, you may find a couple of hours of revenue or jurisprudence in the evening to be light relief!

The revision programme, as well as being realistic in terms of the amount of material which can be covered in a given period, must be realistic in terms of how many hours per day and days per week can reasonably be worked. There is no point in devising a grand scheme under which you get up to start work at 7.00 a.m. with the intention of completing 15 hours revising by midnight. You will not last one day. You need to set targets which can be managed, because there is nothing more depressing than failing to achieve the amount of work you have set yourself, day after day.

It is a good idea to design a programme under which you are working by 8.30 or 9.00 in the morning. In fact, there is something satisfying about being hard at work by 8.30, because it means that you can take a half-hour break for coffee and reading the newspaper mid-morning and still do three hours' work by lunch-time. At lunch-time it is not a good idea to have a 'working lunch'. It is much better to have a complete break for an hour and even take the opportunity of having some exercise. You will then approach the afternoon session in a reasonably refreshed state and in a position to do another three hours' work by tea. Again, take a break at some stage in the afternoon.

Finally, you should try to do a couple of hours' work in the evening, but you should aim to finish completely by 9.00 or 9.30 p. m. at the latest. There is no point in going on longer than this because, if you have worked solidly throughout the day, you will be saturated with the material you have been learning. You will also be tired. It is much better to relax for an hour or so before going to bed. The overriding thing you need to remember is that revising for examinations is like running in a marathon, rather than a 100 metre dash. You need to conserve yourself.

Topic Coverage

Although legal subjects are taught and examined in a variety of ways, one of the common features of most courses is that subjects are separated into discrete topic areas. In some subjects the topic boundaries are much more clear-cut than in others. In the law of evidence there is a considerable, and often unavoidable, overlap between topic areas. Evidence courses are often taught as though the subject does consist of a number of separate and clearly defined topics, but are frequently examined with the 'wires crossed' between the topics. It is probably a little unusual to see all the questions on the paper containing such mixed issues, but it is unrealistic for a student to expect to see every question on a paper confined four-square within the boundaries of a particular topic.

Thorough revision of four topics is unlikely to be enough to get four answers out in an exam. Topics may not appear; they may appear in a particularly unusual or difficult form or they may be mixed in with a topic which you have not revised. On the other hand, you do not want to dilute your revision effort by revising too many topics — being able to answer all

10 questions on the paper is no use if you only need to answer four. You need to strike a happy balance — happy in the sense that you can feel confident before you go into the examination room and happy in that you will be able to do four good answers.

Selecting the areas you are going to cover involves a certain amount of crystal-ball gazing. However, there are a number of sensible guidelines that you can follow in deciding what to revise.

(a) The overall content of the paper will reflect the course that you have been taught. The sum of your tutorial and lecture programme will delimit the boundaries of the subject for the examination.

(b) It is highly likely that those areas on which a lot of time has been spent during the course will get an adequate airing on the paper. Given that the examiner is one of the people who has taught you during the course, anything which he or she obviously enjoys or is particularly interested in is quite likely to feature on the paper.

(c) Examiners are anxious that their students actually pass the paper. Examinations are not games designed to expose the inadequacies of candidates. Accordingly, most examiners will seek to ensure that their paper is essentially fair.

How do you translate these broad assumptions into a working revision strategy?

The first, and most important, point that we must make is that, whatever we say here about topic coverage, you *must* (obviously) be guided wholly by the content and bias of the particular course that you have been following. Most evidence programmes will cover a range of more or less standard issues, but around the fringe of the central areas of evidence there is a lot of scope for individual teachers of the subject to mould their coverage to the topics which are of particular interest to them. In the chapters which follow you will see that we have made no attempt to stray away from mainstream issues, although we hope that the strategies we lay down will be of use to you whatever the particular topic you may be looking at.

A typical evidence course will inevitably cover some or all of the following topics:

(a) The burden and standard of proof.
(b) The competence and compellability of witnesses; the right to silence.
(c) Public policy; privilege.
(d) The course of evidence (including examination in chief, refreshment of memory, unfavourable and hostile witnesses, previous consistent and inconsistent statements, cross-examination).

(e) Evidence of character and the Criminal Evidence Act 1898.
(f) Similar fact evidence.
(g) The rule against hearsay and its exceptions (including confessions).
(h) Opinion evidence and judgments in previous cases.
(i) Documentary evidence.

Any course in which all of the above areas were covered in any depth would be unusually ambitious, but any evidence programme worth its salt will grapple with many of the above issues and in particular will deal in some depth with such fundamental areas as the character of the accused and the rule against hearsay.

If your list of the topics covered during the course looks something like that above, how do you go about selecting the areas you are going to revise? Undoubtedly, if you manage to learn them all you will be very knowledgeable about evidence by the time you have finished. The danger is that it might take you six months to do it. We can offer some tentative advice which may be helpful:

(a) If you feel you have the choice, learn topics which you find interesting.

(b) Some topics should not be studied without mastering other linked areas of the subject.

(c) Some topics can be studied on an independent and free-standing basis, but unless you link your revision to related areas of the subject your overall understanding may be deficient. For example, you may decide that similar fact evidence is one of the topics you will learn. However, unless you have a grasp of the general principles surrounding the use of evidence of character your overall comprehension of the significance of the rules on similar fact evidence will suffer.

(d) Some topics are too fundamental to miss out. Hearsay, character and the rules relating to the course of the trial all come within this category, although for different reasons. Hearsay and character are two of the great issues of evidence. The course of the trial covers a miscellaneous group of rules, none of which may be significant enough to warrant a complete question, but many of which may appear somewhere or other on the paper.

(e) Some topics are viewed as self-contained in the minds of examiners. The burden, standard of proof and presumptions, evidence of opinion and documentary evidence are often examined in such a way. This means that if you are looking for topics to exclude from your revision programme, there may be greater safety in selecting one of these topics than those mentioned in (d) above, although we would emphasise that you will need to understand the significance of these topics, even if you are not prepared to answer an examination question on them.

(f)   Analysis of past papers usually repays the effort. If you look at the papers for the last three or four years you may see a pattern of questions reflected. For example, there may have been a question on confessions in each of those papers, sometimes appearing as a problem and sometimes appearing as an essay. Assuming that the same people are responsible for teaching the course as in those previous years there is a reasonable chance that confessions will appear again. Similarly, you may find that there is either a question on burdens or a question on presumptions on each of the papers. In the light of this you would be reasonably justified in learning these two topics, confident that one or other is likely to appear.

Of course in analysing past papers you need to exercise common sense. If the examiner in the subject has changed over the period of the papers you are looking at, this will inevitably result in some changes in emphasis. However, even if the examiner has changed, past papers have a more general value in that they provide some guidance on the kind of questions which are set, although they are not particularly helpful in the narrower sense of being reliable indicators of the likely topic coverage.

In conclusion on topic coverage, it is worth remembering that if you learn more (in terms of the number of topics) than you predict you will need, that is worth a lot in terms of peace of mind. There is not much to be gained, and potentially a lot to be lost, by cutting things too fine.

EXAMINATION TECHNIQUE

Practical Matters

Your revision for the examination should not continue to the very doors of the examination room and, ideally, should not continue late into the evening before an examination. If you have been sensible and conscientious about your revision programme as a whole you will have enough facts in your head to answer any reasonable question on the paper. If you stay up too late the night before an important examination trying to pack in a few extra details you will probably end up driving out information that was already there. Also, if you get a good night's sleep before the paper it will mean that you will be fresh and alert when you come to do the examination. This is worth a lot more than a few extra facts.

In preparation for actually sitting the examination you should of course ensure that you have an appropriate stock of writing materials and that you have a reliable clock or watch with you (although clocks are always provided for examinations, they are not always particularly visible). You should also have a clean handkerchief with you — to wipe your hands, to mop your brow or to offer to your neighbour who has forgotten to bring one and whose interminable sniffing is driving you mad!

Once you have found your seat in the examination room the first thing you should do is make sure that you have not chosen, or been allocated to, a desk where one leg is shorter or longer than the other three. If you have, then ask for something to be done about it. There is nothing more irritating than trying to write at a desk, the surface of which is pitching and yawing like an Atlantic racer.

Once the invigilator has fired the starting gun, check the rubric of the paper. You will normally know what this will be in advance, but it is something you must double-check, because a failure to answer the number of questions asked is disastrous. It is absolutely crucial that you comply with the rubric of the paper and answer the exact number of questions asked, no more and no less. Some enthusiasts answer more than is required of them. This is a complete waste of time, because the examiner will simply ignore the surplus answer(s). Even worse, candidates far too frequently answer one less question than the rubric demands. Such obvious folly means that, on a paper where you are required to answer five questions and only four are attempted, your paper is being marked out of 80 rather than 100. What is more, you *must* make a proper attempt at your last question. Cryptic little messages like 'Ran out of time' are always interpreted by the cynical and world-weary examiner as 'Ran out of information'. Remember also that because you will always pick up the first few marks on a question relatively easily it is silly to think that you can get better marks by writing longer answers to one fewer question than the rubric requires.

It is very important that you read the examination paper carefully. You might want to skip through the paper first, to reassure yourself that the topics which you have revised have made an appearance, and there is nothing wrong with this, as long as it is not a substitute for a careful examination of the paper's contents.

If you are allowed reading time before the examination begins then make full use of it by methodically reading through the whole paper; if you are not allowed reading time it is nevertheless equally important that you spend a few minutes familiarising yourself with the paper. Make sure that you look at every question — examinees often complain that they failed to spot some question or other that has hidden itself on the last page of the paper.

Once you have gone through the paper you are in a position to begin to assess which four or five questions you are best able to answer. At this point many examinees will want to begin writing their first answer. There is nothing wrong with putting pen to paper straightaway, as long as some thought is given to the structure of your answer and the material which you might incorporate. Other students find it helpful to spend a few minutes in planning their answers, either before attempting any answers at all or before attempting each individual answer. There is no doubt that it is a useful exercise to jot down briefly the key points which you want to make in your answer, together with a list of cases and statutory provisions which you want to use.

You should balance your time more or less evenly between your answers. Unless the rubric provides differently, you can assume that there are equal marks for each question. Your first answer may take you a few minutes over a strictly mathematical allocation as you build up a head of steam, but you will be able to retrieve this over the rest of the paper.

Finally, make sure that your handwriting can be read. Examiners exhibit all kinds of human failings, and boredom and irritation are but two of them. If your examiner has been wading through examination scripts all day, he will find your offering particularly glutinous if he cannot read it. Undoubtedly, if the examiner has to decipher every word on your paper it will mean that he will not be able to follow the threads of your argument, and this will most certainly work to your disadvantage. If your handwriting is suspect, one small thing you can do to assist the examiner (and this applies to candidates whose writing is perfectly legible too) is to underline any cases or statutory provisions you mention. When he is drowning in a sea of words, such highlighted references will be like little beacons, guiding him through your answer.

What are Examiners Looking For?

In setting out a general statement of those matters for which examiners are looking in a script we are conscious that we are stating our own views as to the contents of an ideal examination answer. Your own examiners may have different views from ours, because examiners vary greatly in what they see as a perfect examination answer. Nevertheless, we believe that any student who takes to heart the kind of advice we are giving here will be following a sensible and considered strategy. You should, of course, take every opportunity to winkle out of your examiners their views on how examinations should be tackled.

Law degree examinations in general, and evidence papers in particular, are not designed to test simply your ability to learn and reproduce factual information. Examiners look for a variety of abilities from the examinee, and these include:

(a) the ability to state accurately, and with corresponding understanding, relevant rules of law;

(b) the ability to apply those rules of law to the particular legal issues raised by the questions set;

(c) the ability to use and manipulate the relevant authorities and statutory provisions to support argument in relation to the questions set;

(d)   the ability to carry your discussion beyond a description of the factual information you have used, in order to make informed and critical comment on the law.

Many examinees achieve some of these objectives, but relatively few achieve all of them. In particular, it is very common to see an examination script where the examinee reproduces more or less accurately the relevant law, but makes no attempt to reach any conclusions *about* the law. Often there is little, if any, attempt to assess the present state of the law in anything approaching a critical fashion.

Similarly, candidates will quite often treat the examiner to a lengthy analysis of the law on a particular topic, without addressing themselves to the precise issues which have been raised by the question set.

However, there is considerable disagreement among examiners, even among those who have thought seriously about the matter, as to how examination scripts should be assessed. Some examiners may not be very interested in much more than a blanket coverage of the statutory and case-law material relevant to a particular topic. Others, and in this category we include ourselves, are anxious to see some critical analysis of the relevant law. In such circumstances it is difficult to be dogmatic about how you should approach your own examination, other than to advise you to use your best endeavours to find out just what your own examiner wants.

Writing the Answer

In this section we make some general points about how you should tackle examination questions. Subsequent chapters deal in more detail with some of the specific issues you should keep in mind when dealing with problem or essay questions in a particular area of evidence.

We must emphasise that the approach we take is based on our own experience and details what we think is important. As we have said above, your own examiner in evidence may hold different views and it is up to you to find out, if you can, what different emphasis he or she may have.

The first and overriding rule is that you must answer the question which has been asked, and not one which you had hoped would be asked. Frequently examinees write out pages of completely accurate material which simply does not relate to the question asked. For example, you may see a very general question along the following lines:

'Founded apparently on the proposition that all jurymen are deaf to reason, that all witnesses are presumptively liars and that all documents are presumptively forgeries ... [the law of evidence] has been added to, subtracted from and tinkered with for two centuries until it has become less

of a structure than a pile of builders' debris.' (Harvey, *The Advocate's Devil*, 1958)
    Discuss.

Unless you are very knowledgeable about the law of evidence as a whole, or alternatively desperate for a last question to answer, this sort of question should be avoided. If you do have to answer it, through force of circumstances, you should not use the question as a vehicle for writing all about the burden and standard of proof, or whatever other area you know intimately and have not been able to deploy elsewhere on your script. This kind of question demands that you draw information from all parts of your evidence studies in order to reach a conclusion on the merits of the writer's statement. You simply cannot answer the question by confining your analysis to information from one small area of the subject. Yet this is invariably what candidates do when faced with this kind of question.

In answering the precise question set you should not try to pull the wool over the eyes of the examiner by striking out at a tangent to the question. This ploy is usually quite obvious. Examiners will generally be looking for a particular kind of response to a question — anything too blatantly off target will not get any credit.

The second general principle which you must apply is to use relevant cases, statutes or academic arguments for all they are worth. When marking papers it is very common to see generalised responses without any discussion of relevant authorities. For example, if you are required to judge whether a confession made by an accused to the police in a police station, following protracted periods of questioning without adequate refreshment breaks, during which various ill-defined threats have been made to the accused by his interrogators, is admissible, it is no use writing something like: 'The police should not have behaved in that way. The confession will not be admitted because it was obtained as a result of oppression'.

Although the statement is probably true, it is quite inadequate in the context of an evidence examination. It would be much better to say something like the following:

Under s. 76 of the Police and Criminal Evidence Act 1984 a confession is inadmissible if it is obtained:

    (a)   As a result of oppression.
    (b)   As a consequence of anything said or done likely to render it unreliable.

Section 76(8) defines oppression as including torture, inhuman or degrading treatment and the use or threats of violence. This definition of oppression is based on Art. 3 of the European Convention on Human Rights 1950. Following a number of decisions at common law on the meaning of oppression (see, for example, *Callis v Gunn* [1964] 1 QB 495; *R v Prager* [1972] 1 WLR 260; and *R v Priestley* (1965) 51 Cr App R 1) the question of the meaning of oppression under the Act was considered in *R v Fulling* [1987] QB 426 where the Court of Appeal ...

The difference between these two approaches is striking. Any candidate who writes along the lines of the second approach immediately tells the examiner that he understands completely what is going on. The first approach, in contrast, tells the examiner nothing.

Of course, you must be careful not to let your answer degenerate into a list of cases — although it is perfectly proper, and often desirable, to mention cases in an appropriate context without saying very much about them. The use of *Callis v Gunn*, *R v Prager* and *R v Priestley* above illustrates the point nicely. Inevitably, because of the case-law nature of evidence, you will need to cite and use a large number of cases in most of your answers. In resolving the question of how much detail to put in about these cases, you need to be careful. If you go into too much detail you are wasting time and padding your answer unnecessarily. On the other hand, a series of terse statements of law, supported only by a list of cases, is equally unimpressive. The following example illustrates the point.

Suppose that you are dealing with a problem question involving the issue of whether a witness is allowed to refresh his memory outside the courtroom from a written note of the relevant matters made two days after the event in question by someone other than the witness.

Such a question raises a number of separate issues:

(a)   Can a witness refresh his memory outside the courtroom?

(b)   Was the written note sufficiently contemporaneous to satisfy the normal refreshment of memory rules?

(c)   Can a witness refresh his memory from a written note he has not prepared himself?

One examinee may begin his answer by saying:

One of the issues raised here relates to the question of whether the witness can refresh his memory outside the courtroom. In *R v Richardson* [1971] 2 QB 484 the accused was charged with offences of burglary and attempted burglary. The alleged offences had taken place about 18 months before the date of his trial. Just before the trial of the accused was about to begin four of the prosecution witnesses read over statements which they had made to the police shortly after the alleged offences had taken place. One of the issues on appeal was whether, because the witnesses had been allowed to refresh their memory in this way, their evidence should have been ruled inadmissible.

Another examinee may write:

> On the issue of whether a witness is allowed to refresh his memory out of court see *R v Richardson* [1971] 2 QB 484; held that such refreshment was permissible. See also *R v Westwell* [1976] 2 All ER 812 and *Worley v Bentley* [1976] 2 All ER 449. For a witness to be able to refresh his memory the document must be one drawn up contemporaneously with the events to which it relates: see *R v Richardson* and *R v Simmonds* [1969] 1 QB 586.

There are deficiencies in both of these approaches. The first meanders along too slowly. There is simply not the time to catalogue every detail of all the cases you mention, if you are going to deal with the issues raised in the question properly. The second approach is better than the first in that the relevant authorities are handled much more briskly, but again there are deficiencies in that no attempt is being made to analyse the cases which have been mentioned and there is no critical consideration of the rules being discussed.

The following approach is much more useful:

> In *R v Richardson* [1971] 2 QB 484 the Court of Appeal considered the question of whether a witness was allowed to refresh his memory out of court and held that such refreshment was both permissible, and indeed inevitable. Although the decision was criticised by Howard [1972] Crim LR 351 on the basis that such refreshment is not carried on under the supervision of the court, it is submitted that the better view is that such refreshment should be allowed in the interests of justice. The Divisional Court in *Worley v Bentley* [1976] 2 All ER 449 stressed that it is desirable that the defence be informed where such refreshment takes place, although the Court of Appeal in *R v Westwell* [1976] 2 All ER 812 (while confirming the desirability of such a practice) confirmed that a failure to so inform the defence was not, of itself, a ground for acquittal. However, in *Owen v Edwards* (1983) 77 Cr App R 191 it was decided that the other party is entitled to examine the contents of any statement from which memory is refreshed and is able to cross-examine on it.

This approach tells the examiner, without your having to spell it out, that you are perfectly familiar with the case law on the topic and that you are also aware of such academic debate on the issue as there may be. There has been no detailed treatment of the facts of the cases, yet it is patent from the overall sophistication of the treatment that the examinee understands what they are. There is also some attempt to rebut the academic criticism of the case central to the discussion, which shows the examiner that you have thought about the topic.

Sometimes, of course, it may be necessary to refer to the facts of a case or group of cases to advance the argument you are putting forward. Thus, if you are trying to distinguish different cases decided by the Court of Appeal, the similarity (or, for that matter, dissimilarity) of the facts of the cases maybe of assistance.

CONCLUSION

In this chapter we have set out some of the basic principles which you should follow when revising for and sitting the examination. Many of the issues which we have touched upon here will be explored in more detail in the following chapters, where we will expand on these basic principles in the context of particular topics.

Our parting shot in this chapter is that, ultimately, success in examinations depends to a large extent upon the confidence of the examinee. If you accept the basic premise that examiners will play fair, then, if you have prepared properly, you will be able to approach the examination with a high degree of confidence.

3 COMPETENCE AND COMPELLABILITY; ABROGATION OF CORROBORATION

INTRODUCTION

Issues of the competence and compellability of witnesses are frequently fundamental to a wide range of possible examination questions in evidence. Until the passing of the Police and Criminal Evidence Act 1984 (the 1984 Act) it was certainly possible to set examination questions based entirely on such issues, but it is now much less likely that this will happen, because many of the outstanding problems of competence and compellability have been resolved both by that Act and by subsequent legislation. Nevertheless, the competence and compellability of witnesses is likely to appear on most examination papers somewhere or other, and it is quite possible that you will have to deal with such issues in conjunction with other topics. In addition, the topicality of many of the issues in this area, particularly in the context of child abuse cases, means that these topics are likely to remain fresh in the minds of any evidence lawyers for some time to come.

Corroboration used to be an interesting mainstay in many evidence courses. It had a perennial freshness, largely because of the steady flow of case law occasioned by the way in which issues of corroboration were able to set traps for unwary judges. Issues of corroboration often arose in the same context as questions of competence and compellability and it was, therefore, quite common to see these topics examined together. However, the Criminal Justice and Public Order Act 1994 (CJPOA 1994) has made sweeping changes to the previous law, as a consequence of which most of the law which previously existed is of historical sigificance only. Many of the technical rules which required the so-called corroboration warning have now gone, although there will still be circumstances where judges will wish to warn juries of the possible dangers of acting on the unsupported evidence of particular witnesses. We take the opportunity in this chapter to say a little about the difficulties which led to the changes contained in the CJPOA 1994, but from the point of view of examinations this area must be regarded as being of residual significance only, although in the context of assessed coursework there is undoubtedly some scope for challenging questions based around the developments in the law during the last few years.

COMPETENCE AND COMPELLABILITY

The rules on the competence and compellability of witnesses are relatively straightforward and are easily stated.

The first thing to remember is that, subject to a limited range of exceptions dealt with below, a witness who is competent is also compellable. In other words, a witness who is competent to give evidence in court, but refuses to do so for some reason, risks punishment for contempt of court. For the remainder of this chapter, where we talk about 'competence' then compellability is implied, unless we indicate otherwise.

The second basic proposition is that, in criminal cases, a competent witness is competent for either the defence or the prosecution. The only classes of witness who may not be competent or compellable for one or other of the defence or prosecution are the accused, any co-accused and the accused's spouse. The rules applicable to such witnesses are discussed below.

The third basic proposition is that there are few significant differences between the rules for criminal cases and the rules for civil cases. Because of the greater interest and complexity of the issues in criminal cases, it is generally going to be the case that questions of competence will be asked in the context of a criminal trial.

If we take as the basic working principle the proposition that all witnesses are competent and compellable for either side in either criminal or civil proceedings, there is a limited number of cases where that general principle may be displaced, namely, the cases of the accused, the accused's spouse, the co-accused, children and persons of defective intellect.

The Accused

The appropriate rules for the accused are relatively straightforward to state, although the implications of the changes to the position of the accused introduced by the CJPOA 1994 will, no doubt, take a number of years to work out. The removal of the so-called 'right to silence' previously enjoyed by the accused will have significant tactical implications for accused persons and their advisers in deciding whether an accused should give evidence on his own behalf, and any consideration of the strict legal rules on this matter will need to be balanced by an equally careful consideration of a decision whether or not to give evidence in the circumstances of any particular case.

In so far as the prosecution is concerned the position is absolutely strightforward — an accused person is never a competent witness for the prosecution at his own trial.

Since 1898 the accused has always been a competent witness in his own defence (before that date the most the accused could do was to make an unsworn statement from the dock — a right which was abolished by the Criminal Justice Act 1982). By virtue of s. 1(a) and (b) of the Criminal Evidence Act 1898 it was provided that an accused was not a compellable witness on his own behalf and that his failure to give evidence should not be the subject of any comment by the prosecution. All that has been changed by the CJPOA 1994. The accused remains a competent witness on his own behalf, but s. 1(a) and (b) have been repealed. Technically, the accused still cannot be compelled to give evidence, but ss. 34–37 of the CJPOA 1994 now provide an elaborate framework of provisions dealing with the inferences which may be permissibly drawn on account of the silence of the accused. You need to look at these provisions in detail for yourself and have a good knowledge of their contents. We have more to say on the topic of the right to silence later in the book in chapter 9, but s. 35(3) and (4) are particularly relevant here and provide as follows:

(3)   Where this subsection applies, the court or jury, in determining whether the accused is guilty of the offence charged, may draw such inferences as appear proper from the failure of the accused to give evidence or his refusal, without good cause, to answer any question.

(4)   This section does not render the accused compellable to give evidence on his own behalf, and he shall accordingly not be guilty of contempt of court by reason of a failure to do so.

The accused is not generally competent for the prosecution against a co-accused (see below) but he is competent, although not compellable, *for* a co-accused. Of course, in practice an accused will often not wish to rush into giving evidence for his co-accused, since it may well involve exculpating the co-accused at his own expense. Also, it will give both the prosecution and counsel for the co-accused an opportunity to cross-examine him about his own role in the offence charged. If an accused does not give evidence in his *own* defence, he cannot be so cross-examined by the prosecution or co-accused; the tactical implications of giving evidence *for* the co-accused in such circumstances are accordingly serious, and will not be taken up lightly.

The Accused's Spouse

The position of the accused's spouse was considerably simplified by the 1984 Act. Under the Act a spouse is competent to give evidence for the prosecution in any criminal proceedings against her (or his) husband (or wife). The spouse will only be compellable for the prosecution where the offence charged involved an assault on, injury to, or a threat of such injury to the spouse or to any person who at the material time appears to be under the age of 16. The spouse is also compellable where the offence charged is a sexual offence committed against a person under the age of 16, or, for example, where the offence consists of attempting, conspiring, aiding, abetting, counselling, procuring, or inciting to commit any of the above offences. You should examine s. 80 carefully, where you will find the complete list of the exceptional cases.

A spouse is always competent for the accused or any co-accused. She is compellable for the accused (except where she is jointly charged with him, unless the case against her has already been concluded) but she is only compellable for a co-accused where the accused is charged with one of the offences mentioned above.

The position of the divorced spouse is now clear. A divorcee is regarded as competent and compellable, as if she had never been married to the accused.

The overall effect on competence and compellability of the changes introduced by the 1984 Act was to simplify and clarify the law and a number of strange anomalies were removed.

The Co-accused

The position of the co-accused is slightly more complex. His position remains unaltered following the 1984 Act and is governed by the common law and the Criminal Evidence Act 1898.

From the point of view of general principle, the co-accused is not a competent witness for the prosecution, either with regard to the case against himself or with regard to the case against the accused. Nevertheless, there are a number of ways in which the co-accused can find himself competent against the accused:

(a) Following an acquittal after a decision to offer no evidence.

(b) Following a plea of guilty. You should note that it used to be thought that as a matter of principle the co-accused should not only have pleaded guilty, but should also have been sentenced. The Court of Appeal has cast some doubt on this principle (R v Weekes (1982) 74 Cr App R 161). However, the question is always one of discretion for the court, since the trial judge may not be in a position to sentence until he has heard the whole case.

(c)   Following the grant of a *nolle prosequi* (literally 'let us not proceed') by the Attorney-General. A *nolle prosequi* is an undertaking (which in practice is complied with) not to continue the proceedings against the co-accused. The effect is to remove the issue of his guilt or innocence from the jury, as a result of which the co-accused becomes a competent prosecution witness.

(d)   Following a separation of the trials of the accused and the co-accused (note the strong criticism of this practice in *R* v *Pipe* (1967) 51 Crim App R 17) but contrast the different approach in *R* v *Turner* (1975) 61 Cr App R 67).

Perhaps more importantly, it is worth realising that although the co-accused may not technically be a competent prosecution witness, there are several ways in which the evidence which the co-accused gives in his own defence can be utilised by the prosecution, both as regards the case against the co-accused and as regards the case against the accused. Thus, if the co-accused gives evidence in his own defence he can be cross-examined on it by the prosecution. This cross-examination might elicit evidence which implicates both the co-accused and the accused.

It may be that the essence of the evidence of the co-accused is to place the blame for the commission of the crime squarely on the shoulders of the accused. Such evidence is entirely admissible, and is evidence for all purposes in the case, including that of being evidence against the accused. The accused has some measure of protection against such allegations by the co-accused, in that he can call to his aid s. 1(f)(iii) of the Criminal Evidence Act 1898 and cross-examine the co-accused on his previous criminal record (if he has one) in order to destroy the credit of the co-accused (see chapter 7). Unfortunately for the accused, this may be too late because the damage might have already been done.

In the context of an examination question the important thing to remember when two or more people are tried jointly is that the question may be posing clear issues of competence.

Children

The whole question of the giving of evidence by children has been the subject of considerable discussion and debate in recent years. The reasons behind this have been centred on the growing appreciation of the difficulties of obtaining convictions in cases of child abuse, and the realisation that the evidence of children can, when subject to certain safeguards, form a reliable basis on which a conviction can stand. Of central significance was the enactment of the Criminal Justice Act 1991 (CJA 1991).

The Act provides for the evidence of all children under the age of 14 to be given unsworn (see CJA 1991, s. 52, and CJA 1988, s. 33A). Some commentators have argued that there are difficulties in interpreting the precise effect of this provision: see, for example, Spencer (1990) 140 NLJ 1750. However, the provision has the considerable merit of establishing a clear line between those cases where evidence is given sworn, and those where it is given unsworn.

The question of whether a child is competent to give evidence does not depend on whether the child has reached a particular age. Under s. 33A(2A) of the CJA 1988 it is provided that a child's evidence shall be received unless it appears to the court that the child is incapable of giving intelligible testimony.

Finally, you should note that children are now able to give unsworn evidence in civil cases should they fail to satisfy the judge that they are competent to give evidence on oath. This is provided for by s. 96 of the Children Act 1989 which states that if a child does not understand the nature of the oath he may give unsworn evidence if (a) he understands it is his duty to speak the truth; and (b) he has sufficient understanding to justify the evidence being received. The whole issue of child abuse and the rules of evidence relating to children is likely to continue to feature in evidence examinations. In this context you should be aware of certain related provisions already in force (for example, the possibility of 'live-link' testimony and the more liberal provisions for the admissibility of documentary hearsay under the CJA 1988). In addition, you should familiarise yourself with the additional provisions contained in the CJA 1991, most notably those allowing the substitution of a pre-recorded interview with a child witness for the child's evidence in chief in certain cases. For an analysis of the implications of all of this, see Birch's review in [1992] Crim LR 262.

Persons of Defective Intellect

The competence of persons of defective intellect to give evidence is governed by *R* v *Bellamy* (1986) 82 Cr App R 222. Essentially the matter is one for the judge, who must determine whether the witness has sufficient capacity to give evidence.

ABROGATION OF CORROBORATION

Background

Until the enactment of the CJPOA 1994 the law of corroboration was an area which always seemed to be topical. Its boundaries were constantly being redefined by the courts and it was always relatively easy to say something about the topic beyond a conventional recitation of the bare legal rules. The basic rules, which were subject to a number of relatively unimportant exceptions or variations, were well known. Historically the general principle was that the evidence of a single witness was enough, if believed, to justify a finding by a court. In other words, as long as the evidence was of good quality, it did not need to be confirmed by any supporting evidence. However, this basic rule was modified in three situations:

(a) Those cases where, as a matter of law, the corroboration of the evidence of certain witnesses was required.

(b) Those cases where, although corroboration was not required as a matter of law, a warning of the dangers of acting without corroboration had to be given to the jury. Textbooks often referred to these cases as cases where corroboration was required as a matter of practice. A warning of the dangers of acting on uncorroborated testimony was mandatory, even though a jury may have ultimately decided to convict without suitable corroborative testimony.

The principal situations where a corroboration warning was required were:

(i)   With regard to the evidence of accomplices testifying for the prosecution in criminal cases.

(ii)   Generally in sex cases (against victims of either sex) with regard to the evidence of the complainant.

(c) Those cases, on the fringe of the topic, although not falling within categories (a) or (b) above, where a trial judge may have felt it necessary, in the exercise of his discretion, to give a jury some kind of warning about the dangers of acting on the evidence of certain categories of witness. It was difficult, if not impossible, to categorise comprehensively the situations where such a discretionary warning might have been called for.

The Effect of the CJPOA 1994

The law in this area was completely recast by the CJPOA 1994. In the years leading up to the passage of the Act there had been a growing volume of criticism of the ways in which the rules on corroboration were inherently self-contradictory and problematic. There was also an ever-present risk, given the complexity of the traditional corroboration warning, that a trial judge might fall into error in his direction to the jury. Lord Ackner characterised the complexities involved in the following way in *R v Spencer* [1987] AC 128:

> The warning to be sufficient must explain why it is dangerous so to act . . . The jury are, of course, told that while as a general rule it is dangerous so to act, they are at liberty to do so if they feel sure that the uncorroborated witness is telling the truth. Where, however, there is evidence before the jury which they can properly consider to be corroborative evidence the

position becomes less simple. The trial judge has the added obligation of identifying such material and explaining to the jury that it is for them to decide whether to treat such evidence as corroboration.

The matter could also be very much more complicated than outlined above. Following the recommendations of the Law Commission in its Report 'Corroboration of Evidence in Criminal Trials', in 1991, s. 32(1) of the CJPOA 1994 now provides:

Any requirement whereby at a trial on indictment it is obligatory for the court to give the jury a warning about convicting the accused on the uncorroborated evidence of a person merely because that person is—

(a) an alleged accomplice of the accused, or
(b) where the offence charged is a sexual offence the person in respect of whom it is alleged to have been committed,

is hereby abrogated.

Section 32(3) goes on to provide:

(3) Any requirement that—

(a) is applicable at the summary trial of a person for an offence, and
(b) corresponds to the requirement mentioned in subsection (1) ...,

is hereby abrogated.

The straightforward effect of the above provisions is that the old style full corroboration warning rules have now been abrogated. However, if you have given some consideration in your course of study to the extent to which any of the pre-1994 law persists in this area, you will need to set this in the context of the overriding duty of a judge to put the case of the defendant fairly to the jury. This may require the judge to warn the jury where the credibility of a witness against the accused is doubtful. The Law Commission (*op. cit.*, paras. 4.11–4.15) gave consideration to the issue of how judges might address the need to give such warnings once the actual *requirement* of a corroboration warning was abolished. Its view was that with the abolition of the obligation to give a corroboration warning, the rules as to what is capable of being corroboration in law will have no continued standing or purpose. Following abolition of the requirement to give the classic corroboration warning judges are now free, in the exercise of their general discretion, to warn in terms which are appropriate to the facts of a case, but also to make use (or not) of any of the concepts and distinctions previously embodied in the detailed law on the meaning of 'corroboration' and dealing with what evidence was capable of being corroborative.

The abolition of the corroboration rules in the categories dealt with by s. 32 of the CJPOA 1994 does not, of course, directly impact on those situations where, before 1994, there was an obligation on a trial judge to warn the jury of the dangers of acting on certain types of evidence without exercising particular care. The two main areas which you should consider are, first, identification evidence and, secondly, the more general situation where judges are directing juries on how to deal with the evidence of witnesses who may have a purpose of their own to serve. In relation to the law relating to this aspect of identification evidence, the minimum you will need to know will be some kind of critique of the pre-1976 law on identification evidence (preferably culled from the report of the Devlin Committee on Evidence of Identification in Criminal Cases), a good understanding of the principles emerging from the decision of a full Court of Appeal in *R* v *Turnbull* [1977] QB 224, together with an appreciation of the way the law has developed in the years since *Turnbull*. You should be prepared, in revising this area, to come to some conclusions on such questions as the following:

(a)   Why was there a need, by 1976, to do something about evidence of identification?

(b)   Why is the Devlin Committee Report unlikely ever to receive legislative effect?

(c)   What are the differences between the proposals of Devlin and the legal regime which now applies following *Turnbull*?

In relation to the situations where judges direct juries in cases of witnesses who may have a purpose of their own to serve, there has been some discussion in recent years of the rules which should (or should not) apply where a prosecution witness has an undoubted purpose of his own to serve while giving evidence. The evidence of such a witness may be very suspect. What do the courts do to protect the accused from its use? Historically, accomplices did not form part of this category, simply because there was, before 1994, a mandatory corroboration warning requirement in respect of accomplices. Post-1994, fairness will inevitably require that, in some cases, an appropriate warning is given to the jury. Thus, in *R* v *Makanjuola* (1996) Crim LR 44 the Court of Appeal ruled that a judge retained a discretion as to what, if any, warning should be given. The decision whether or not to give a direction to the jury depends on the circumstances of the case, the issues raised and the contents and quality of the evidence of the relevant witness or witnesses. The Court also indicated that there needs to be an evidential basis for suggesting that a witness is unreliable — in other words, there needs to be something more than a suggestion to that effect by counsel.

Witnesses with a purpose of their own to serve may have very strong motives for giving perjured evidence but it was clear, following the decision in *R v Beck* [1982] 1 All ER 807, that a traditional corroboration warning as classically understood was not required. A case establishing a similar point in a slightly different context was *R v Wilkins* [1985] Crim LR 222. These cases were part of a wider pattern of cases which emerged during the 1980s which indicated the great reluctance of the courts to extend the requirement of a corroboration warning beyond the then existing categories: see also *R v Spencer* [1987] AC 128.

Two very useful articles where the impact of the CJPOA 1994 is reviewed are Mirfield, 'Corroboration After the 1994 Act' [1995] Crim LR 448 and Birch, 'Corroboration — Goodbye to all that' [1995] Crim LR 524. Both subject the effect of abolition by s. 32 to extensive critical analysis and review in full the continuing importance of *R v Beck*.

PLANNING YOUR REVISION

Competence and Compellability

The overriding thing to remember when learning this topic is that essentially you are concerned with a group of rigid rules which must be learnt. Much of the controversy in this area in the past centred on the anomalous rules governing the position of the accused's spouse and divorced spouse and in the attempts to try to reconcile those rules with the underlying principles which were supposed to explain why the rules were as they were. The Police and Criminal Evidence Act 1984 and subsequent legislation have introduced a welcome measure of rationalisation into this topic and have resolved many of the difficult problems which had subsisted. As a consequence much of the attraction of competence and compellability as an examination topic, at least in its own right, has disappeared. This does not mean, however, that these topics can be safely ignored. This is because any question which involves a discussion of the evidence of various kinds of witness (as opposed to a question requiring a discussion of various kinds of evidence) will quite possibly need some kind of discussion of these rules. Admittedly, such issues may be no more than preliminary matters which have to be cleared out of the way before going on to discuss the real heart of the particular question which has been asked, but it would be foolish to sacrifice marks on an examination question on matters so straightforward as these.

Clearly, in approaching your revision of these areas, you will need to take into account any particular emphasis which your course has taken, but whatever particular bias your course has had, you ought to know at the very least the basic rules discussed above. Following the legislative activity of the last decade most of the previously existing difficulties have been resolved and probably the most complex rules which subsist are those which govern the position of the co-accused. These rules are to be found in the Criminal Evidence Act 1898 and in the common law. In dealing with the position of the co-accused you should tie in with your revision in this area the rules covering the cross-examination of a person when being tried in the same proceedings as the accused under s. 1(f)(iii) of the Criminal Evidence Act 1898. This last matter is dealt with in chapter 7.

You will need to have a good understanding of the effect of ss. 34–37 of the CJPOA 1994 in relation to inferences which juries may be entitled to draw from the accused's failure to mention facts when questioned or charged (s. 34), from his failure to give evidence at his trial (s. 35) or from his failure to account for objects in his possession or his presence at a particular place (ss. 36 and 37). It is quite likely that you may have covered this area as a special topic in its own right, but it is equally possible that these matters have been covered in the context of competence and compellability, or in the context of the law relating to confessions. We return to these matters later in the book in chapter 7, but two points you need to keep in mind are that, first, this is a new, topical and controversial area of law which is a very likely examination topic for some time to come and secondly, that it is an easy matter for an examiner to slip issues relating to the right to silence into a wide range of possible problem questions as one of the issues to be considered. You need to be prepared for this.

ABROGATION OF THE CORROBORATION RULE

The enactment of the CJPOA 1994 marked the culmination of a long period of growing dissatisfaction with the arbitrary and confusing nature of the traditional rules on corroboration. The clear abrogation of those rules by the Act has, at a stroke, removed a great deal of arcane and dated jurisprudence from the law of evidence. The residual matters which are left — such as the kind of warning and comment which a judge may need to give in cases of disputed identification, or more generally where a witness may be unreliable because he has a purpose of his own to serve — will be areas of judicial evolution in the future.

In relation to identification evidence the central case which you will need to use is, of course, R v Turnbull [1977] QB 224. As part of your revision of this topic you will have mastered the basic guidelines to judges which spring from the case and you will understand when the Turnbull principles can and cannot be brought into play.

The essential rules which emerge from Turnbull are clear. First, whenever the case against the accused depends wholly or substantially on the correctness of identification evidence (even though it comes from more than one witness) which the accused alleges is mistaken, the trial judge must warn the jury of the special need for caution before they convict in reliance on the identification evidence. Additionally, he must go on to tell the jury why there is such need for caution and point out to them that a mistaken witness (or witnesses) can be convincing. There is no particular formula which the judge has to use. The judge must then go on to direct the jury to examine closely the circumstances in which the identification was made.

Where the identification evidence is of good quality (e.g., where there was a long observation by the witness, and his view was not obstructed by passing traffic, the light was good, etc.) this can be left to the jury, after the warning outlined above has been given. However, where the identification evidence is poor then, unless there is other evidence which supports the correctness of the identification, the case should be withdrawn from the jury.

The fact that two witnesses have made the same identification does not affect the position, although following *R v Weeder* (1980) 71 Cr App R 228 an identification by one witness may be used to support identification by another, as long as the jury are warned that a number of honest witnesses can be mistaken.

You will probably realise that there has been a steady stream of reported cases since *R v Turnbull* where particular aspects of identification evidence have been raised. By all means look at these cases, but we would emphasise the need to be completely familiar with *R v Turnbull* itself, where the law is subjected to a thorough and helpful appraisal by the Court of Appeal.

In the context of considering the kind of warning, if any, which a judge may now have to give following the abrogation of the corroboration rules, *R v Beck* and *R v Spencer* [1987] AC 128 are important decisions and will provide you with a solid foundation on which you can build your consideration of the subsequent development of the law; you should also look at the decision in *R v Cheema* (1994) 98 Cr App R 195.

POSSIBLE EXAMINATION QUESTIONS

The major changes which have been introduced by the CJPOA 1994 will undoubtedly lead to a steady stream of case law in the future as the new principles which have been introduced are tested and developed. As always, your revision of these topics will need to be informed by the weight and emphasis which your particular programme of study has followed. Prior to the abrogation of the corroboration rule, complete problem questions linking issues of competence, compellability and corroboration were commonplace and often explored many of the detailed complexities surrounding the classic corroboration warning. All this has now changed and in the future it is much more likely that issues of competence and compellability will appear as just one element of a larger question in which other issues are examined. However, the newness of the law under which juries are able to draw inferences from the silence of the accused, and its continuing topicality, mean that this is an area which is very likely to appear in one form or another on the paper. As with other issues relating to competence and compellability, these matters may arise in the context of a more wide-ranging problem question, but you should also be prepared for a focussed and testing essay on this issue.

As far as the abrogation of the corroboration rule is concerned, the consequence has been a considerable simplification in this area of law. Unless the course you have followed has taken a particular historical emphasis, or has concentrated on the changes in the law over the passage of the CJPOA 1994, the old categories of case where a full corroboration warning was required are now only of residual interest. Nevertheless, the nature of warnings which judges will continue to give juries in the cases of witnesses who may have a strong motive not to tell the truth will, no doubt, continue to exercise the courts for some time to come and may well provide a fertile ground for appeals in the future. In this context you should certainly be aware of the particular problems which surround the admission and use of disputed evidence of identification — this is a matter which frequently appears in problem questions and, once again depending on the focus of your particular course, may well form the subject of a dedicated essay question. You should also understand the nature of an obligation on a trial judge to warn the jury of the potential unreliability of a witness with a purpose of his own to serve.

We would offer the same advice in this area, as in others, with regard to the need to use and refer to the academic literature on the subject. We have set out below some of the key recent articles in this area and we recommend that you make full use of them.

CONCLUSION

We have not been able in the space of this chapter to deal with the multitude of issues which these topics can generate, but the approach we have taken above gives an insight into the way in which you can apply your knowledge to the relevant issues. The point to remember about the topics dealt with in this chapter is that they can be analysed and learned in a logical and ordered way. Many of the rules we have discussed are firmly established, while a few are a little more open textured. But they all contribute to an orderly legal structure which you can readily understand. If there are any easy marks to be picked up in an evidence examination, this is one of the places where you will find them.

FURTHER READING

Birch, 'Corroboration — Goodbye to All That' (1995) Crim LR 524.

Jackson, 'The insufficiency of identification evidence based on personal impression' [1986] Crim LR 203.

Jones, 'The evidence of a three-year-old child' [1987] Crim LR 677.

Mirfield, 'Corroboration After the 1994 Act' (1995) Crim LR 448.

Spencer, 'Child witnesses, video technology and the law of evidence' [1987] Crim LR 76.

Corroboration of Evidence in Criminal Trials (Law Commission Report No. 202, Cmnd 1620).

Report to the Secretary of State for the Home Department of the Departmental Committee on Evidence of Identification in Criminal Cases (Chairman: Lord Devlin) (House of Commons paper No. 338, Session 1975-76).

4 THE BURDEN AND STANDARD OF PROOF

THE BURDEN OF PROOF

All evidence courses deal with the law relating to the burden of proof. It forms the basis of the whole subject, determining which party to any proceedings is required to prove the facts in issue in order to succeed.

Most of the difficulties which students experience in this area arise from the fact that the one term 'burden of proof' has been used in more than one sense. Further, the courts have often not made it clear in which sense they are using the term. The textbook writers have, it is true, used several different terms, but unfortunately have differed from each other in the meaning they have given to them! As Hoffmann puts it, 'There is probably no part of the law of evidence more in need of a linguistic purge' (*South African Law of Evidence*, 3rd ed. (1981), p. 385). There has been much academic debate on the whole question. This, however, provides very little consolation to the student studying evidence for the first time who is looking for a secure base from which to obtain a grasp of the fundamentals of the subject, a base from which to examine deeper questions. Where do you start? There is one safe starting point; there are two kinds of burden which must be kept distinct the legal burden and the evidential burden.

THE LEGAL BURDEN

This is the obligation which lies upon one party to prove the truth of a particular fact which is in issue in the case and is vital to the success of his case. It follows that if that party fails to discharge this burden this will be fatal to his case. In other words, the incidence of the legal burden decides which party will fail on a given issue if, after hearing all the evidence, the court is left in doubt. We shall refer to this burden as the legal burden, as being the most popular and useful term. You should note, however, that several other terms have been used to refer to it, for example the 'persuasive burden', the 'burden of proof on the pleadings', the 'fixed burden of proof', the 'ultimate burden', the 'probative burden', the 'burden at the end of the day' or simply the 'burden of proof proper'. The latter has much sense in it, since as we shall see the discharge of the other burden proves nothing. Always examine closely the usage of these terms in judgments and textbooks. Is the writer using them consistently?

It becomes crucial to decide which party bears the legal burden when all the evidence on both sides has been presented. This is because it is at this point that the trial judge must direct the tribunal of fact (which may, of course, be himself) as to who bears this burden on each of the facts in issue. If, at that point, the tribunal of fact is in doubt on an issue it must find against the party who bears the legal burden. Of course, most cases involve more than one issue, and the legal burden upon the different issues may, as we shall see, be variously distributed between the parties.

THE EVIDENTIAL BURDEN

'The evidential burden is the obligation to show, if called upon to do so, that there is sufficient evidence to raise an issue as to the existence or non-existence of a fact in issue, due regard being had to the standard of proof demanded of the party under such obligation' (*Cross and Tapper on Evidence*, p. 122).

The stages at which this obligation has to be considered are, first, at the start of the trial to decide which party should begin on a particular issue and, second, at the close of that party's evidence, to decide whether enough evidence has been shown on his behalf to require the other party to produce evidence in reply.

Suppose A has been charged with theft and has elected trial before judge and jury. The prosecution bears both the evidential and legal burden with regard to the elements of theft. This means that with regard to each of these elements it must (a) produce enough evidence to prevent the judge from withdrawing the issue from the jury; and (b) convince the jury. It follows from this that if the judge rules that there is not enough evidence on any one of the elements of theft to justify its being considered by the jury, then if the prosecution, as here, also bears the legal burden on that issue, it must inevitably fail on that issue. It cannot possibly discharge the legal burden.

Now, suppose that the judge rules that the evidence adduced by the prosecution is enough to go to the jury. Does that mean that it must win the case? Of course not. The jury still have to be convinced and they might not be. There are many possible reasons for this. Perhaps they will not draw the necessary inferences from the evidence, or perhaps they simply do not believe that the prosecution witnesses are telling the truth or that their perceptions were accurate and reliable. It is true, however, that once the prosecution has discharged the evidential burden, then the defendant, if he adduces no evidence on the issue in question, does run the risk of losing. This is simply common sense and has led writers to talk about this bearing a 'tactical' burden (yet another term!) to adduce some counter-evidence. At the end of the day, however, the issue will go to the jury as one of fact.

The term 'evidential burden' is being used more frequently by the courts, as is the term 'burden of adducing evidence', which is equally sound. Wigmore's reference to 'the duty of passing the judge' illustrates the essence of the matter. (*Treatise on the Anglo-American System of Evidence*, 3rd ed., vol. 9, para. 2486).

WHERE THE LEGAL BURDEN LIES

Civil Cases

It is a basic principle of our legal system that if a person desires a court to take action on his behalf he must prove his case to the court's satisfaction. This is usually expressed in the maxim 'He who asserts must prove' and means that the burden of proving any vital fact in issue lies on the person who must establish the issue in order to succeed. As to discovering what are the facts in issue in a particular case you must look at the substantive law and also at the pleadings since the latter will show whether any particular fact is admitted or denied. Each party must prove any fact which is a necessary element of his case.

Let us illustrate this by some straightforward examples. Suppose that A (the plaintiff) is suing B (the defendant) for negligence. Here, A bears the legal burden of proving the duty of care, breach of that duty by B and consequential loss to A. If B's defence is a mere denial of A's case then no burden rests upon him. He is simply putting A to proof of his case. However, if B's defence is to raise a specific defence, for example to plead contributory negligence, then the burden of proving that defence is upon him. Similarly, if C is suing D for breach of contract, then C must prove the existence of the contract, the due performance of conditions precedent, breach of contract by D and consequent loss to C. Again, if D raises a specific defence, say infancy, then he must prove it. In many civil actions, therefore, the burden of the issues may be divided, each party having one or more imposed upon him.

There is much good sense to be found on these general matters in the judgment of Brown LJ in *Abrath v North Eastern Railway Co.* (1883) 11 QBD

440, as well as an illustration of the point that a necessary element of a case may occasionally consist in the proof of a negative fact rather than a positive one.

If it is unclear on the decided authorities as to where the burden of proof lies on a particular issue, then it is a question of construction of, for example, the relevant statute, if any, or contract. If this yields no answer, then on the whole considerations of public policy have been treated by the courts as decisive.

'In such cases, the courts have inclined to require proof of the party to whom the least difficulty or embarrassment will be caused by the burden, and in deciding this, a sound rule of thumb is to require proof of a positive rather than a negative proposition' (*Murphy on Evidence*, p. 90).

There are many examples in the law reports of the approach of the courts. We suggest that the following should be examined: *Joseph Constantine Steamship Line Ltd* v *Imperial Smelting Corporation Ltd* [1942] AC 154; *Levison* v *Patent Steam Carpet Cleaning Co. Ltd* [1978] QB 69; *The Glendarroch* [1894] P 226; *Munro, Brice & Co.* v *War Risks Association Ltd* [1918] 2 KB 78.

Criminal Cases

The general rule

Here there are no pleadings by which a defendant may raise separate issues and so assume legal burdens. In a criminal case a plea of 'not guilty' puts in issue every material fact.

The general rule in criminal cases is that the legal burden of proving every element of the crime charged is on the prosecution and remains there throughout the trial. This is of course only in accordance with the notion that 'he who asserts must prove'. Every person is presumed innocent until proved guilty. The general rule was finally laid down definitively by the House of Lords in *Woolmington* v *DPP* [1935] AC 462. You will recall that the defendant was charged with the murder of his wife from whom he was separated. He gave evidence to the effect that whilst endeavouring to induce her to return to live with him by threatening to shoot himself, he had shot and killed her accidentally. The jury were directed that, once it was proved that the defendant shot his wife, it was for him to prove the absence of *mens rea*, although *mens rea* was an essential element of the charge of murder. Lord Sankey LC expressed the crucial point in this way: 'Throughout the web of the English Criminal Law one golden thread is always to be seen, that it is the duty of the prosecution to prove the prisoner's guilt subject to . . . the defence of insanity and subject also to any statutory exception.' Please try not to repeat the performance of a student mentioned by Professor Glanville Williams in his *Textbook of Criminal Law* who referred instead to the 'cobweb' of English criminal law!

Incidentally a few moments of entirely innocent humour can be obtained from a perusal of the note allegedly written by Reginald Woolmington and found in his pocket. You will find it reproduced at p. 464 of the report.

Exceptions

The *legal* burden is put on the *accused* in the following situations:

(a) *Insanity*. This is the sole common law exception and was mentioned specifically by Lord Sankey in *Woolmington*. Therefore, if an accused person raises the defence of insanity to a charge, he must prove it. As we shall see, however, the standard of proof required of him is less than that generally required of the prosecution.

(b) *Express statutory exceptions*. In a number of cases statute expressly imposes a legal burden of proving a particular issue upon the accused. There are many such instances, those most commonly dealt with in evidence courses being:

(i)   The defence of diminished responsibility (which is a defence only to a charge of murder) under s. 2 of the Homicide Act 1957.

(ii)   Charges of possessing an offensive weapon, where lawful authority or reasonable excuse must be proved by the accused.

(iii)   Charges under the Prevention of Corruption Act 1906, where gifts to an official are deemed to have been given and received corruptly unless the contrary is proved. So, if the jury are in doubt on this fact, they must convict!

It is very unlikely that you would be asked a question involving some other express statutory exception unless this had been dealt with specifically by your lecturer. The above are simply illustrations of some practical significance.

Remember, of course, that the burden imposed by these exceptions applies only to the issue dealt with by the statute. The prosecution's duty to prove all the other elements of the offence is quite unaffected.

An express, statutory reversal of the legal burden which is of more general significance is s. 101 of the Magistrates' Courts Act 1980:

Where the defendant to an information or complaint relies for his defence on any exception, exemption, proviso, excuse or qualification, whether or not it accompanies the description of the offence or matter of complaint in the enactment creating the offence or on which the complaint is founded, the burden of proving the exception, exemption, proviso, excuse or qualification shall be on him; and this notwithstanding that the information or complaint contains an allegation negativing the exception, exemption, proviso, excuse or qualification.

What is this cumbrous section designed to do? It is not so difficult as it seems. It means that where the offence charged is made by the enactment creating it to be subject to limited exceptions, permitting the behaviour in question when it is committed by persons of a certain class, possessing certain qualifications or holding certain licences, a legal burden rests on the accused. An obvious example would be the offence of driving a motor vehicle on a road without being the holder of a current driving licence. In order to decide whether s. 101 is applicable it is necessary to decide whether the words of the statute alleged to amount to an exception etc. are an integral part of the definition of the offence, or rather the equivalent of a defence. In practice, the application of s. 101 has been somewhat hit-and-miss (see Smith, 'The Presumption of Innocence' (1987) 38 NILQ 223, at pp. 231–236).

Section 101 is confined in its application to magistrates' courts. However, in *R v Hunt* [1987] AC 352, the House of Lords held that s. 101 sets out the common law rules on the subject. This is very doubtful historically, but obviously it makes sense that the question of which party bears the burden of proof on an issue should not depend on whether the offence is tried summarily or on indictment.

(c) *Implied statutory exceptions*. Even where there is no express statutory reversal of the golden rule it may be held that the legislature has impliedly reversed the legal burden. This is a subject on which the authorities have been fraught with uncertainty. In previous editions of this book we dealt at some length with the controversial case of *R v Edwards* [1975] QB 27. In order to understand this area properly, you still need to be familiar with the significance of that decision, and with some of the academic literature which it spawned. However, there is now a House of Lords, decision, *R v Hunt* [1987] AC 352, referred to earlier, which recognises the possibility of an implied statutory reversal of the burden of proof. What does remain in some doubt is exactly when it may be said that such an exception arises, and whether the approach in *R v Hunt* is the appropriate one. We return to this on p. 56.

WHERE THE EVIDENTIAL BURDEN LIES

The general rule, which applies to both civil and criminal cases, is, as one would expect, that the party bearing the legal burden on an issue also bears the evidential burden on that issue. As far as civil cases are concerned there is, for our purposes, nothing further to say since no problems arise.

As far as criminal cases are concerned, the general rule can be illustrated by looking again at *Woolmington v DPP* [1935] AC 462. If the facts of that case were to recur, the prosecution would have to adduce evidence fit to be left to the jury of the essential elements of the crime of murder, i.e., that the accused killed the victim and did so with malice aforethought.

Similarly, where the accused, as an exception to the general rule, bears the legal burden of proving a defence, e.g., insanity, then he will also bear the evidential burden on the issue.

This is all straightforward. What is a little more complicated, but backed by sound reason, is the fact that with regard to most common law defences it is settled that, although the prosecution bears the legal burden of disproving them, the accused must 'lay a proper foundation' for them. In other words, an evidential burden is put on him. The reason behind this is that it would be unfair and totally impracticable to require the prosecution to anticipate defences which may or may not be raised. As Hale CJ once put it, this would be 'like leaping before one come to the stile' (*Sir Ralph Bovy's case* (1684) 1 Vent 217).

The most important of such cases are:

(a) provocation;
(b) self-defence;
(c) duress;
(d) non-insane automatism;
(e) use of force in the prevention of crime;
(f) intoxication;
(g) mechanical defect (as a reason for an accident rather than careless driving);
(h) reasonable excuse for failing to supply a specimen for a laboratory test in excess-alcohol cases;
(i) impossibility as a defence to common law conspiracy.

You would do well to read Lord Goddard CJ's judgment in *R* v *Lobell* [1957] 1 QB 547. In addition, you will find a clear statement of the relevant issues in the judgment of Devlin J in *Hill* v *Baxter* [1958] 1 QB 277.

The examples in the list above are well settled. There may be others, but this is a more difficult question which will be examined later. What must be kept clearly in mind is the distinction between defences for which the accused bears an evidential burden and the defences we examined earlier for which the *legal* burden is put on the accused. Failure to draw this distinction may lead to difficulties in the examination.

Finally, just a note that in addition to these common law cases, a statute will often be interpreted so as to place an evidential burden on a particular issue on the accused. An example is s. 25 of the Theft Act 1968.

THE STANDARD OF PROOF

There is no point whatsoever in mastering the law relating to the burden of proof in civil and crimnal cases without also understanding what standard of proof is required.

We have seen that one party to any proceedings must persuade the court of the truth of any fact in issue on which he bears the burden of proof. It follows then that the evidence which this party calls must be more persuasive than that of his opponent if he is to succeed. If the evidence is equally balanced then the party bearing the burden of proof will lose on that issue. But, how *much* more persuasive must his evidence be, in order to succeed?

> There are few things about which anyone can say that he feels absolutely certain, but short of this point there is a wide spectrum of possible degrees of conviction. One may say that, on the evidence, the happening of an event was remotely possible, reasonably possible, more probable than not, very probable, almost certain. (Hoffmann, *The South African Law of Evidence*, pp. 363-4.)

The standard of proof is going to differ in different cases and is likely to depend on the consequences of a positive finding in the particular proceedings. Therefore, we could expect a higher standard in criminal cases where the consequences of a conviction may be so serious for the accused. This is reflected in the present law. However, civil matters, such as those involving the possible future welfare of children, can be vitally important and some regulatory offences, although given the label 'criminal', are arguably not so serious. In these factors lies the main problem for those looking for certainty in the law. What can be said for now is that different standards are recognised for civil and for criminal cases. As for their exact statement and application, this is far less certain, and we shall return to this question.

A helpful statement is that of Denning J in *Miller v Minister of Pensions* [1947] 2 All ER 372:

> [The degree of cogency required in a criminal case before an accused person is found guilty] is well settled. It need not reach certainty, but it must carry a high degree of probability. Proof beyond reasonable doubt does not mean proof beyond the shadow of a doubt. The law would fail to protect the community if it admitted fanciful possibilities to deflect the course of justice. If the evidence is so strong against a man as to leave only a remote possibility in his favour which can be dismissed with the sentence 'of course it is possible, but not in the least probable', the case is proved beyond reasonable doubt, but nothing short of that will suffice. . . .
>
> [The degree of cogency required to discharge a burden in a civil case] is well settled. It must carry a reasonable degree of probability, but not so high as is required in a criminal case. If the evidence is such that the tribunal can say: 'We think it more probable than not', the burden is discharged, but if the probabilities are equal, it is not.

This clearly indicates the existence of two standards. In civil cases, the party bearing the burden must simply tip the scales in his favour. In criminal cases, although scientific certainty is not required, there must be proof beyond reasonable doubt.

Directions to the Jury in Criminal Cases

What continues to remain in some doubt is precisely how the criminal standard should be explained to the jury. The hallowed expression, of course, is proof 'beyond reasonable doubt' but an alternative formulation now well recognised is 'satisfied so that they feel sure' (or more simply 'sure of guilt'). The courts have stated further that there is no set form of words. What matters is whether the judge has succeeded in stressing that high standard which the jury must seek.

> If the jury are made to understand that they have to be satisfied and must not return a verdict against a defendant unless they feel sure, and that the onus is all the time on the prosecution and not on the defence, then whether the judge uses one form of language or another is neither here nor there (Lord Goddard CJ in *R* v *Kritz* [1950] 1 KB 82, approved in *Walters* v *R* [1969] 2 AC 26).

It is possible, however, to state categorically that certain formulae are not adequate. Examples would be: 'satisfied' (by itself); 'pretty certain'; 'reasonably sure'; 'satisfied so that you are reasonably sure'.

It is quite clear that in those cases where the accused bears the legal burden on an issue, the standard of proof is the civil standard (*R* v *Carr-Briant* [1943] KB 607).

PLANNING YOUR REVISION

This topic is one that is fairly self-contained. It is true that an examiner may ask about the burden and standard of proof as a minor part of a question concerned chiefly with other matters. More often the topic is dealt with on its own. You should remember, however, that the question of presumptions, which is dealt with in the next chapter, may affect the burden of proof in a particular case. The two topics should be studied together.

With regard to revising burdens and standards, you must first master the basic distinction between the legal and evidential burdens. As to the rules concerning the incidence of the legal burden, and those concerning the standard of proof, these are easily assimilated. There are two revision matters which we would stress on this topic.

(a) It is essential to know precisely when the accused bears the *legal* burden of proof and also when he merely bears an evidential burden. These two situations are frequently made the subject of a problem question. An example is considered later in this chapter.

(b) As we have tried to make clear elsewhere, an examiner is looking for something outside the ordinary run-of-the-mill answer. He is looking for critical awareness on the part of the candidate, an ability to examine the rationale behind the rules and the policy implications which may be involved in them. The subject-matter of this chapter may give you an opportunity to exploit this. Questions in this area will often be of either an essay type or part essay, part problem. The actual rules of law can generally be quickly stated or applied to the facts of a problem. These are the matters which we suggest that you might examine in more detail:

(i) As we mentioned briefly earlier, with regard to the standard of proof, certain occurrences are inherently more improbable than others and are fraught with more serious consequences if proved. Therefore, depending on the issue, there may be within each standard variations in the amount of evidence required. This was first stated with some precision by Denning LJ in *Bater* v *Bater* [1951] P 35:

> It is of course true that by our law a higher standard of proof is required in criminal cases than in civil cases. But this is subject to the qualification that there is no absolute standard in either case. In criminal cases the charge must be proved beyond reasonable doubt, but there may be degrees of proof within that standard....
>
> So also in civil cases, the case may be proved by a preponderance of probability, but there may be degrees of probability within that standard. The degree depends on the subject-matter. A civil court, when considering a charge of fraud, will naturally require for itself a higher degree of probability than that which it would require when asking if negligence is established. It does not adopt so high a degree as a criminal court, even when it is considering a charge of a criminal nature; but still it does require a degree of probability which is commensurate with the occasion.

The view expressed here was adopted by Morris LJ in *Hornal* v *Neuberger Products Ltd* [1957] 1 QB 247:

> Though no court and no jury would give less careful attention to issues lacking gravity than to those marked by it, the very elements of gravity become a part of the whole range of circumstances which have to be weighed in the scale when deciding as to the balance of probabilities.

This approach has been accepted in subsequent cases (see, for example, *Re Dellow's Will Trusts* [1964] 1 WLR 451; *R* v *Secretary of State for the Home Department (ex parte Khawaja)* [1984] AC 74; *R* v *Hampshire County Council (ex parte Ellerton)* [1985] 1 WLR 749; but cf. the note of caution expressed by Edmund Davies LJ in *Bastable* v *Bastable* [1968] 1 WLR 1685).

Closely associated with this issue is the question of the proof of crimes in civil cases. On occasions one party to a civil matter may be alleging conduct that amounts to a crime. For instance, suppose that A has referred to B as a 'bigamist' and B has sued him for defamation. A now raises the defence of justification. This involves him in proving that B was guilty of bigamy, a criminal offence. What standard of proof applies, the criminal or the civil? The answer is the latter (*Hornal* v *Neuberger Products Ltd*), but again you must bear in mind what we have said earlier, that the more serious the allegation the more cogent is the evidence required to overcome the unlikelihood of what is alleged and thus to prove it.

Other common situations are where a plaintiff sues for damages for conspiracy to defraud, or where a plaintiff claims on a fire insurance policy and the defendant alleges that the plaintiff started the fire and was guilty of the crime of arson.

Analogous to these cases is the question of the standard of proof in matrimonial causes. At one time the rule was that matrimonial offences had to be proved to the criminal standard of proof. However, this rule was weakened by the decision of the House of Lords in *Blyth* v *Blyth* [1966] AC 643 that condonation as a bar to matrimonial relief need not be disproved beyond reasonable doubt. Further, the replacement of the idea of the matrimonial offence by the doctrine of the irretrievable breakdown of marriage also implies a different approach. As Ormrod J stated in *Pheasant* v *Pheasant* [1972] Fam 202:

> It would be consistent with the spirit of the new legislation if this problem were now to be approached more from the point of view of breach of obligation than in terms of the now outmoded idea of the matrimonial offence.

There is a useful review of the authorities in *Bastable* v *Bastable* [1968] 1 WLR 1684. Although there is no direct decision overruling the older authorities, this question now seems to be a dead issue. It would be wise, however, for you to examine whether any particular emphasis is given to it on your particular course. If not, then our advice is not to go any further than obtaining an outline knowledge of the courts' approach to it.

With respect to criminal cases, Professor J. C. Smith (*Criminal Evidence*, p. 37) expresses well the difficulty of the theory that there may be many different standards of proof:

It may well be true that in practice the trier of fact will be less ready to find the case proved where the charge is very grave than where the offence is relatively trivial; but it is difficult to see how this can be translated into a rule of law. A rule of law must be capable of communication to a jury. If an idea is incapable of articulation, it cannot be a rule of law. A judge cannot direct a jury that they must be 95 per cent sure of this and 90 per cent sure of that.

(ii) Another question which you might examine in more detail concerns the difficulties involved in directing the jury in a criminal case on the standard of proof. One may note the campaign of Lord Goddard in the 1950s to abolish the use of the phrase 'beyond reasonable doubt' though he later tempered this opinion to the extent of saying that the traditional formula was *one* of those which were acceptable, although he did not personally prefer it. The attempt of judges, given this new freedom, to invent new ways of expressing the standard of proof was something of a catastrophe. In 1961 the Court of Criminal Appeal expressed disapproval of the formula used by the trial judge in no fewer than seven cases!

Quite often in setting problem questions, examiners put a particular inadmissible form of direction in the mouth of a trial judge. It is useful then also to be aware of formulae which have been disapproved by the courts. Here are some of them: 'pretty certain'; 'reasonably sure'; 'satisfied so that you are reasonably sure'; 'satisfied'.

Yet, suppose that the jury return to ask for further guidance from a trial judge on this matter. Is he to say nothing? If not, how can he avoid devising a new way of expressing the standard and does this not cause uncertainty in the law and risk of injustice? Certainly, trial judges have not been loath to make such attempts. For example, a reasonable doubt was said to be 'something to which you can assign a reason.... [T]he sort of matter which might influence you if you were to consider some business matter. A matter, for example, of a mortgage concerning your house' (*R* v *Ching* (1976) 63 Cr App R 7.) This direction was upheld. In *Walters* v *R* [1969] 2 AC 26 the Privy Council approved the reference to the personal affairs of the jurors, but added a qualification that the comparison must be with affairs of importance in their lives. Can the matter of the mortgage really be equated with a question of murder?

Remember, also, that the law must be seen in context. How do jurors in reality approach questions of this kind? There are research studies both in this country and abroad. An excellent short account, together with much else that is of value, is given by Professor Eggleston in his book, *Evidence, Proof and Probability*, ch. 9. Related to this are the recent attempts to apply mathematics and probability theory to the assessment of the standard of proof. A lot has been written on this question, much of it accessible only to the mathematician, but there is a useful short account in *Cross and Tapper on Evidence*, pp. 172–75.

Finally, how do we justify the high standard in criminal cases? The great majority of those who stand trial are guilty. Should doubts therefore be resolved in the favour of the prosecution? *Is* it in fact better that 10 guilty men should escape than one innocent man should suffer? It is generally accepted that the present rule in criminal cases is appropriate, but, if so, does this not reflect on other areas of the law of evidence? If the standard is to be so high, should it also continue to be possible for the accused to have the right not to testify and so shield himself from cross-examination by the prosecution? The question is tempered, of course, by the recent reforms in the so-called 'right to silence'. These matters are discussed by Professor Cross (1970) 11 JSPTL 66, and by Stephen, *History of the Criminal Law*, vol. 1, pp. 354, 438.

Knowledge in depth of these matters on the part of a student indicates an ability to look further than simply at the paper rules of the subject, and is evidence of a critical awareness. These things are given credit by an examiner.

EXAMINATION QUESTIONS

Questions on the burden and standard of proof come in all shapes and sizes. They may be very narrow or range over the whole subject. We have even seen recently the following question: 'Compare the rules as to the burden and standard of proof in civil matters with those in criminal proceedings, with reference to decided cases'. Just how on earth this is meant to sort out the able student from the plodder we do not know. In its present form it is likely to inhibit both. The good candidate, however, has it in his power to deal with it successfully, by simply passing on to the next question. Alternatively, he may decide to tackle it but use it as an invitation, not to write about the whole of this area, but rather to examine in detail one particular aspect of it. This can be dangerous. An examiner who is capable of setting such a question is perhaps capable of penalising the student on the grounds that he has failed to answer the whole of the question.

It is possible to indicate the more important matters that are frequently examined.

(a)   With regard to essay questions, these usually take one of the following forms. This may consist of an invitation to discuss the famous words of Lord Sankey in *Woolmington* v *DPP* [1935] AC 462:

'Throughout the web of the English Criminal Law one golden thread is always to be seen, that it is the duty of the prosecution to prove the prisoner's guilt.' Discuss.

Alternatively, it may involve the question of implied statutory exceptions which we have touched upon above. The following is an example:

'The importance of the presumption of innocence is such that, apart from insanity and express statutory reversals of the burden of proof, there should be no erosion of this principle.' Discuss.

These two questions seem at first sight to be different, but they are not. They overlap considerably, because the significance of implied statutory exceptions is their impact upon the golden rule as expressed in *Woolmington*.

Quite frequently, this interrelationship is made clear within the question itself, for example:

'To search for the golden thread today is to search in vain.' Discuss.

All of these questions are concerned with the present status of the *Woolmington* principle and the inroads that have been made upon it. It is true, of course, that even Lord Sankey, in delivering his famous judgment, expressed the principle to be subject to two exceptions, insanity and cases under statute. Some would see these two exceptions to *Woolmington* as anomalous and ripe for abolition. Thus, the Criminal Law Revision Committee in its 11th Report (1972) proposed that burdens on the defence should be evidential only (subject to certain exceptions which are not relevant here). Similarly, in relation to the express case of insanity, the Butler Report on Mentally Abnormal Offenders (1975) made the same recommendation. The Criminal Law Revision Committee gave several reasons, of which two are particularly important. First:

In the typical case where the essence of the offence is that the offender has acted with blameworthy intent, and the defence which the accused has the burden of proving implies that he had no such intent but acted wholly innocently, it seems to us repugnant to principle that the jury or magistrates' court should be under a legal duty, if they are left in doubt whether or not the accused had the guilty intent, to convict him. For this is what the law requires.

Secondly, the Committee felt that it was confusing to a jury to be given the complicated direction on the difference between the burden on the prosecution of proving a matter beyond reasonable doubt and that on the defence of proving a matter on a balance of probabilities. You would be well advised to read the full argument put forward by the Committee in its report (pp. 87–91).

These recommendations, however, remain merely proposals for legislation, and since the publication of the report giant steps have been taken in the opposite direction. Parliament has continued on occasion expressly to place the legal burden on the accused. But the courts have also added to the exceptions to *Woolmington*.

At one time it was thought that a statutory reversal could be implied only in two narrowly defined situations. The first was where part of the prosecution's case consisted of a negative averment about a matter which was peculiarly within the knowledge of the defendant. This is cumbersome language but it was the terminology used in *R v Turner* (1816) 5 M & S 206. The second was where an excuse was not contained in the definition of the offence but was added afterwards as a proviso. Even where one of these two exceptions applied, it was generally thought that the burden cast upon the defendant was no more than an evidential one.

However, in *R v Edwards* [1975] QB 29, the Court of Appeal stated the scope of the exception in much wider terms. Lawton LJ, delivering the judgment of the court, expressed it as follows:

> It is limited to offences arising under enactments which prohibit the doing of an act save in specified circumstances or by persons of specified classes or with specified qualifications or with the licence or permission of specified authorities. Whenever the prosecution seeks to rely on this exception, the court must construe the enactment under which the charge is laid. If the true construction is that the enactment prohibits the doing of acts subject to provisos, exceptions and the like, then the prosecution can rely upon the exception.

The offence in question was that of selling intoxicating liquor by retail without holding a justices' licence authorising the accused to do so, an offence to which the 'peculiar knowledge' argument could not apply since an easily accessible register of licences had to be kept by the clerk to the justices. It was also made clear by the court that when the *Edwards* principle applied, the defendant bore the *legal* burden of proof. This was irrelevant to the case before the court because in it the accused gave no evidence at all and called none on his behalf: if the burden upon him had been held to have been an evidential one only, the result would still have been the same. It seems harsh that if the court is left in doubt about a particular issue it must convict. Several other criticisms of the decision are fully developed in important articles by Zuckerman (1976) 92 LQR 402 and Glanville Williams (1976) 126 NLJ 1032. It is not at all easy to accept the statement of Lawton LJ in *Edwards*, who stated that the burden of proof had to be placed on the accused 'to ensure that *justice* [our emphasis] is done both to the community and to defendants'. Does the decision square with your ideas of justice?

Whatever the merits or otherwise of the *Edwards* principle, the House of Lords has widened the law still further in this area. You must read *R v Hunt* [1987] AC 352 very carefully. The House of Lords there confirmed the existence of cases where the legislature has not expressly reversed the burden of proof but has done so impliedly. Whether it has done so in a particular case is a question of construction of the particular statute. Where does *Edwards* stand in all this? The answer, according to the House of Lords, is that cases where an implied statutory reversal would be recognised would only rarely fall outside the *Edwards* principle. Yet, the House saw this principle as an excellent guide to construction rather than as an exception to a rule. In the final analysis each case must turn upon the construction of the particular legislation. The House went on to give guidance on the factors to be taken into account. If linguistic construction did not clearly indicate upon whom the burden should lie, the court should look to other considerations to determine Parliament's intention. These would be matters of policy and might involve looking at the mischief at which the statute was aimed and the ease or difficulty that the respective parties would encounter in discharging the burden. In addition, the fact that an offence is both very serious and of strict liability would be a reason for resolving any ambiguity in favour of the defendant. On the question of construction, examine the judgments of Lords Griffiths and Ackner.

The decision in *Hunt* leaves the law in a very uncertain state. The importance of the policy factors referred to leaves it very difficult to predict which way the court will jump in a particular case.

The doctrine of implied statutory reversal of the burden of proof does have one important limitation: it does not apply to common law defences, which remain covered by the golden rule in *Woolmington*.

Patrick Healey in [1987] Crim LR 355 brings out the ambiguities within *Hunt* and the way in which the case conflates issues of substantive and adjectival law. His article also looks at deeper questions involving the nature of judicial decision-making, but he brings out the way in which the *Woolmington* principle is being eroded.

This is a difficult area, but an examination of the literature referred to will indicate the opportunity open to you to exhibit your awareness of the wider ramifications of the subject. You will find a particularly useful summary of the whole debate in Zuckerman, *The Principles of Criminal Evidence*, pp. 142–9.

We should perhaps add that the House of Lords in *Hunt* also held that the burden, once cast on the defendant, would be a legal one, not merely evidential. This is the same approach as was taken in *Edwards* and confirms that if a burden of proof is placed on the defendant it is the same burden whether the case be tried summarily or on indictment, to be discharged on the balance of probabilities.

(b)   Questions are also commonly set concerning the relationship between the legal and evidential burdens, in the context of a criminal case. Quite often a whole question, or part of one, is set in which the accused might raise several defences to an allegation and you are required to advise him on how best to present his case, especially with regard to the burden and standard of proof. Alternatively, on similar facts, you might be asked to put yourself into the shoes of the trial judge and direct the jury with regard to the burden and standard of proof. Here is an example:

> Leonard is charged with murdering Mary. His defence is that he was showing her his new garden scythe when he accidentally tripped and fell, and the scythe severed her jugular vein. He further alleges that he is subject to blackouts, and pleads this as an alternative reason for his losing control of the scythe.
>
> How should the jury be directed on the question of the burden and standard of proof?

Here, the charge being one of murder, the prosecution will have to prove all the essential elements of the crime. Therefore it will bear both the evidential and legal burden of showing that Leonard killed Mary and did so with the necessary intention to kill or do grievous bodily harm. The requisite standard of proof will be that beyond reasonable doubt. If then, the jury cannot make up their minds as to whether the accused is guilty or innocent, they must find him not guilty. They must still acquit even if they believe him to be guilty, if after hearing the evidence, they are left with any reasonable doubt as to his guilt. These points you should make very briefly. They are straightforward and need little expansion.

Turning then to the possible defences, the accused is claiming that the death of Mary was accidental or alternatively was a result of automatism, either insane or non-insane. Before dealing with these defences, a more general issue arises here. That is that problem questions of this kind often raise implicitly issues of substantive law as well as issues of evidence. As we shall see the various defences involving some form of what might be called 'mental disorder' differ from each other in respect of whether the accused bears only an evidential burden or whether he bears the legal burden of proving the defence in question. Therefore, this area is something of a favourite for examination questions. You may feel that it is unfair of the examiner to introduce issues of substantive law into a procedurally based subject. The answer to this is that the subject of evidence presupposes the existence of the substantive law and issues of the latter kind must inevitably arise in many questions. However, such matters are usually treated in a straightforward way and require no specialised knowledge of the substantive law in question. Further, as far as the criminal law is concerned, the great majority of students who study evidence will previously have studied criminal law. It must be confessed, however, that the relationship between automatism and insanity is a difficult one. We would advise you to re-read your materials on insanity, diminished responsibility and automatism, together with the related issue of the accused's fitness to plead. You should remember that the primary interest of the examiner is in your ability to apply the rules of evidence. He will understand if you are not precisely on the mark concerning a complicated issue of criminal law, especially if it is a matter of recent development.

The distinction between the defence of insanity and that of automatism rests upon whether the condition is produced by a disease of the mind. According to the latest authority (*R v Sullivan* [1984] AC 156), the word 'mind' here is used in the ordinary sense of the mental faculties of reason, memory and understanding. If the effect of a disease is to impair these faculties so severely that as a result the accused did not know the nature and quality of the act he was doing, or, if he did know, that he did not know he was doing what was wrong, then the defence of insanity is available. It matters not whether the cause of the impairment itself is permanent or transient and intermittent. However, if temporary impairment (not being self-induced by consuming drink or drugs) resulted from some external physical factor such as a blow on the head causing concussion, then the defence of automatism would apply. The judge must rule as to whether the defence arising on the evidence is insanity or automatism. This is an important decision for the accused because if it is decided that only insanity is available, then this defence must, as we have seen, be proved by the accused, albeit only to the civil standard. It should also be noted that under the Criminal Procedure (Insanity and Unfitness to Plead) Act 1991, s. 1, a jury must not return a verdict of not guilty by reason of insanity, except on the evidence of two or more medical practitioners, one of whom is approved under the Mental Health Act 1983. However, with reference to automatism the evidential burden in respect of the issue of intent is placed upon the accused. Medical evidence must generally be given, and is essential where the accused says only that he had a black-out. The accused himself, surprisingly, is not under an obligation to testify. If there is sufficient evidence (and, of course, this may come from the prosecution witnesses in addition to the defence) to lay a foundation for the defence of automatism, then the judge must direct the jury that the legal burden of proving *mens rea* on the part of the accused rests on the prosecution. Many cases have been fought around whether the condition from which the accused suffers arises from insanity or from non-insane automatism. The former may result in mandatory commitment (although a range of possible sentences is now available under the Criminal Procedure (Insanity and Unfitness to Plead) Act 1991, whereas the latter results in a complete acquittal.

Incidentally, while we are discussing the question of mental disorder we would briefly offer you two further pieces of advice, even though they do not actually arise on the facts of the present question. First, it is useful to have some knowledge of the Criminal Procedure (Insanity) Act 1964, s. 6. This provides that if on a charge of murder the accused raises diminished responsibility as a defence then the prosecution may adduce evidence of insanity on the part of the accused, or vice versa. In this event, the prosecution bears the legal burden of proving the issue on which it has adduced evidence (and to the criminal standard). Secondly, there are even some examiners around (rumoured to be related to the Marquis de Sade!) who are quite prepared to set questions involving the burden and standard of proof on the question of whether the accused is fit to stand trial. Thankfully it is rare these days to see questions requiring knowledge of matters of this kind.

We come now to the defence of accident. Here we enter more uncertain territory. Some judges have implied that the accused bears an evidential burden in respect of every explanation that he advances in order to demonstrate his innocence (see, for example, Lord Morris of Borth-y-Gest in *Bratty* v *Attorney-General for Northern Ireland* [1961] 3 All ER 523 at p. 537). In principle, it would appear that a distinction must be drawn between what might be called the prosecution elements of the offence, in other words those relating to the essence of the charge, with respect to which the prosecution bears the evidential burden, and defence elements. A defence element would be, say, self-defence, provocation or duress and in such cases the accused does bear an evidential burden, as we have seen earlier. It is sometimes suggested that the so-called defence of accident comes into this last category. This is almost certainly untrue. Professor Glanville Williams has explained the true distinction to be drawn, in the course of discussing *Mancini* v *DPP* [1942] AC 1, where it was assumed that the defences of accident and provocation were in the same position in relation to the duty of the judge to leave the issue to the jury:

> They are in the same position in that the persuasive burden in both respects lies on the prosecution; but they are not in the same position in respect of the evidential burden, which rests on the defendant in respect of provocation but not in respect of accident. The difference is that the defence of provocation does not deny the positive essentials of the crime of murder, but adds a further element by way of confession and avoidance (as it would be called in civil pleading), whereas the defence of accident does deny an essential positive element, as does (in most cases) the defence of mistake. If the crime charged requires the prosecution to prove an intent, the defences of accident and mistake take issue on the intent, and the jury must be instructed in the usual way on the necessity for proving intent. It is not incumbent on the defendant to raise the issue, and his defence that he lacked the requisite intent must be left to the jury however weak the evidence in support of it. ((1977) 127 NLJ at pp. 157-8)

Professor Williams argues that it is logically impossible for both sides to bear an evidential burden on the same issue. This is an attractive argument. Professor Williams proceeds to apply it to the defence of alibi, gaining support from the decision in *R* v *Denney* [1963] Crim LR 191.

What can be said against this argument? Well, there is Bratty itself, where Viscount Kilmuir LC said that the accused bears the evidential burden with regard to accident; and there is *Mancini*, of course.

In addition, Professor Smith sets the issue in its practical context:

In every murder case the judge must direct the jury that they must be sure that D intended to kill or to cause GBH; but in a case like *Woolmington* where all that the prosecution proves is that D shot V while they were alone in a room together, the judge does not have to tell the jury that they must be sure that the gun did not go off by accident as D was getting it out from under his coat, unless some evidence has been given that this is what happened. If D wishes the jury to consider the particular facts which he claims are inconsistent with the prosecution's case, he must tender evidence of them. There is no duty on the court to speculate as to possible explanations of the case, of which no evidence has been given. (*Criminal Evidence*, p. 29)

Further, in *R v Johnson* [1961] 1 WLR 1478, the Court of Appeal suggested that alibi should be treated in the same way as self-defence and provocation (see, in addition, *R v Preece* (1993) 96 Cr App R 264). Also, where an accused raises non-insane automatism, where we know that there is an evidential burden on the accused, is he not merely saying that the prosecution elements of *actus reus* and *mens rea* have not been proved? Perhaps the answer in relation to automatism is that, since the defence is easy to raise and difficult to rebut, there are policy reasons for placing an evidential burden on the accused.

All these matters, plus much other useful information may be found in two articles by Professor Williams: 'The evidential burden: some common misapprehensions' (1977) 127 NLJ 156; and 'Evidential burdens on the defence' (1977) 127 NLJ 182. You might also wish to refer to the draft Criminal Code Bill (Law Com. No. 177, 1989), where, in clause 13, it is recommended that the legal burden of disproving any defence should as a general rule be on the prosecution.

CONCLUSION

We have covered the major issues arising on the topic of burdens and standards. It is not practicable to deal with every possible matter. In particular examiners do on occasions set out in a question two or three statutory provisions and ask for a consideration of the burden of proof in each case. Much depends on the exact wording of the particular statute. Your lecturer may have considered certain of them in the course of the lectures and you would be wise to concentrate on these.

FURTHER READING

Birch, 'Hunting the Snark: the elusive statutory exception' [1988] Crim LR 221.

Criminal Law Revision Committee, *11th Report: Evidence (General)* (Cmnd 4991) (London: HMSO, 1972).

Healey, 'Proof and policy: no golden threads' [1987] Crim LR 355.

Home Office and Department of Health and Social Security, *Report of the Committee on Mentally Abnormal Offenders* (Chairman: Lord Butler) (Cmnd 6244) (London: HMSO, 1975).

Mirfield, 'The legacy of *Hunt*' [1988] Crim LR 19.

Mirfield, 'An ungrateful reply' [1988] Crim LR 233.

Smith, 'The presumption of innocence' (1987) 38 NILQ 223.

Stein, 'After *Hunt*: the burden of proof, risk of non-persuasion and judicial pragmatism, (1991) 54 MLR 570.

Williams, 'Placing the burden of proof', in E. Campbell and L. Waller (eds), *Well and Truly Tried* (Sydney: Law Book Co., 1982).

Williams, 'Statutory exceptions to liability and the burden of proof' (1976) 126 NLJ 1032.

Williams, 'The evidential burden: some common misapprehensions' (1977) 127 NLJ 156.

Williams, 'Evidential burdens on the defence' (1977) 127 NLJ 182.

Zuckerman, 'The third exception to the *Woolmington* rule' (1976) 92 LQR 402.

5 PRESUMPTIONS

One of the major problems faced by a student coming to the law of evidence for the first time is that of terminology. The subject has for the most part grown up in a piecemeal fashion. There are very few precise definitions of the most commonly recurring terms. Nowhere is this problem felt more pressingly than in relation to the question of presumptions. Your first acquaintance with this topic is likely to be followed by a feeling of total exasperation. You will be faced with presumptions of law, presumptions of fact, conclusive presumptions, evidential presumptions, provisional presumptions, irrebuttable presumptions — in fact, presumptions of all shapes and sizes, to suit every possible taste. These feelings are not confined to students.

One writer has brought out the characteristic feelings very clearly: 'Every writer of sufficient intelligence to appreciate the difficulties of the subject-matter has approached the topic of presumptions with a sense of hopelessness and has left it with a feeling of despair' (Morgan (1937) 12 Wash L Rev 255).

What is likely to arouse these feelings of despair is that the distinctions drawn between these disparate species appear not to have a solid connecting link. It is not that a particular presumption has an uncertain area of application. It is rather that the term 'presumption' has been applied indiscriminately by the courts to a series of things which are fundamentally different in kind from each other.

On first confronting this factor, you may decide to avoid this area altogether for the purposes of the examination. You may be wise, however, to persevere, for two reasons:

(a)   Once this initial problem of classification is overcome (which it can be with effort), then the statement of the rules relating to this area of the law is relatively straightforward.

(b)   Questions in evidence examinations concerned with presumptions are usually fairly self-contained. The major difficulty with evidence, then, i.e., its integrated nature to which we have referred previously, is less obvious here. Of course, you may have to tackle other matters in the one question. Presumptions do have an effect on the question of the burden of proof. Therefore, if you decide to revise presumptions, then you must also be prepared to deal with the question of the burden and standard of proof. The two interrelate.

It is necessary first to tackle this question of classification and structure. Then we shall set out the essential requirements of the law of presumptions.

CLASSIFICATION

The term 'presumptions' is used in the authorities to refer to several things which seem to have very little in common with each other. The traditional classification of presumptions has been heavily criticised, but we may use it as a starting-point, remembering, however, to treat it with caution.

Presumptions are said to fall into three categories:

(a)   presumptions of fact;
(b)   irrebuttable presumptions of law;
(c)   rebuttable presumptions of law.

Presumptions of Fact

These are merely commonly recurring examples of circumstantial evidence and most commentators recognise them as such and treat them as illustrations of evidence that is relevant to the facts in issue. For example, if a person is found in possession of recently stolen goods and he fails to give a credible explanation of how he came by them, then the court is entitled to infer that either he stole them or that he dishonestly handled them, knowing or believing them to be stolen. Similarly, if a person destroys or conceals evidence then the court may infer that the evidence was unfavourable to him. This is all simply a matter of common sense and there is no magic involved. What has happened is that since some of these fact situations occur over and over again, the textbook writers have tended to list them and refer to them as presumptions of fact.

In addition to the two examples already mentioned, you should be aware of two others. First, the so-called presumption of continuance. All that this means is that any proved state of affairs may be presumed to have continued for some time. For example, if it is proved that A was alive in 1982 it may well be inferred that he was still alive at some later date. How much later will depend upon the circumstances, such as his age and state of health. Again, if the speed of a car at a certain point is in issue, evidence of its speed a few moments earlier is admissible.

The second case is that of s. 8 of the Criminal Justice Act 1967 which makes it clear that a court may infer the intention of the accused from the fact that generally a person intends the natural consequences of his actions.

A court or jury, in determining whether a person has committed an offence:

(a)   shall not be bound in law to infer that he intended or foresaw a result of his actions by reason only of its being a natural and probable consequence of those actions; but

(b)   shall decide whether he did intend or foresee that result by reference to all the evidence, drawing such inferences from the evidence as appear proper in the circumstances.

You should approach these so-called presumptions of fact, therefore, as being simply illustrations of the basic principle of the law of evidence that before an item of evidence can be admissible it must be relevant. The vital point to grasp here is that although the inference *may* be drawn by the court, it is *not bound* to draw it. As we shall see, it is this factor which primarily marks out the difference between 'presumptions' of fact and what we shall refer to as true presumptions.

Irrebuttable Presumptions of Law

It is often said that there is a presumption that a child under 10 cannot commit a criminal offence. This is true enough, but it does not follow from the application of any presumption, as that term is generally understood. These so-called presumptions are in reality rules of substantive law or procedure masquerading as rules of evidence. You will know of them, if at all, from your studies in criminal law, and they play no part in the law of evidence. It is a contradiction in terms to talk about something as being a presumption (which implies that it is a conclusion which is drawn only conditionally) and then to go on and say that it can never be rebutted. The truth is that these are fixed rules of law.

Rebuttable Presumptions of Law

Now we reach those matters which are of importance to us in the present context, those which play an important role in the law of evidence. But, first, we can dispose of two other uses of the word 'presumption'. These are the terms 'presumption of innocence' and 'presumption of sanity'. These are merely ways in which commentators have referred to the question of the burden of proof. They are simply a shorthand way of saying that in criminal cases the burden of proof generally is on the prosecution; and that if the accused raises the defence of insanity, then he has the burden of proving that defence. We have examined these questions in chapter 4.

Rebuttable presumptions of law are presumptions where on proof of certain facts certain prescribed conclusions must be drawn in the absence of rebutting evidence. Notice immediately the difference between this and, for example, the doctrine of recent possession. In the case of the latter, the inference of guilt *may* be drawn, but in case of a rebuttable presumption of law the inference specified in the presumption *must* be drawn, there is no option (provided, of course, that there is no evidence to the contrary). These, then, are true presumptions for the purposes of the law of evidence. Their hallmark is that they always require two things:

(a)   Certain facts must be proved. These are called the *primary* facts or the *basic* facts. We shall use the first term henceforth.

(b)   On (a) being proved, some other fact (we can call it the *presumed* fact) must in law be taken by the court to be true if there is no evidence to the contrary.

It follows, therefore, that with regard to all true presumptions of this kind, you must be aware of two matters concerning them:

(i)   The *primary* facts which have to be proved; what are they?
(ii)   The amount of evidence needed to rebut the presumption.

Having defined the characteristics of a true presumption, the question arises, which ones do you need to know? There are many of them throughout the law, the majority being statutory. Several of them are taught in other legal subjects; for example, the presumption of a resulting trust and the doctrine of *res ipsa loquitur*. However, certain of them are of more general application and these are the ones that are usually examined as part of an evidence course. The following four are obvious candidates:

(a)   the presumption of marriage;
(b)   the presumption of legitimacy;
(c)   the presumption of death;
(d)   the presumption of regularity.

Of course, as always, everything depends on the exact ground covered in the evidence course which you are studying. Additional ones may be included within the examinations or it may be made clear that certain ones are omitted from the syllabus.

Below we have set out briefly the legal requirements for the application of these four presumptions. Later, when we come to look at some specimen examination questions on presumptions, we shall take account of certain matters of detail which frequently have to be considered.

The Presumption of Marriage

This presumption is a source of much misunderstanding. There are, in reality, three situations capable of operating here, and they are frequently run together by students.

(a) On proof of the celebration of a marriage ceremony, in other words one which is capable of producing a valid marriage according to the local law (these are the primary facts), the law will presume the *formal* validity of the marriage, that is to say that the various formalities (for example, a special licence if celebrated in a private house) were complied with. As illustrations you should examine the cases of *Piers* v *Piers* (1849) 2 HL Cas 331 and *Mahadervan* v *Mahadervan* [1964] P 233. Notice that with regard to the presumption of formal validity, cohabitation of the parties is not required; it is not one of the primary facts. So, the presumption of formal validity will apply to a deathbed marriage.

How much evidence is needed to rebut this presumption? The traditional view is that it is a strong presumption and that in order to rebut it there must be proof beyond reasonable doubt that there was no valid marriage. Once again, however, note that the authorities date from the time when a more stringent attitude was taken towards the standard of proof required in matrimonial cases. They must be read in the light of the more recent developments in that field outlined in chapter 4.

(b) On proof of the celebration of a marriage ceremony (the same primary facts as before), the law will presume the 'essential validity' of the marriage, that is that the parties had the necessary capacity of marrying and that their consents were real.

Here it seems that a lesser standard of proof will suffice to rebut the presumption. The cases seem to establish that some evidence of incapacity is enough to do so (see, in particular, *Tweney* v *Tweney* [1946] P 180) although there is some conflict.

What we have said so far with regard to rebutting the presumption of marriage applies to civil cases. Whatever the standard is there you must remember that in all probability it is different in a criminal case. To take the almost universal example, if the accused is charged with bigamy, where the prosecution is seeking to prove a valid first marriage, then it seems clear that all that the accused need do is to raise doubts as to the validity of that marriage. That arises simply out of the fact that the prosecution in general bears the burden of proof of all the elements of a crime.

(c)   On proof that a couple lived together as husband and wife and were generally regarded as married (primary facts), the law will presume that they were living together in consequence of a valid marriage. This presumption may only be rebutted by evidence of the most 'cogent' kind. Further, it seems not to apply to criminal cases (*Morris* v *Miller* (1767) 4 Burr 2057). Therefore, if in a bigamy prosecution the validity of the first marriage is in issue, the prosecution must bring evidence of an apparently valid ceremony, and then it may rely on the presumption of marriage dealt with under (a) and (b) above. Proof or admission of cohabitation supported by the production of a marriage certificate does suffice for these purposes (*R* v *Birtles* (1911) 6 Cr App R 177).

The Presumption of Legitimacy

Where a child is born or conceived in lawful wedlock, the husband not being separated from his wife by an order of the court (primary facts), the law will presume the legitimacy of the child. If, however, the husband and wife are separated by a court order (which refers to a decree of judicial separation or the equivalent order in the magistrates' court), the presumption is that any child conceived by the mother during such a period is *illegitimate*. Note, then, that provided there is no such court order in force, the presumption of *legitimacy* does apply, even though the parties are, say, living apart at the material time, or if proceedings for divorce have commenced, or even if a decree nisi of divorce has been granted, although of course it is likely to be easier to rebut the presumption in such cases.

The evidence needed to rebut the presumption of legitimacy must go to show that the child's mother and her husband did not have intercourse by which the child could have been conceived. We will say more later about the kind of evidence which may be used to do this.

Any presumption of legitimacy or illegitimacy in civil cases may be rebutted on the balance of probabilities (Family Law Reform Act 1969, s. 26).

Of course, the presumption has little practical application in criminal cases, but if it did arise, then the analogy with the general rule regarding the burden of proof in criminal matters, already referred to in relation to the presumption of marriage, would apply. Thus, if the prosecution sought to rebut the presumption, it would have to do so beyond reasonable doubt, while the accused need only point to a reasonable possibility of illegitimacy.

The definition of the necessary primary facts which we have given means that the presumption of legitimacy applies even in the case of a child born to a woman shortly after her marriage at such a time that it must have been conceived before the marriage. Further, the presumption applies to children who, though conceived in lawful wedlock, are born after the termination of the mother's marriage (either by divorce or by the death of the husband).

The Presumption of Death

There is a common law presumption of death, plus several statutory provisions. We shall look at the common law first. Here the primary facts are as laid down in the leading case of *Chard* v *Chard* [1956] P 259. They are:

(a)   no acceptable affirmative evidence that the person in question was alive at some time during a continuous period of seven years or more;

(b)   that there are persons who would be likely to have heard of him over that period;

(c)   that those persons have not heard of him; and

(d)   that all due enquiries have been made appropriate to the circumstances.

On proof of these facts, the law will presume that the person in question died at some time within that period. Of course, if the period is less than seven years, the court (depending on the circumstances) may be prepared to infer death as a matter of fact if he has not been heard of by those who would be likely to have done so. The significance of the seven-year period is that it brings a presumption of *law* into operation, rather than merely one of fact. The presumption casts only an evidential burden on the other party; therefore, all that is needed to rebut the presumption is acceptable evidence to the contrary.

As we have indicated, in addition to the common law presumption of death, you will need to know certain specific statutory provisions. There are three of importance, the first two applying to civil cases, the third to certain criminal prosecutions.

(a)   *Law of Property Act 1925, s. 184.* Under this section where two or more persons have died in circumstances rendering it uncertain which of them survived the other(s), then for all purposes affecting *title to property*, there is a presumption that the persons died in order of age, the eldest dying first. You must note here one important exception to this section, the case of an intestate and his or her spouse. In this case there is no such presumption.

(b)   *Matrimonial Causes Act 1973, s. 19(3).* Section 19(1) of this Act enables any married person who alleges that reasonable grounds exist for supposing that the other spouse is dead, to petition for a decree dissolving the marriage and presuming the death of such spouse. Section 19(3) provides that in such petitions the facts that (i) for a period of seven years or upwards the other party to the marriage has been continuously absent from the petitioner, and (ii) the petitioner has no reason to believe that the other party has been living within that time, shall be evidence that he or she is dead until the contrary is proved. Notice how generous this presumption is compared with the common law presumption of death:

(i)   no enquiries need have been made;
(ii)   the fact that the petitioner would be unlikely to hear of the person is immaterial;
(iii)   in deciding whether the petitioner had no reason to believe in the person's continued existence, only events taking place within the last seven years are relevant.

(c)   *Proviso to s. 57 of the Offences against the Person Act 1861.* This provides a statutory defence to a charge of *bigamy* (and, note, only to such a charge) if at the time of the second ceremony the former spouse had been continually absent for the last seven years and was not known by the accused to have been living during that time.

The Presumption of Regularity

The matters dealt with under this heading only rarely appear in evidence papers, although there are three that it may be helpful to be aware of.

(a)   Proof that a person acted as the holder of a public office is evidence of his right to do so. The usual examples here are judges, magistrates and police officers.
(b)   There is a presumption that mechanical instruments which are usually in order (for example, traffic lights, speedometers) were in order when they were used.
(c)   On proof that necessary business transactions have been carried out, which require to be effected in a certain order, it is presumed that they were effected in that order.

The presumption in all these three cases is obviously useful and time-saving in practice, although weak and, therefore, rebutted by quite slight evidence to the contrary. There is some uncertainty with regard to the operation of the presumption in criminal cases, but an outline knowledge of the kind we have indicated is more than sufficient for the vast majority of evidence papers.

PLANNING YOUR REVISION

We have little to say here. The topic of presumptions is a relatively self-contained one. It is generally unpopular with students, who see it as 'dry' when compared with the more controversial and 'glamorous' areas like similar fact evidence, character and confessions. Neither is it a major area of interest for most lecturers who find it difficult to say anything fresh or original about the topic. Some evidence courses give it a perfunctory treatment, and in some it is not touched upon at all. If that is so in your case, then there is nothing further to say. If it has been dealt with fully, however, then there is a choice to be made. If you are revising the burden and standard of proof, as will almost certainly be the case, then it is essential to have at least a fair knowledge of presumptions. As we have seen in this chapter, a presumption quite often operates as a device for fixing the burden of proof in relation to certain facts. Also, as we have indicated above, once the problems of terminology have been sorted out, the topic is not unduly difficult. However, students generally perform better where they find the particular subject to be interesting. If you find that the topic of presumptions is as exciting as the day-to-day life of *Lumbricus terrestris* (the earthworm), then you would probably be well advised to concentrate on something else.

In revising the different presumptions, concentrate on the basics. You must become familiar with the exact primary facts which it is necessary to prove in each case, and with the amount of evidence which is needed to rebut each presumption. You do not need to know the detailed nuances of this topic (unless, of course, your lecturer has indicated that he considers them to be of the greatest importance).

As we shall see, the difficulties involved in unravelling the facts of problem questions mean that a very detailed answer will not generally be required.

It is useful also to be aware of the sort of evidence which is commonly adduced in order to rebut the presumption in question, but remember that this is essentially a question of fact and any authorities on the point do not lay down fixed rules of law.

There is no substitute on this topic (or on the others for that matter) for hard work. Wrap your head in a wet towel, *learn* the appropriate rules and examine how they are applied in the various cases.

EXAMINATION QUESTIONS

1   Comment on one of the two following quotations:

(a) 'Presumptions of law are nothing else than natural inferences or presumptions of fact which the law invests with an artificial or preternatural weight.' (Gulson)

(b) 'Does the classification of presumptions into conclusive, persuasive, evidential and provisional do more to assist an understanding of the subject than the orthodox classification?'

2   Martin and Ruth lived together from 1970 until February 1977. Throughout this period they were known to those living in the area as Mr and Mrs Goodbody. In February 1977, Ruth left Martin and went to live with David. On 6 October 1977, Ruth gave birth to a daughter, Nicola. In 1986, Martin, who still lived in the same area, met and married Olga. Recently Martin has been visited by the police and in January 1996 he was charged with two offences: (a) bigamy in relation to his marriage to Olga, (b) incest with Nicola. Martin states that he has indeed had sexual intercourse with Nicola. However, he is adamant that Nicola is not his daughter because, he claims, he and Ruth always used contraceptives. He adds that David must be the father of Nicola since Ruth and David were already having sexual intercourse at the time when Nicola must have been conceived.

Discuss.

Question 1

Essays on presumptions are quite rare in evidence papers. Occasionally, a straightforward account of a particular presumption is asked for, perhaps coupled with a problem question. Such an essay does very little to sort out the good student from the merely average one. More demanding are the two essay questions above which raise more fundamental issues.

These questions are both concerned with the theoretical basis of the doctrine of presumptions and with its rationale. The majority of students will not be able to tackle such questions other than superficially. An examiner is suitably impressed with a candidate who is able to make a good attempt at them and will be relatively generously disposed towards him. Also, the points that are relevant here would enhance any answer to the more straightforward essay question referred to at the start of this section.

The first question is concerned with the rationale of the doctrine of presumptions. It requires you to examine the reasons why presumptions exist. There are several things which may be said. Sometimes the presumed fact is a logical inference from the primary fact. Certainly, this will always be the case with respect to the so-called presumptions of fact, because, as we have seen, these are merely commonly recurring items of circumstantial evidence, the strength of which derives entirely from their relevance to the facts in issue. Similarly, to take one of the presumptions of law, in deciding whether two persons are married it would be relevant to ask whether they went through a ceremony of marriage, or lived together and were regarded as married, although the answer would not be conclusive on the issue. Yet in the case of this and of other presumptions logic may play a minimal part. As Sachs J stated in *Chard* v *Chard* [1956] P 259, when speaking of the seven-year period in relation to the presumption of death: '[T]here can hardly be a logical inference from any particular set of facts that a man had not died within 2,555 days but had died within 2,560'.

It is matters of this kind that the quotation from Gulson's work draws attention to. Another illustration may be found in the fact that the evidence supporting the primary fact may be relatively weak where the rebutting evidence is strong. Yet, if the latter is not sufficiently weighty as to reach the standard that is required to rebut the presumption (this, remember, may vary), then the presumed fact must still be taken by the court to be true.

A very powerful factor in the recognition of presumptions is that of public policy, a matter which is not necessarily related to logic. Heydon (*Evidence: Case and Materials*, p. 49) gives a useful series of illustrations as follows:

> It is undesirable that children be held illegitimate lightly, so there is a presumption of legitimacy; the stigma of illegitimacy retains some shock, even if the accusation of non-paternity against a man married to the mother of a child has more. Ownership is inferred from possession because stability of title is desirable. The driver of a car is presumed to be driving with the owner's consent in order to give anyone injured by the driver a better chance of recovery and also to encourage road safety by giving an inducement to owners to select careful drivers. Deaths are presumed to be due to accident rather than suicide partly so that life insurance contracts for the deceased's family will be performed rather than avoided by the insurer. The accused is presumed innocent because it is thought important not to convict men wrongly and this is one way of ensuring that the trier of fact takes care.

Other reasons may lie behind particular presumptions. It may be easier for one party to prove a particular fact than for the other party to prove the opposite. There may be other reasons for general convenience. The application of a presumption may save time at the trial or serve a variety of procedural purposes. Examine the major presumptions again and consider what reason(s) lie behind their recognition. Heydon has a short but vigorous discussion on this point (pp. 48-9).

The second essay question above focuses on the attempts which have been made by various commentators to devise a new classification of presumptions. In our exposition of presumptions earlier in this chapter, we referred to the traditional classification, although we did point out the artificiality of this. In practical terms, a very important aspect of presumptions is the amount of evidence required to rebut the presumption. The new classification concentrates on this and analyses presumptions relative to this factor subdividing them into the following four kinds:

(a)· Conclusive presumptions. Here, no evidence of any kind can rebut the truth of the presumed fact. This category is equivalent to what are usually referred to as irrebuttable presumptions of law. We have also referred to the incongruity of referring to them as presumptions at all.

(b) Persuasive presumptions. These are cases where the effect of the presumption is to put the legal burden of disproving the presumed fact on the party against whom it operates. This category would include certain of what are traditionally called rebuttable presumptions of law, as for example the presumption of legitimacy.

(c) Evidential presumptions. This is where the effect of the presumption is to place an evidential burden on the party against whom it operates. The traditional approach as we have seen, is to lump them together with (b) above. An example would be the presumption of death.

(d) Provisional presumptions. Here, the court is not bound to believe the presumed fact even if no evidence at all is adduced in rebuttal. These are equivalent then to presumptions of fact.

Any answer on this question must state accurately the differences between the orthodox classification and the new one. As to the value of the new terminology, it does at least draw attention to the fact that rebuttable presumptions of law are not all of the same kind. However, conclusive and provisional presumptions are little, if at all, different from the equivalent older terms. As for persuasive and evidential presumptions, the distinction that exists between them is irrelevant in criminal cases because of the general requirement at common law that the prosecution proves its case beyond reasonable doubt. 'Proof of the basic facts of a common law presumption can cast nothing more than an evidential burden on to the accused and nothing less than a legal burden on to the prosecution' (*Cross and Tapper on Evidence*, p. 140). Even in civil cases, the requisite standard for rebutting each particular presumption varies greatly according to the different strength of each presumption, so as to blur the distinction that is drawn between persuasive and evidential presumptions.

There is no general agreement even on the revised classification.

These matters were dealt with in a series of important writings (see Denning, 'Presumptions and burdens' (1945) 61 LQR 379; Bridge, 'Presumptions and burdens' (1949) 12 MLR 273; Williams, *Criminal Law (The General Part)*, 2nd ed. (1961), p. 877). A more recent attempt at a new classification can be found in Carter, *Cases and Statutes on Evidence*, pp. 77-9.

There is a danger in any attempt to create a fixed terminology in this area:

The categories just discussed do not constitute an iron hierarchy; presumptions are essentially guides to probability, and presumptions vary in this respect, both intrinsically and on the facts of particular cases. More evidence may be needed to rebut an improbable persuasive presumption than a highly probable provisional presumption. It is therefore more important for courts to remember this than to work out an accurate hierarchy of presumptions, which is perhaps one reason why no clear classification has been developed or accepted. (Heydon (above), p. 48)

Question 2

The problem question set out earlier is a typical one on presumptions. Students do not generally write good answers to such questions. Frequently they feel inhibited by the many dates referred to and the relationship of the several events to each other. A common occurrence is for a student to recognise this question as concerned with presumptions and then to throw down on to the paper any scrap of information he may have on that topic with no more than a token glance in the direction of the actual facts of the problem. All the more chance, then, for a student who is well prepared in this area to make a good impression with the examiner by comparison with other candidates.

The examiner is looking for the ability to apply the various rules (here predominantly concerned with presumptions) with some precision to the actual facts of the problem. Questions of this kind on an evidence paper may safely be said to be of a less academic nature than some others. Of course, the examiner will give credit to you if you show that you have read the critical literature in this field and are able to examine and perhaps question the rationale of the rules. But, remember, he does appreciate that it takes time to unravel the facts and relationships of the parties in this question, more time than would usually be required in a problem question where the facts are more unstructured, involving less precise rules, as with many problems, for example, on similar fact evidence. Therefore, simply to give a precise account of the bearing of the present law on these facts will almost certainly take up the whole of the time allotted to the question.

So, how should you approach this question? First, it is essential for you to have a clear grasp of the various dates involved and their relationship to each other. Although this may take a little time, time in which you will not actually be writing your answer to the question, it will be time well spent, because frequently in such questions the exact time at which particular events take place is crucial to which legal rules apply. We therefore set out a synopsis of the facts of this question in chronological order:

1970 to February 1977: Martin and Ruth live together.
February 1977: Ruth leaves Martin to live with David.
6 October 1977: Ruth gives birth to Nicola.
1986: Martin marries Olga.

January 1995: Martin is charged with bigamously marrying Olga and with committing incest with Nicola.

As always you must look next at what is required of you by the question. The general word 'discuss' means that you must consider any relevant matters contained within the particular syllabus of the course. This question may be divided into two sub-questions:

(i)   Evidential matters relating to the charge of bigamy against Martin.
(ii)   Those matters relating to the charge of incest.

The charge of bigamy
Since you are told the specific charge you need only examine the elements of bigamy and then consider the problems of proof in this particular case. The effect of s. 57 of the Offences against the Person Act 1861 is that whoever, being married, goes through a ceremony of marriage with any other person during the life of his or her spouse is guilty of bigamy, subject to certain defences. The prosecution must therefore prove three things: the existence of a valid marriage; its subsistence at the time of the second ceremony; the second ceremony. (It is sensible for you to point out briefly here that the legal burden of proof will be, as is usual in criminal cases, on the prosecution; and that it must prove its case beyond reasonable doubt.)

(a)   *The validity of the first marriage.* The prosecution will seek to show first that Martin was validly married to Ruth. You are told that Martin and Ruth lived together from 1970 until February 1977; but also that during that period they were known to their neighbours as Mr and Mrs Goodbody. How then will the prosecution prove a valid marriage between Martin and Ruth? As stated above, for many purposes the law will presume a marriage from evidence that the parties cohabited with the reputation of being married. However, despite the fact that there is cohabitation and repute here, it will not assist the prosecution since, as we have also seen, this aspect of the presumption of marriage seems not to apply to bigamy prosecutions. So the prosecution will have to prove that Martin and Ruth went through a *ceremony* of marriage. This can be done by producing the marriage certificate, if that is available, and calling someone who was present at the ceremony to identify the parties. If necessary, it is sufficient to call the identifying witness without any proof of the registration of the marriage or of any licence. Of course, Ruth, as the injured spouse, is a competent, although not compellable, witness for the prosecution on a bigamy charge (Police and Criminal Evidence Act 1984, s. 80). If she is willing to give evidence, this makes the prosecution's task here that much easier.

Once it has been proved that Martin and Ruth went through a ceremony of marriage, then there is a presumption of law that they are validly married. This is, of course, rebuttable. The question itself says nothing in this connection and you should content yourself with stating merely that as this is a criminal case, then the better view is that in order to rebut the presumption the defence needs only to raise a doubt as to the validity of the marriage. If the examiner had wanted you to look in detail at the evidence needed to rebut the presumption, he would have given more detail relating to this matter.

Coming back for a moment to the question of cohabitation and repute, the better student might make the point that where there is such cohabitation, it is almost inevitable that Martin will have acknowledged Ruth as his wife. The acknowledgement would be admissible against Martin as being an admission and it has been held (*R v Birtles* (1911) 6 Cr App R 177) that the production of a marriage certificate coupled with an acknowledgement is sufficient evidence of the first marriage.

There is much law on the distinction between void and voidable marriages and their application to the law of bigamy; also on the question of polygamous and potentially polygamous marriages. These involve complicated questions of substantive law and it would be very harsh of an examiner to include them within an evidence paper.

(b) *The subsistence of the first marriage.* The prosecution must in addition prove the subsistence of the first marriage (i.e., that it was still existing at the time of the second ceremony in 1986). This means establishing that Ruth was still alive in 1986. All that the question states is that Ruth left Martin in February 1977 to live with David. We are not told whether Ruth is available to give evidence or whether she has disappeared and her whereabouts are unknown. If the latter, then the court may be able to infer from her age and state of health that she was alive in 1986. If this is done, then the court will be drawing an inference from the facts, perhaps relying on the so-called presumption of continuance, to which we have referred previously.

(c) *The second ceremony.* Here, all that is necessary is for the prosecution to prove the ceremony, which it will do by producing the marriage certificate, if that is available, together with evidence to identify Martin as one of the parties. This evidence will in all probability come from a person who was present at the ceremony. No question of a presumption will arise, since, of course, the second 'marriage' will, in the nature of things, be void.

(d) *Defences.* On the facts given, Martin would clearly seek to raise the statutory defence to bigamy provided by the proviso to s. 57 of the Offences against the Person Act 1861. In other words, he will argue that for the space of the last seven years (1979–86) Ruth was continually absent and was not known to have been living within that time. We have stated the elements of this defence above and it is only necessary to add two things:

(i)   This proviso is more than a presumption since it applies even if there is conclusive evidence that the former spouse *was alive* at the relevant time.

(ii)   Although the defence is contained in a proviso, it has been held that if evidence is given of seven years' absence, the prosecution has the legal burden of proving that the accused had in fact heard of his spouse during that period (*R* v *Curgerwen* (1865) LR 1 CCR 1).

The charge of incest

A man who has sexual intercourse with a girl whom he knows to be his daughter, as is alleged here, is guilty of incest. We are told that Martin admits having sexual intercourse with Nicola so that the only question at issue is whether Nicola is in fact Martin's daughter.

The legal burden in relation to proving this fact will lie upon the prosecution (*Woolmington* v *DPP* [1935] AC 462), who must establish its case beyond reasonable doubt. The relationship of the parties may be proved, of course, by oral evidence or by certificates of marriage and birth, coupled with identification. Again, proof that Martin and Ruth went through a ceremony of marriage raises a presumption that the marriage was valid.

If it is possible for the prosecution to prove a valid marriage between Martin and Ruth, then they may proceed to show that Nicola was Martin's daughter. If they can show that Nicola was born in lawful wedlock, then the presumption will arise that she was a legitimate child of Martin and Ruth and therefore the daughter of Martin for the purposes of the charge of incest. Since this is a criminal matter, in order to rebut the presumption, it would be enough for Martin to raise a reasonable doubt in the mind of the jury about whether Ruth and he had intercourse by which Nicola could have been conceived. This will generally be a question on which the evidence will be circumstantial. We are told here both that Martin claims that he and Ruth always used contraceptives and that Ruth and David were already having sexual intercourse at the time Nicola must have been conceived. These are both items of relevant evidence and may be considered and given the appropriate weight by the jury provided they can be proved by admissible means. It must be remembered, however, that proof that Ruth committed adultery with any number of other men is not, by itself, conclusive. This is for the simple reason that she could also have had sexual intercourse with Martin. However, such evidence may be enough to raise a doubt in the mind of the jury as to Martin's guilt.

It may be helpful for you if we note down at this point common methods of seeking to rebut the presumption of legitimacy which are used in practice and are often referred to in problem questions in this area:

(a)   proof that the husband was abroad at the time of conception;
(b)   proof that the husband was impotent;

(c) proof that the mother had been living for a long time with another man;

(d) proof that the husband's opportunities were slight;

(e) proof of the conduct of the wife and the other man with regard to the child;

(f) proof of the appearance of the child;

(g) evidence of blood groups;

(h) proof that the circumstances were such as to make sexual intercourse unlikely.

These are simply items of circumstantial evidence relevant to the question in issue. As to the appropriate weight to be given to them, this will depend on the particular circumstances of the case.

Shortage of space precludes our discussing a problem question on presumption involving civil matters. The technique required is the same though you should bear in mind two matters in particular. First, when answering a question on the civil law, it is important to know exactly how much evidence is needed to rebut each presumption. In criminal cases, however, we have seen already that the general application of the *Woolmington* principle means that an accused need only raise a reasonable doubt in the mind of the jury in order to rebut a presumption that is operative against him.

The second matter relates to the presumption of death. With regard to this presumption, there is a conflict between the cases on an important point. The stricter approach is that the presumption is only that death occurred before the proceedings; and that death on any particular day will not be presumed. There are, however, authorities supporting a more relaxed approach. In some cases the exact date of death may not be of significance, as, for example, where a person claims on a policy of life insurance. However, there are many cases in which one of the parties must prove that death occurred before or after a particular date (as, for example, for the purposes of succession to property). Problem questions are often concerned with this issue and you must be familiar with the case law. The authorities supporting the stricter approach are: *Re Phene's Trusts* (1870) LR 5 Ch App 139; *Re Rhodes, Rhodes v Rhodes* (1887) 36 ChD 586; *Lal Chand Marwari v Mahant Ramrup Gir* (1925) 42 TLR 159. Those supporting the less strict approach are: *Re Westbrook's Trusts* [1873] WN 167; *Re Aldersey, Gibson v Hall* [1905] 2 Ch 181; *Chipchase v Chipchase* [1939] P 391. There is no authoritative resolution of this issue as yet.

CONCLUSION

For the very capable student, the topic of presumptions has some important limitations which must be recognised. There is little that is controversial in this area and no real interplay between law and policy. It is, therefore, difficult to show any originality in your answer. Even for the average student the topic demands a disproportionate amount of effort to overcome its relative dullness. However, you must remember that an outline knowledge of presumptions may be necessary, depending on your course coverage of burdens and standards.

FURTHER READING

Bridge, 'Presumptions and burdens' (1949) 12 MLR 273.
Denning, 'Presumptions and burdens' (1945) 61 LQR 379.
Morgan, 'Presumptions' (1937) 12 Wash L Rev 255.

6 SIMILAR FACT EVIDENCE

INTRODUCTION

In 'The young person's guide to similar fact evidence' [1983] Crim LR 284, Professor Elliott remarked:

> It would be the rashest presumption to offer anything so concrete or definite as a *guide* to a judge in a criminal trial faced with the notoriously difficult question which arises when he is asked to admit evidence of former misconduct by the accused for the purpose of proving that he committed the crime with which he is being charged....
>
> [The student] is often rather unfairly asked to dilate on what for long eluded the best minds on or off the bench.

This neatly summarises the essential problem a student faces in this topic. It *is* difficult to grasp those factors which have determined the differing judicial approaches to this issue. Even if you can grasp the essential principles it is often difficult to translate them into the workable rules which you need when grappling with the typical examination question on this topic. Nevertheless, similar fact evidence is a popular area on any conventional evidence syllabus. The cases, in what is an almost entirely case-law topic, tend to have colourful and easily remembered facts. There has also been sufficient judicial inconsistency to provide a fertile medium for vigorous academic discussion. Accordingly, similar fact evidence often comes up on examination papers.

Similar fact evidence is concerned with one aspect of the general question of the admissibility of the character of the accused in criminal proceedings.

The basic rule is that evidence of other offences which may have been committed by the accused is not admissible for the prosecution (either in chief, or through the cross-examination of the accused or his witnesses) in order to show that he is guilty of the offence charged. There are some exceptional cases under s. 1(f) of the Criminal Evidence Act 1898 where such evidence becomes admissible, but in these circumstances it is generally only allowed to relate to the credibility of the accused as a witness. This is discussed fully in the next chapter.

The broad rationale for the general exclusion of similar fact evidence is easy to understand: there is a great danger that such evidence would have an overwhelmingly prejudicial effect on the mind of the jury. Any jury hearing that the accused has a long criminal record for the commission of offences similar to that with which he is presently charged will inevitably be influenced by that knowledge and would be much more likely to convict: the accused would be being tried not just for the offence with which he is charged, but for other offences with which he is not charged. Nevertheless, a point comes where the distinctive similarities between the offence charged and other crimes committed by the accused become so marked and compelling that it would be an affront to common sense to exclude such evidence. Accordingly the law of evidence draws a line between that evidence of bad character which has insufficient probative value when weighed against its prejudicial effect (and which is accordingly inadmissible) and that evidence whose probative value is so strong as to compel admissibility. Some simple examples illustrate the point:

(a)   X has a criminal record for offences of dishonesty. He is charged with indecently assaulting a little girl. In this example the previous criminal record of X may have some relevance to his credibility as a witness on the basis that such a person is more likely to be a liar than a person of unspotted character. However, even on the issue of the credibility of the accused, such evidence would not be admitted unless the provisions of s. 1(f) of the Criminal Evidence Act 1898 applied. It is quite obvious that his criminal record has no relevance whatsoever in relation to the crime charged and accordingly would be completely inadmissible on the issue of guilt.

(b)   X has previous convictions for importuning in a public place. He is charged with indecently assaulting a small boy. Once again the previous criminal record may have some relevance on the issue of credibility. It may even be argued that X's previous criminal record is relevant to the proof of the actual crime which has been charged. However, common sense tells us that there are grave dangers of prejudice to X if his previous record became known to the jury and it is quite clear that such prejudice would greatly outweigh any relevance it may have. On the issue of guilt such evidence should be excluded.

(c)   X has previous convictions for stealing from parked cars. He is charged with theft from a car. Once again it may be argued that the previous record of X has some relevance to the crime charged, if only because human behaviour tends to repeat itself. But the relevance of such evidence would be relatively slight while its prejudicial effect would be substantial. Accordingly, such evidence would be excluded.

(d)   X has three previous convictions for rape. All these offences involved a peculiar *modus operandi* whereby the assailant committed the offence while dressed as a Roman soldier and wearing roller skates. There is evidence from the complainant that the man who raped her was dressed as a Roman soldier and was wearing roller skates. The prosecution wishes to lead evidence of X's previous convictions as part of the case against him.

Undoubtedly if any ordinary jury were convinced that the rapist in the instant case had committed the offence while wearing such eccentric garb and that X had previous convictions for the same kind of offence in which similar clothing had been worn, X would probably be convicted. He would be convicted because the jury would be satisfied that the rapist in the instant case was the same man as the rapist in the earlier cases, namely X. The dramatic similarities between the offence charged and the previous offences are too marked to be discounted on the basis of coincidence and although the prejudicial effect on X's case of the earlier convictions would be overwhelming, so would its relevance. In this situation it is likely that the evidence of the other offences committed by X would be admitted as part of the prosecution case on the issue of guilt.

The problem which the law of evidence has had to face in this area has been that of drawing up some kind of rule, the formulation of which has to have the effect of excluding the kind of evidence referred to in examples (a), (b) and (c) above, while allowing in evidence which falls under example (d). The attempts which judges have made to draw this line have not been wholly consistent. For a period following the decision of the House of Lords in *DPP* v *Boardman* [1975] AC 421 it was possible to state the overriding principles with a reasonable degree of certainty, even though it may still have remained difficult to state on which side of the admissibility/inadmissibility line any particular fact situation fell. However, in commenting on two subsequent House of Lords' decisions (*DPP* v *P* [1991] 2 AC 447 and *R* v *H* [1995] 2 All ER 865) Tapper has stated that '... the House of Lords has so reduced the threshold of admissibility as to force a reconsideration of the position' ((1995) NLJ 1223).

Most conventional treatments of similar fact evidence have traditionally begun with the judgment of Lord Herschell LC in *Makin* v *Attorney-General for New South Wales* [1894] AC 57 where the applicable principles were stated in the following way:

In their Lordships' opinion the principles which must govern the decision of the case are clear, though the application of them is by no means free from difficulty. It is undoubtedly not competent for the prosecution to adduce evidence tending to show that the accused has been guilty of criminal acts other than those covered by the indictment, for the purpose of leading to the conclusion that the accused is a person likely from his criminal conduct or character to have committed the offence for which he is being tried. On the other hand, the mere fact that the evidence adduced tends to show the commission of other crimes does not render it inadmissible if it be relevant to an issue before the jury, and it may be so relevant if it bears upon the question whether the acts alleged to constitute the crime charged in the indictment were designed or accidental, or to rebut a defence which would otherwise be open to the accused.

The two strands of this formulation meant first, that if the evidence of other criminal acts committed by the accused would do no more than show that the accused is someone who has a general criminal disposition, then such evidence is not admissible; secondly, that if the evidence goes further and 'is relevant to an issue before the jury' then it may be admissible.

In the 80-year period between *Makin* and *Boardman* the courts sought to apply the second limb of Makin by working out, in the form of a number of categories, those situations where similar fact evidence could be admitted. Elliott ([1983] Crim LR 284 at p. 285) has described the consequence:

The perhaps inevitable result ... was the generation of an enormous volume of case law on when similar fact evidence could and when it could not be deployed. That in turn was followed by what was meant to be helpful exegesis by commentators, involving elaborate systemisation and employing an arcane vocabulary wherein terms originally coined merely to aid exposition took on a life of their own. This epistemology was adopted in and to that extent legitimated by some judgments, and the building of the Tower of Babel went on apace.

Not very comforting for the frightened examinee!

It is not our intention to give an extended explanation of the various ways in which the introduction of similar fact evidence was justified in the pre-*Boardman* cases, but it is important for an examinee to realise that it is very difficult to analyse the significance of *Boardman* and the effect of the subsequent decisions without at least a nodding acquaintance with pre-*Boardman* law. The extent to which you will feel it necessary to delve into the law before 1975 will be dictated to a large extent by the views of those who teach you, but some knowledge of the evolution of the topic is essential to enable you to understand the present position.

THE LAW BEFORE BOARDMAN

The key to the development of the pre-1975 law is to be found in the two limbs of Lord Herschell's elegant formulation in *Makin v Attorney-General for New South Wales* [1894] AC 57. Although the general principle as set out in the first limb is an exclusionary one, under the second limb similar fact evidence may become admissible where it is relevant to an issue before the jury. The examples used by Lord Herschell to illustrate such relevance were where the evidence was being adduced to demonstrate whether the commission of the offence was deliberate or accidental or where it was admitted to rebut a defence otherwise open to the accused. In other words, the evidence became admissible if an acceptable purpose justifying admissibility could be identified. It did not take the courts long to establish that the purposes enumerated by Lord Herschell were not exhaustive, and the next 80 years saw the creation of a number of categories of case which satisfied the necessary purpose test. The following are examples:

(a) *To show 'design'* (or rebut the defence of accident). In *R v Smith* (1915) 11 Cr App R 229 (the 'brides in the bath' case) the question was whether the circumstances of the deaths of two women to whom the accused had at some time been married, were admissible to prove his guilt on a charge of murdering a third woman to whom he had also been married. The Court of Criminal Appeal adopted the following:

And then comes in the purpose, and the only purpose, for which you are allowed to consider the evidence as to the other deaths. If you find an accident which benefits a person and you find that the person has been sufficiently fortunate to have that accident happen to him a number of times, benefitting him each time, you draw a very strong, frequently irresistible inference, that the occurrence of so many accidents benefitting him is such a coincidence that it cannot have happened unless it was design.

(b) *To prove 'system'* (negativing accident or mistake). In *R v Bond* [1906] 2 KB 389 the issue was whether the evidence of a girl who alleged that the accused had performed an illegal abortion on her was admissible when the accused was charged with a similar offence against someone else. By a majority the Court for Crown Cases Reserved admitted the evidence. A variety of justifications for admissibility were given, variously described as 'negativing innocence of intent', 'negativing accident or mistake', and 'proof of system'.

(c) *To prove 'guilty passion'* (rebutting defence of innocent association). In *R v Ball* [1911] AC 47 a brother and sister were indicted for incest. The prosecution sought to adduce evidence of other earlier acts of carnal knowledge (committed before the Punishment of Incest Act 1908) to show that the accused had a guilty passion towards each other. Lord Loreburn LC said in the House of Lords:

> I consider that this evidence was clearly admissible on the issue that this crime was committed ... to establish the guilty relations between the parties and the existence of a sexual passion between them.

(d) *To identify the accused*. In *R* v *Straffen* [1952] 2 QB 911 the accused was charged with murdering a little girl near Broadmoor. The child had been killed during a short period of a few hours when the accused had escaped from Broadmoor. The issue was whether evidence of two other murders committed by the accused (with similar features to the killing in the instant case and for which he had been committed to Broadmoor) was admissible. The Court of Criminal Appeal stated:

> In the opinion of the court that evidence was rightly admitted ... for the purpose of identifying the murderer ... as being the same individual as the person who had murdered the other two little girls in precisely the same way.

A particularly significant illustration of the way in which the courts have used the 'identity' category to allow in similar fact evidence was in *Thompson* v *R* [1918] AC 221 where possession by the accused of powder puffs and indecent photographs of boys was admitted to identify him as a person who had committed acts of gross indecency with boys on a particular occasion. Lord Sumner opined that:

> Persons ... who commit the offences now under consideration seek the habitual gratification of a particular perverted lust, which not only takes them out of the class of ordinary men gone wrong, but stamps them with the hallmark of a specialised and extraordinary class as much as if they carried on their bodies some physical peculiarity.... It was accordingly admissible evidence of his identity with that criminal.

The cases and categories referred to above provide, of course, only the crudest outline of the pre-1975 law. However, they serve to illustrate the general approach taken by the courts. If a *purpose* for which the evidence was relevant could be identified, that provided a gateway to admissibility.

DPP v BOARDMAN AND AFTER

The significance of the decision in *DPP* v *Boardman* [1975] AC 421 lay in the fact that, while the House of Lords did not openly state that the earlier cases were decided for the wrong reasons, the whole theoretical basis of the admissibility of similar fact evidence was recast. Some extracts from the judgments show this to be the case:

> The basic principle must be that the admission of similar fact evidence ... is exceptional and requires a strong degree of probative force. This probative force is derived, if at all, from the circumstance that the facts testified to by the several witnesses bear to each other such a striking similarity that they must, when judged by experience and common sense, either all be true, or have arisen from a cause common to the witnesses or from pure coincidence. (per Lord Wilberforce)
>
> Circumstances, however, may arise in which such evidence is so very relevant that to exclude it would be an affront to common sense.... [T]he question as I see it must be one of degree. (per Lord Cross of Chelsea)
>
> [I]f the crime charged is committed in a uniquely or strikingly similar manner to other crimes committed by the accused the manner in which the other crimes were committed may be evidence upon which a jury could reasonably conclude that the accused was guilty of the crime charged. The similarity would have to be so unique or striking that common sense makes it inexplicable on the basis of coincidence. (per Lord Salmon)

A clear message shone through these extracts, and indeed through the whole of the judgments of the House of Lords, and it was this: *categories of relevance* were unimportant; what mattered was the *degree of relevance*. In other words, the purpose for which one might wish to adduce the evidence did not matter. What did matter, according to the House of Lords, was whether the evidence was of such a high degree of relevance that it satisfied the 'unique or striking similarity' test. Viewed in this light, it was possible to return to the pre-*Boardman* authorities and look at them again from the new perspective. Take, for example, the case of *Straffen*. After *Boardman* it was no longer necessary to resort to the notion of identity to provide the avenue for admissibility. As was expressly recognised in relation to *Straffen* by Lord Cross of Chelsea in *Boardman*, the question was whether such evidence was so very relevant that to exclude it would have been an affront to common sense.

Hoffmann ('Similar facts after *Boardman*' (1975) 91 LQR 193) explained the significance of *Boardman* as follows:

> Despite what appears to have been further approval of Lord Herschell's rule in *Boardman*, the reasoning of their Lordships contains the seeds of its downfall. A careful reading of the speeches of Lord Morris, Lord Wilberforce and Lord Cross leads one to the conclusion that Lord Herschell was guilty not so much of obscurity as of error. Quite simply, the lucid

antithesis is wrong. The repeated efforts of the courts to persuade themselves that it accords with their actual decisions on the admissibility of similar fact evidence are directly responsible for the confused state of the law throughout the present century. It is perhaps significant that Lord Wilberforce and Lord Cross, the two Law Lords in whose speeches the reasoning in *Boardman* is most fully articulated, do not mention *Makin* in all.

So what of the 20 years or so since *Boardman* was decided? Did the case represent a new dawn of understanding in this area? The answer is a qualified 'yes'. Subsequent decisions did approve of and apply the 'striking similarity' test, but there were soon a number of indications that the courts, and particularly the Court of Appeal, felt uneasy with that single formulation. Thus in *R v Rance and Herron* (1975) 62 Cr App R 118 Lord Widgery CJ explained that one must be careful not to attach too much importance to Lord Salmon's vivid phrase 'uniquely or strikingly similar'. He said that the gist of that test is that similar fact evidence is admissible if, and only if, it goes beyond showing a tendency to commit crimes of this kind and is positively probative in regard to the crime charged. Similarly in *R v Scarrott* [1978] QB 1016 Scarman LJ said:

> Positive probative value is what the law requires, if similar fact evidence is to be admissible. Such probative value is not provided by the mere repetition of similar facts; there has to be some feature or features in the evidence sought to be adduced which provides a link.

In several cases decided after *Scarrott*, the Court of Appeal applied the 'striking similarity' test in combination with the warning given in that case that it was merely a label and that what was needed was positive probative value. The difficulty with *Boardman* was that it gave the impression of a single, all-embracing standard, to be applied in all cases. By contrast, the later analysis in the Court of Appeal suggested that the actual test of admissibility in a given case would inevitably turn on such matters as the other evidence in the case and the nature of the defence being run by the accused. In *DPP v P* [1991] 2 AC 447, the House of Lords confirmed that 'striking similarity' is only one way of establishing what is needed in similar fact cases, namely a high degree of probative force. Lord Mackay, with whom the rest of the House concurred, expressed the central principle as follows:

> ... [T]he essential feature of evidence which is to be admitted is that its probative force in support of the allegation that an accused person committed a crime is sufficiently great to make it just to admit the evidence, notwithstanding that it is prejudicial to the accused in tending to show that he was guilty of another crime. Such probative force may be derived from

striking similarities in the evidence about the manner in which the crime was committed.... But restricting the circumstances in which there is sufficient probative force to overcome prejudice of evidence relating to another crime to cases in which there is some striking similarity between them is to restrict the operation of the principle in a way which gives too much effect to a particular manner of stating it, and is not justified in principle.... Once the principle is recognised, that what has to be assessed is the probative force of the evidence in question, the infinite variety of circumstances in which the question arises demonstrates that there is no single manner in which this can be achieved. Whether the evidence has sufficient probative value to outweigh its prejudicial effect must in each case be a question of degree.

The precise question which the House of Lords was asked to consider in *DPP* v *P* was as follows:

Where a father or step father is charged with sexually abusing a young daughter of the family, is evidence that he also similarly abused other young children of the family admissible (assuming there to be no collusion) in support of such charge in the absence of any other 'striking similarities'.

The essence of the actual decision in the case was that the evidence *is* admissible if the similarity is sufficiently strong *or* there is other sufficient relationship between the events described and the evidence of the other young children of the family that the evidence, if accepted, would so strongly support the truth of the charge that it is fair to admit it notwithstanding its prejudicial effect.

The issues considered in the case of *R* v *H* [1995] 2 All ER 865 also illustrate the way in which the reasoning of the House of Lords has moved on since the decision in *Boardman* in a way which is very clear. In *R* v *H* the accused was charged with committing a number of sexual offences against his adopted daughter and his step daughter who were aged 9 and 14 respectively. The essential issue in the case was whether the evidence relating to the charges in respect of one daughter was admissible in relation to the charges respecting the offences committed against the other. The context in which this issue had to be considered was that of a potential risk that the two girls had put their heads together and concocted their respective stories. Lord Griffiths was quite explicit in his judgment in explaining why the law on this matter has moved on in the last century. He referred to the many restrictive evidential rules which had been fashioned in the past and which were designed to protect the accused at a time when juries were less well-educated and more likely to be illiterate, and when the penalties for even minor criminal offences were very severe. He contrasted that with the present position where many of the old rules are being re-evaluated or discarded, and he stated the application of the newly developed principles of similar fact evidence in the following way:

> There is no dispute in this case that if the statements of the two sisters were truthful, accurate accounts of their stepfather's sexual misconduct towards them, they showed such similarities as to render them similar fact evidence in the more relaxed sense of that term now to be applied as a result of the recent decision of the House in *R* v *P*, and therefore prima facie admissible both as probative and corroborative evidence.

It should perhaps be noted that Tapper ((1995) NLJ 1223) remarked that 'There seems to have been no suggestion that the offences were of striking, or indeed any, similarity. No application seems to have been made to sever the indictment. The issue related simply to the use of the evidence adduced in relation to the one daughter on the counts relating to the other'. He concluded (at p. 1264) that 'The result in *H* was to remove the last vestiges of the breakthrough made by *Boardman* in relation to the admissibility of similar fact evidence. After *P* it seems that the relevance of evidence of allegations of other offences is to be assumed without explanation of the reasoning process involved, and after *H* the evidence is to be assumed to be true'.

As the above extracted quotations demonstrate, the decisions in *R* v *P* and *R* v *H* have given rise to considerable criticism, and these are useful cases for you to consider in depth and on which you should seek to work out your own position.

PLANNING YOUR REVISION

The number of reported cases on this topic seems endless and the most difficult aspect of your revision will be to avoid total confusion. It is helpful to appreciate that in a standard examination you will only have time to analyse properly a very small proportion of the quantity of material available. Accordingly, you should not try to learn everything. The essence of your task is to try to understand in outline the way the law developed before *DPP* v *Boardman* perhaps with some knowledge of the landmark cases of the past, and couple that with a relatively detailed appreciation of the direction in which the law has evolved in recent years, and in particular the significance of *DPP* v *P* and *R* v *H*.

The selectivity of your treatment must depend upon the emphasis the course you are studying adopts. Thus, for example, if you have concentrated on the problems of similar fact evidence in the context of homosexual assaults upon children then a detailed knowledge of both the pre- and post-*Boardman* cases on this area would be invaluable. On the other hand, if the treatment has been more generalised, then you will need to broaden your examination of the case law, with some corresponding sacrifice of depth. In any event, it is usually helpful to try to break the topic down into a number of constituent elements. This will assist you in penetrating the gloom and will lend some structure to the revision of the topic. We have suggested below a number of headings under which it may be useful to collect your material.

Makin's Case

There may be something to be said for discarding *Makin* v *Attorney-General for New South Wales* [1894] AC 57, and all it stood for, from your materials on this topic. A close analysis of the recent decisions inescapably leads one to the conclusion that the first limb of *Makin* has not survived, even if the case had managed to retain some identity after the bombardment represented by the decision in *Boardman*. However, it is undoubtedly useful to know where the whole story began. Lord Herschell's dictum is a useful starting point for answers to a wide range of questions which can be asked on similar fact evidence and therefore you should know it. This does not need to be a verbatim recollection, but a clear understanding and recollection of the two limbs of the formulation is useful. The actual facts and decision of the case are almost incidental.

Development of the Law 1894 to 1975

You must be wary here. We would suggest that if you attempt to assimilate and learn the vast quantity of law generated during this period then you are in grave danger of concentrating too much on an area of law which is no longer so important. Where you really need to be concentrating your effort is in mastering the post-*Boardman* developments and the modern academic debate on the subject; you will get bogged down if you try to probe too deeply into the old cases. However, this does not mean that you can abandon the older material completely; you need to have some knowledge of it, if only to be able to locate any discussion of the modern issues within some kind of context. We have already given a brief sketch of the older cases earlier in this chapter; many students may feel that a treatment along these lines (without necessarily using the same authorities) will be adequate enough. Nevertheless, if you feel that it is likely that you will have to grapple with examination questions which seek to probe the theoretical foundations of the subject, it is desirable to have some familiarity with the landmark cases. You will find that *Thompson* v *R* [1918] AC 221 is a particularly useful decision in that it provides an interesting point of comparison with some of the recent decisions on similar fact evidence in homosexual offence cases.

Boardman and the Consequent Academic Discussion

It must be obvious from what we have said that *Boardman* is a case of critical importance. You need to know this case well and be familiar with the various tests of admissibility adopted by the members of the House of Lords. You will find Lord Hailsham's judgment particularly useful because he uses some vivid examples (which are easily understood and remembered) to illustrate parts of his argument. A detailed understanding of the facts of *Boardman* is needed, not for the purposes of repetition on the examination paper but to understand the vital issues of cross-corroboration with which the case was concerned. Corroboration is no longer of significance, in its traditional academic sense, following the Criminal Justice and Public Order Act 1994, but you need some understanding of these issues in order to be able to understand properly the discussion of the similar fact questions in *DPP* v *P* and *R* v *H*. You should also be aware of the things *Boardman* does not say; in particular you should look at the treatment (or non-treatment) of *Makin*. Finally, think about the precise question of law which was referred by the Court of Appeal to the House of Lords. What does that tell you of the view of the Court of Appeal about the state of the law immediately prior to *Boardman*? What does the response of the House of Lords tell you about the importance of *Boardman*?

As far as the academic debate on *Boardman* is concerned there are two articles which we regard as being of keynote importance: Hoffmann, 'Similar facts after *Boardman*' (1975) 91 LQR 193 and Elliott, 'The young person's guide to similar fact evidence' [1983] Crim LR 284, 352. You will find these articles to be of particular value, Hoffmann's because he exposes the unstable theoretical foundation on which the post-*Makin* law was constructed, and Elliott's, because it is a scholarly and detailed treatment of some of the important issues. Neither of these two articles is simple: you will need to think long and hard about the points the authors are making. Remember the advice given in chapter 1: do not go overboard in trying to compile extensive notes from these materials. What you need to understand are the key points being made, with a corresponding appreciation of the main strands in the arguments employed.

DPP v P and R v H

You will have spent some time in your course considering the impact of these two cases. You need to spend time on them and familiarise yourself, not just with the particular questions which the House of Lords had to address and its responses to them, but also with the much wider significance of these cases in terms of the overall evolution of the law on this topic. A detailed knowledge of and a critical attitude towards them is essential. We will be making reference to these two cases in the context of a specific examination question later in this chapter but in our view it is very important at the revision stage to try to formulate some ideas of your own about the way in which this topic is moving. As we suggest in other chapters of this book, we believe that all examinees should actually have something to say about the topic on which they are writing. It is only through such an approach that you can inject some kind of distinctive contribution of your own into an otherwise standard product of an examination answer. You will undoubtedly find that if you try to work out some conclusions for yourself as to what is currently happening in the law, that exercise will both help you to understand and to remember the topic. As we have said elsewhere, no one expects a dramatic and original theoretical construct which exposes the one true rationale of similar fact evidence from an undergraduate student, even one of first-class ability. But any student who aspires to a good examination performance will have to do more than simply reproduce material which has been learnt. Remember that it does not matter greatly if your analysis of the area leads you to a conclusion which is in fact wrong, as long as you can make a reasonable and reasoned effort in justifying your particular viewpoint.

What then, if anything, is there to be said about similar fact evidence that has not been said before? Probably very little, but we would suggest that the following are the key points around which you could construct your thinking:

(a)   Make sure you know the major trends in the development of the law.

(b)   Relevance is the basic test of admissibility. In the context of similar fact evidence, admissibility is all dependent on the degree of relevance the evidence has and given the relatively sparse information often contained in an examination question, it will often be difficult to determine accurately which side of the line the evidence falls.

(c)   Because of the generality of the test, the question of admissibility will turn on the particular facts in question.

(d)   A useful guide to relevance is to look at the purpose for which the evidence is sought to be admitted. You cannot categorise cases, as used to happen before *Boardman*, but purpose lends relevance to the evidence, and may therefore provide a helpful signpost to you.

(e)   'Striking similarity' is just one way in which the evidence may show the degree of relevance which is required. But striking similarity is particularly important in cases where the other evidence in the case is sparse: e.g., *R* v *Straffen*. Conversely, if the other evidence in the case is substantial, then provided that the similar fact evidence has sufficient probative value, the similarities may be relatively commonplace: e.g., *R* v *Rance and Herron*; *R* v *H*.

Whatever approach you take towards analysing the law in this area, it must be done on the solid foundation of a good understanding of contemporary academic argument juxtaposed with modern judicial practice. We have already referred to some of the relevant literature, but other contributions which you should consider are Mirfield, 'Similar facts — *Makin* out' [1987] CLJ 83, Zuckerman, 'Similar fact evidence — the unobservable rule' (1987) 104 LQR 187 and Tapper, 'The Erosion of *Boardman* v *DPP*' (1995) NLJ 1223.

EXAMINATION QUESTIONS

Similar fact evidence lends itself to both essay and problem questions. It is also a topic which can be combined reasonably easily with other areas of the law of evidence and, in particular, it is often combined with questions of a more general nature on character evidence and on s. 1(f) of the Criminal Evidence Act 1898. Essay questions on similar fact evidence are usually very easy to identify: the presence of the word 'similar fact evidence' or 'disposition' or 'propensity' will usually be enough to remove any lingering doubts you may have about what the subject-matter of a particular question is. Problem questions may cause some difficulty, particularly if the similar fact issues are submerged under a number of other matters. Students sometimes become confused between identifying those issues which relate to similar facts and those which relate to more general aspects of the character of the accused. However, a useful point to remember is that if the issue in the question involves a discussion of whether the particular item of disputed evidence can be used by the prosecution, in chief, and for the purposes of proving guilt (as opposed to merely destroying credibility) then it is almost certain that the question is concerned with similar facts.

In our experience, wherever a question which is concerned wholly or mainly with similar facts appears on a paper it will usually involve a discussion of the mainstream arguments on the admissibility of such evidence. Inevitably you will need to display a good understanding of the theoretical foundation of *DPP* v *Boardman* and of necessity you will have to be familiar with the post-1975 case law. Indeed, many typical essay questions are concerned with the impressive (if rather impenetrable) dicta which have emerged from some of the recent cases.

Problem Questions

Problem questions on similar fact evidence are quite common, partly because it is a very easy topic on which to create a problem question and partly because there is no real difficulty in pulling in issues from other areas of the law of evidence. A typical problem question might look something like this:

James is on trial for the attempted buggery of three boys. Ian, Steven and Clive, who are aged 8, 11 and 15. The three boys all give evidence at the trial that James, who was a leader at an annual cub and scout camp, approached them in their tents in the early hours of the morning, suggested that they return to his tent for a cup of tea and that when each went, he attempted to commit buggery with them. James denies these allegations and says that the boys were asked to come to his tent because they had been smoking in their tents. He alleges that they have colluded and made up the stories. The prosecution wishes to use the evidence of each of the boys to confirm the evidence of the others and wishes also to bring the evidence of three other scouts who allege that similar events took place at the previous summer camp, although no actual attempts at buggery took place. Discuss.

This is not a particularly difficult question of its type but you should not rush headlong into writing your answer. It is important to identify the central issues raised by the problem, both because you will get some credit for identifying what the issues are and because you will be able to write a more carefully structured (and pleasing) answer to the question. The best way to start an answer to a problem of this kind is to work out in rough form the issues you have spotted, jotting down at the same time those cases which you think you may wish to use in your answer. There is no need to spend a long time in doing this, but it will help to avoid the risk of forgetting to deal with some matter once your answer has got under way.

If you can properly do so within the confines of any problem question you should make a determined effort to use the question as a vehicle for any fundamental theoretical knowledge you may have, any relevant academic arguments you can bring to bear and any views you have formulated on the topic. We are not suggesting that you should corrupt or distort the question or give it some kind of fanciful interpretation simply to force in what may be the product of a considerable amount of study and thought, but if you have a legitimate opportunity to take account of such wider issues then you should use that opportunity if you can.

In the context of this question it may fairly be said that an opportunity for an exploration of the theoretical basis of similar fact evidence is available, given that much of the evolution of the subject has centred on sexual offences of one type or another.

You should *not* begin your answer by rewriting in your own words the question which has been set. This may seem a fairly obvious point, but a common fault among examinees is to launch themselves rather too gently into their answer by a simple recitation of the facts. A much better way to begin is to identify, in the first paragraph of your answer, the central issues in the problem. This tells the examiner that you know what you are doing and that you have accurately identified what the question is about. Do not worry that you may not have spotted every issue in the problem. Some questions may raise a large number of issues, but it is a mistake to think that a good mark depends on pinpointing each and every issue and side issue that can be squeezed out of the words of the question. You will get a good mark if you deal with those matters lying at the heart of the question in a full and intelligent manner, even if you miss (or even consciously decide not to deal in any detailed way with) one or two of the less important points.

In this question it is quite legitimate, and indeed highly desirable, to regard some of the points raised as being of less importance than some of the others. We are told, for example, that the purpose for which the prosecution wish to adduce the disputed evidence is to confirm the testimony of the boys. Accordingly, it is entirely proper to assume that the question is *not* searching for a detailed explanation of the historical position concerning the corroboration rules which used to relate to the kinds of offences with which the question is concerned. You may feel uneasy at the prospect of passing by such matters, but if you spend time on a necessarily brief explanation of such matters, it is quite possible the examiner will see that as no more than a padding out of the answer. Although the question raises questions of competence (see chapter 3), the basic issue in the problem in the context of this chapter is whether the evidence of each of the boys in relation to the offence committed against him is admissible for the prosecution in relation to the offences committed against the other boys. Such evidence will only be admissible if it gets in under the similar fact principles. You should make the following general points in your answer:

(a)   From an early date (*Thompson* v *R* [1918] AC 221) homosexual offences, particularly when committed against children, have always appeared to satisfy the appropriate admissibility test for similar fact evidence more readily than other types of offence.

(b)   The above point was confirmed by the way in which the Court of Appeal framed the question that the House of Lords was asked to consider in *DPP* v *Boardman*.

(c)   The House of Lords in *DPP* v *Kilbourne* [1973] AC 729 and more emphatically in *DPP* v *Boardman* disposed finally of the suggestion that there was a special rule or principle applicable to sexual, or to homosexual, offences.

(d)   The post-*Boardman* position depends on the evidence being received by virtue of a general principle. This general principle received various formulations in *Boardman*, but can be summarised in the propositions enunciated by Lord Wilberforce, to the effect that the admission of similar fact evidence requires a strong degree of probative force. Such probative force is derived, if at all, from the striking similarities which the various events bear to each other.

(e)   Their Lordships in *Boardman* found the case to be very borderline, and it is even arguable that having established a rigorous test of admissibility, they then failed to apply it on the facts of the case. The relevant similarity related to the passive, rather than the active role which *Boardman* took in the proceedings.

(f)   There are clear signs that the formal rigour, at least, of the *Boardman* formulation has been diluted by subsequent authority from the Court of Appeal, and now from the House of Lords in *DPP* v *P* and *R* v *H*.

Thus, in *DPP* v *P* Lord Mackay was able to state that the essential feature of evidence which is to be admitted is that its probative force in support of the guilt of the accused is sufficiently great to make it just to admit the evidence, notwithstanding that it is prejudicial to the accused.

Unless the facts of an examination problem on this topic are so distinctive and extraordinary, it is not really practicable to speak in anything other than fairly general terms of whether the test of a sufficiently high degree of probative force has been satisfied, given that in the few words of an examination problem it is impossible to detail enough information to enable such a positive conclusion to be reached. Accordingly, in the context of this question, it is not altogether desirable to reach dogmatic conclusions on whether evidence of the offences with which the defendant is charged satisfies the general test of admissibility. However, it is probably worth making the point that there is little in the facts of this problem which is unusually distinctive. Following the decision in *R* v *H* this does not appear to be a significant problem; see also, for example, *R* v *Barrington* [1981] 1 WLR 419, where relatively commonplace similarities were sufficient.

What of the evidence of scouts from the earlier camp? It should be noted that the facts of the problem disclose that no criminal offences were committed against this group and the problem here invites you to assess what, if any, difference that may make. There are really two separate issues here:

(a)   Is behaviour which is not of itself criminal, but which forms part of the surrounding circumstances of a crime, admissible under the similar fact principles, or is that doctrine confined only to conduct which is of itself criminal?

(b)   If the above question is answered in the affirmative, can one take the argument further and admit evidence of conduct which is not criminal and which does not form part of the circumstances surrounding the relevant crimes?

You can bring a number of interesting cases to bear on these questions. On the first of the two questions, it is quite clear that the similar fact principle is wide enough to embrace evidence of surrounding circumstances, which may not be in themselves criminal. Thus, for example, in *R v Scarrott* [1978] QB 1016 Scarman LJ said:

> [O]ne cannot isolate, as a sort of laboratory specimen, the bare bones of a criminal offence from its surrounding circumstances and say that it is only within the confines of that specimen, microscopically considered, that admissibility is to be determined.... Some surrounding circumstances have to be considered in order to understand either the offence charged or the nature of the similar fact evidence which it is sought to adduce and in each case it must be a matter of judgment where the line is drawn. One cannot draw an inflexible line as a rule of law.

A moment's reflection will convince you that this is true. Many of the cases on similar fact evidence involve the admission of evidence of all kinds of matters which did not form part of the crime itself. A mass murderer may kill his victims in a relatively ordinary way, but his preparations for the crimes, his motives, or the way he disposes of the bodies could all contribute to a unique and strikingly similar pattern. Thus, in the case of *Makin* v *Attorney-General for New South Wales* [1894] AC 57 the fact that the Makins had taken in a number of children after they had promised to look after them during childhood, but had only demanded a token payment from the mothers of the children, was part of the similar fact evidence. Similarly, in *R v Smith* (1915) 11 Cr App R 229 (the 'brides in the bath' case) the court had regard to the facts that the accused had married the women who were ultimately his victims and that he had taken out insurance policies on their lives shortly before he disposed of them.

Were the position otherwise there would be very few cases on similar fact evidence.

The second question posed above brings us much nearer to the facts of our problem. The scouts from the previous summer camp did not have any offences committed against them, although they were still subject to the same preliminaries as I, S and C. The principal arguments against the admissibility of such evidence is that it is really too remote from the alleged crimes with which J is charged, that it is too prejudicial and that in any event it does not satisfy the present test of admissibility. In addition, such acts were entirely non-criminal in their nature. However, in *R v Barrington* [1981] 1 WLR 419, it was held that the fact that the proposed similar fact evidence was not evidence of criminal activity was not a barrier to admissibility.

As with all examination questions, you should try to structure your answer so that it contains a beginning, a middle and an end. One of the common faults with answers, and particularly answers to problem questions, is that they tend to stop in full flow, without any attempt to draw the strands of discussion together and without any considered conclusion. You will have noticed that the instruction on the question we have been considering invited you to 'discuss' the issues raised. Unlike an instruction which requires you to 'advise' one or more of the parties, the requirement to discuss the issues raised can quite legitimately be interpreted as an invitation to say something relevant about the matters raised in the question, yet which may lie outside the narrow matters of concern to the various parties in the problem. One good way of rounding off your answer to this question would be to pull together those aspects of your discussion of the law which can be utilised to illustrate some of the thinking and ideas which you may have on the topic as a whole. Some candidates may find it unnecessary to formalise such matters in the way which we are suggesting here, because the overall sophistication of their treatment of the problem may have already indicated their views on the present, somewhat confused, state of play. However, for most candidates a good way of concluding their answer would be to write a final paragraph or so in which the opportunity is taken of displaying evidence of a depth of appreciation which may not be altogether apparent from the earlier, and more functional, part of the answer. This particular problem provides an easy route into such a conclusion. This is because the nature of the issues raised directs you squarely to an examination of *Boardman*, *DPP* v *P* and *R* v *H*. In the light of the issue with which *Boardman* was concerned and given the particular question certified by the Court of Appeal for the House of Lords, you have the freedom to contrast the recent development of the subject with some of the canons of the past. In particular, some mention of the various academic analyses and the way in which the recent cases would stand up to such analytical scrutiny would bring ample evidence for the examiner to be fully convinced that your perception of the topic was one of quality. In addition, you should try to include your own assessment of the present state of play. Back it up by reference to authority, rather than by stating some bold, but unreasoned conclusion. And do not write 'Ran out of time'!

Essay Questions

We do not propose to say very much about essay questions on this topic. Many of the general points that any typical essay question on similar fact evidence will raise have already been touched upon in our general outline of the operative principles and current problems. In practice, essay questions on this topic will tend to be directed towards a general treatment of the effects of *DPP* v *P* and *R* v *H*. The following are typical examples of the kinds of questions which can be set:

'[E]vidence is admissible as similar fact evidence if, but only if, it goes beyond showing a tendency to commit crimes of this kind and is positively probative in regard to the crime now charged.' (per Lord Widgery CJ in *R v Rance and Herron* (1976).) Comment.

'The demise in appreciation of the rational principles which underpinned the decision of the House of Lords in *Boardman* v *DPP* has reduced similar fact evidence to an incoherent body of law.' Comment.

'The rules adopted in *DPP* v *P* and *R* v *H* adopt a test of admissibility for similar fact evidence which is too low in the context of preventing the risk of undue prejudice to the accused when such evidence is admitted.' Do you agree?

All these quotations, real or invented, have the common feature that at their heart lies a requirement of a full and critical treatment of *Boardman*, *DPP* v *P* and *R* v *H*. They require an assessment of where the rule lies today, together with a detailed commentary on the post-1975 decisions. We hope that we have said enough in the earlier parts of the chapter to give you a clear indication of the kind of approach you should employ in handling this kind of question. You will find the article by Elliott, 'The young person's guide to similar fact evidence', to be of inestimable value in providing an interesting and coherent attempt to pull together some of the various strands of the topic since *Boardman*. This article will provide you with a foundation on which you should build your own consideration of *DPP* v *P* and *R* v *H*.

FURTHER READING

Acorn, 'Similar fact evidence and the principle of inductive reasoning: *Makin* sense' (1991) 11 OJLS 63.

Allan, 'Similar fact evidence and disposition: law, discretion and admissibility' (1985) 48 MLR 253.

Carter, 'Forbidden reasoning permissible: similar fact evidence a decade after *Boardman*' (1985) 48 MLR 29.

Cross, 'Fourth time lucky — similar fact evidence in the House of Lords' [1975] Crim LR 62.

Elliott, 'The young person's guide to similar fact evidence' [1983] Crim LR 284.

Hoffman, 'Similar facts after *Boardman*' (1975) 91 LQR 193.

Mirfield, 'Similar fact *Makin* out' [1987] CLJ 83.

Tapper, 'The Erosion of *Boardman* v *DPP*' (1995) NLJ 1223, 1263.

Zuckerman, 'Similar fact evidence the unobservable rule' (1987) 104 LQR 187.

7 EVIDENCE OF CHARACTER

INTRODUCTION

Evidence of character is the most difficult of all topics on any conventional course. It is one of those irritating and elusive subjects where one moment you think you have grasped what it is all about and the next you feel totally at sea. Yet it is a topic on which you can really shine in an examination if you finally manage to master its fundamental secrets. Furthermore, there is really no alternative to studying character, since it makes an appearance in virtually every evidence paper.

The key to success in this area is to approach it in a logical and ordered way (which is something that the textbooks sometimes fail to do). We think that the way to deal with this subject is to begin by breaking the subject down into its constituent parts. You should then master the principles which apply to each of those elements, before putting the subject back together again and viewing it as an integrated whole. You will find, once you have understood the basic principles, that each aspect of the topic is closely interrelated. We think it is helpful to approach the study of character in the following way:

(a) Identify the meaning of 'character', first at common law, and secondly under the Criminal Evidence Act 1898 (the 1898 Act).

(b) Understand the rules relating to the admissibility of evidence of character in the case of witnesses other than the accused.

(c) Understand the rules relating to the character of the accused at common law.

(d)   Understand the problems faced by the draftsman of the 1898 Act in dealing with the special position of the accused as a witness.

(e)   Learn verbatim s. 1(e) and (f) of the 1898 Act.

(f)   Analyse the crucial question of the relationship between s. 1(e) and s. 1(f).

(g)   Appreciate the nature of the prohibition on questions as to character on the cross-examination of the accused established by s. 1(f).

(h)   Learn the exceptions to that prohibition in s. 1(f)(i), (ii) and (iii) and appreciate the evidential purpose of such cross-examination.

(i)   Understand the nature of the discretion of the judge to disallow or limit such cross-examination, even where it is technically permissible.

We deal with these nine critical stages in turn.

MEANING OF 'CHARACTER'

Conventional treatments of this issue usually begin by saying that 'character' has one of three possible meanings in the law of evidence. 'Character' can mean:

(a)   the disposition of a person; for example, that he is in the habit of acting in a particular fashion, going to church, assaulting old-age pensioners etc;

(b)   the reputation of a person in a neighbourhood;

(c)   particular good or bad acts of a person, for example, that he restored a wallet he had found to the owner or conversely a previous conviction for stealing a wallet.

At common law it was established in the important case of *R v Rowton* (1865) Le & Ca 520 that in the law of evidence 'character' meant 'reputation'. In other words, if evidence is being given of the character of a person, that evidence must be confined to details of his general reputation. Character witnesses cannot depose to specific good or bad acts, or to the disposition of the person, to prove his character.

The most important question you need to consider is whether the narrow *Rowton* principle still applies generally today. The answer to that question is that, in theory at any rate, it does, and there are occasional examples of where the courts insist on its application. A good illustration is *R v Redgrave* (1982) 74 Cr App R 10, where the accused was charged with persistently importuning other men for an immoral purpose. He sought to give evidence of various heterosexual relationships to rebut the inference that he had been making homosexual approaches. The Court of Appeal ruled that although the accused could give evidence that he had not committed the acts alleged against him, he was not allowed to give evidence of particular facts to show that he did not have a disposition to behave in the way alleged by the prosecution. In other words, only evidence of general reputation would have been admissible.

However, whatever theory (and occasionally the Court of Appeal) may say, there is no doubt that in practice the rule in *Rowton* is more honoured in the breach than in the observance. Frequently the accused is allowed to state his own character as widely as he pleases — he is allowed to testify to his disposition (to help old ladies across the road) or to specific good acts he may have performed (returning a lost grant cheque to an impecunious student).

It is well nigh impossible for the *Rowton* principle to apply in the context of the 1898 Act. The Act, for the first time, permitted the accused to give evidence on his own behalf (which was simply not possible at the time when *Rowton* was decided). This means, *inter alia*, that the accused himself can now testify as to his character, as opposed to calling character witnesses to speak on his behalf. The problem is how an accused can give evidence as to his reputation in the neighbourhood when reputation is nothing other than 'that which people say about him when he is not there' (as Professor Cross once said). The answer is, of course, that he cannot. He can only testify as to his own disposition or to specific acts that he has done. This has been accepted, if only implicitly, by the courts. Thus in *R v Samuel* (1956) 40 Cr App R 8 the accused, who had been charged with larceny by finding, testified that on several previous occasions he had returned lost property which he had found to its true owner. As a consequence he was cross-examined as to his previous convictions under s. 1(f)(ii) of the 1898 Act on the basis that he had put his character in issue. Such cross-examination was held to be perfectly proper, despite the fact that the accused had only deposed to specific good acts, and not his general reputation in the neighbourhood. Another case you can usefully look at is *R v Dunkley* [1927] 1 KB 323.

CHARACTER AND WITNESSES OTHER THAN THE ACCUSED

It is quite permissible to attack the credibility of any ordinary witness in order to discredit his evidence. This can be done in a variety of ways, one of which is to question the witness on his character. For example, if the witness has 15 previous convictions for perjury this must surely, at the very least, leave the court in some doubt as to the trustworthiness of his evidence. The position is not so clear-cut where the previous convictions are for cruelty to his pet dog, but at any rate the jury is entitled to know that he is not a person of unspotted character. You should remember that if an accused attacks the credit of a prosecution witness in this way, he may open up his own character to cross-examination under s. 1(f)(ii) of the 1898 Act. We discuss this further below.

THE CHARACTER OF THE ACCUSED AT COMMON LAW

As a general rule, at common law an accused may adduce evidence of his good character, despite the fact that the prosecution may not generally adduce evidence of his bad character. Where evidence of good character is adduced, this goes primarily to the credibility of the accused, and is also capable of going to the issue of innocence of the crime charged. A potentially tricky aspect of this arises in the case of joint trials of two or more accused where not all of the accused are of previous good character. Where this is the case a direction by the judge as to the good character of one accused will treat that accused more favourably than the others. The whole question of directions to the jury concerning the good character of an accused was reviewed by the Court of Appeal in *R* v *Vye* [1993] 1 WLR 471, where guidelines are laid down. You must read this case. In addition, you should also look at *R* v *Aziz* [1995] 3 All ER 149 where further guidance is given by the House of Lords.

Once the accused has taken advantage of this common law right to adduce evidence of his good character, the prosecution is entitled, by way of rebuttal, to lead evidence of his bad character. A classic illustration is *R* v *Rowton* (1865) Le & Ca 520.

DRAFTING THE 1898 ACT

The draftsman must have found this very difficult. In making the accused competent for the first time the problem had to be faced of how to control his cross-examination by the prosecution. Was he to be treated in exactly the same way as any other witness? If so, his credit as a witness could have been attacked by questioning him on his previous character (such as previous convictions). Such a consequence would be highly prejudicial to an accused with anything in the nature of a criminal record, and to prevent the jury hearing of his record the accused might well have declined to give evidence in the first place. His new-found competence to testify on his own behalf would have been worthless. Was he to be given preferential treatment over other witnesses, so that he was to be immune from cross-examination on his character? If so, he would have been able to perjure himself quite happily in his evidence in chief about his own character without any fear of a come-back in cross-examination. He would also be able to blacken the character of his accusers with impunity.

Consequently the draftsman compromised. The accused was given an immunity (often referred to as a shield) against cross-examination on his character. This immunity is not absolute, and can be lost in certain circumstances. These circumstances are set out as the provisos to s. 1(f) of the

Act. You will find a short explanation of this by Glanville Williams, *The Proof of Guilt* (1963), pp. 216-18, but what is probably the definitive account is that of Tapper in *Crime, Proof and Punishment: Essays in Memory of Sir Rupert Cross* (1981), p. 296.

It is important to remember throughout that these provisions are concerned with the cross-examination of the accused. The accused who does not give evidence cannot be cross-examined. In the case where an accused seeks to adduce evidence of his good character, either by calling witnesses or cross-examining the prosecution witnesses, but does not give evidence himself, the common law allows the prosecution to lead evidence in rebuttal, as we have seen earlier.

SECTION 1(e) AND (f)

If you have not already learnt these provisions by heart, do so now. You will probably not need to recite them in an examination, but you will find it impossible to answer questions on character without a detailed knowledge of them.

Section 1(e) and (f) states:

(e) A person charged and being a witness in pursuance of this Act may be asked any question in cross-examination notwithstanding that it would tend to criminate him as to the offence charged.

(f) A person charged and called as a witness in pursuance of this Act shall not be asked, and if asked shall not be required to answer, any question tending to show that he has committed or been convicted of or been charged with any offence other than that wherewith he is then charged, or is of bad character, unless:

(i) the proof that he has committed or been convicted of such other offence is admissible evidence to show that he is guilty of the offence wherewith he is then charged; or

(ii) he has personally or by his advocate asked questions of the witnesses for the prosecution with a view to establish his own good character, or has given evidence of his good character, or the nature or conduct of the defence is such as to involve imputations on the character of the prosecutor or the witnesses for the prosecution or the deceased victim of the alleged crime; or

(iii) he has given evidence against any other person charged in the same proceedings.

THE RELATIONSHIP BETWEEN SECTION 1(e) AND 1(f)

This is one of the most awkward aspects of character to understand and you will find yourself floundering in a morass of difficult terminology and dicta which serve to darken, rather than illuminate, your understanding of the issue. The best academic treatment is in *Cross and Tapper on Evidence*, but you will find that his account presupposes a considerable depth of understanding. Accordingly, we have set out below a simplified version of the relationship.

The essential problem of the relationship between the two subsections is that they appear, at first sight, to conflict with each other. Professor Smith in [1962] Crim LR 244 puts the matter as follows:

Proviso (e) provides that the accused may be asked '*any question* in cross-examination notwithstanding that it would tend to criminate him as to the offence charged'. Proviso (f) provides that he shall not be asked, *inter alia*, any question tending to show that he has committed or been convicted of any other offence. Now it is apparent that a question which shows that the accused has commited or been convicted or some other offence may also tend to criminate him as to the offence charged. Proviso (e) apparently allows such a question, proviso (f) apparently forbids it. One or other must give way.

There has been considerable uncertainty as to the resolution of this difficulty.

At one time the case law on these sections permitted two possible views to be taken as to the relationship between the provisions. Essentially these opposed views were (a) that s. 1(e) was paramount (a 'wide' view, in the sense of the range of permissible questions) or (b) that s. 1(e) must be read subject to s. 1(f) (a 'narrow' view, in that the range of permissible questions was cut down).

A case which is conventionally used to illustrate the narrow view is *R* v *Cokar* [1960] 2 QB 207, where the accused was charged with burglary. His defence was that he had entered the house in question only for warmth and in order to sleep. The prosecution cross-examined him as to the fact that he had been acquitted previously in similar circumstances, in order to show that Cokar knew that it was not an offence to be on private premises for an innocent purpose — in other words, to destroy his defence. The accused appealed against conviction on the ground that the cross-examination was prohibited by the words of s. 1(f) as 'tending to show that he has ... been charged with any offence other than that wherewith he is then charged'. The Court of Criminal Appeal, in quashing the conviction, interpreted s. 1(f) very tightly. Unless any of the provisos applied, the question was clearly prohibited under the section. Provisos (ii) and (iii) obviously did not apply and the wording of proviso (i) did not extend to cases where the accused has previously been charged, but acquitted. In other words, once the question falls foul of the prohibitive part of s. 1(f), and is not permitted under any of the provisos, it is not saved by s. 1(e).

A case usually cited to support the wide view of the relationship between the sections is *R v Chitson* [1909] 2 KB 945. The accused was charged with having had unlawful sexual intercourse with a girl aged 14. The complainant gave evidence at the trial that on the day after the alleged offence the accused had told her that he had previously done the same thing with another girl. There was no evidence of the age of the other girl. The trial judge allowed the accused to be asked in cross-examination whether he had made any such statement. On appeal, the Court of Criminal Appeal ruled the question permissible. If the reasoning adopted in *Cokar* had been applied in this case, the question would have been disallowed under the prohibitive words of s. 1(f), and would not have been let in by any of the provisos. However, the court took the line that the question 'would tend to incriminate him as to the offence charged' under s. 1(e) as tending to confirm the complainant's story. In other words, s. 1(e) overrode s. 1(f). Another useful illustration of this approach is *R v Kurasch* [1915] 2 KB 749.

Much of the difficulty of reconciling the effects of the differences between these two views was removed by the decision of the House of Lords in *Jones v DPP* [1962] AC 635. The accused was arrested following the rape of one girl guide and the murder, one month later, of another. He was first tried for the rape and was convicted. He was then tried for the murder. The circumstances of the murder were very similar to those of the rape, but the prosecution did not seek to adduce evidence under the similar fact rule as this would have involved the surviving girl guide having to go through the ordeal of testifying again. When the accused was first questioned he set up a false alibi. At his trial for murder, he testified instead that he was with a prostitute, whom he was unable to identify, on the night in question and related a conversation with his wife on his return home. He accounted for the change in alibi by saying in his evidence in chief that he 'had been in trouble with the police before' and therefore had been reluctant to give an alibi which could not be corroborated. His testimony about the new alibi was very similar to that given by him at an earlier trial at which he was convicted of raping a girl guide. He was cross-examined with regard to these similarities on the basis that it was an extraordinary coincidence that he should have an identical alibi for the two occasions on which he had been in trouble. He was convicted of murder and appealed on the ground that the cross-examination was inadmissible because the questions were prohibited by s. 1(f). The House of Lords ruled that the questions were permissible. It did this by attaching a particular interpretation to the words 'tending to show' in s. 1(f). We return to this aspect of the decision later under the next heading, but for present purposes it is sufficient to appreciate that by a majority of 3 to 2 the House preferred the narrow view of the relationship between s. 1(e) and s. 1(f).

THE PROHIBITION IN SECTION 1(f)

Conventional textbook treatments of the prohibition in s. 1(f) involve breaking the provision down into its constituent parts and examining them in succession. We recommend that you do this, and all that we have done in the section is to pick out the most significant matters. You will find that familiarity with the detail of the prohibition is very useful when you come to answering examination questions on this topic.

One of the most important aspects of s. 1(f) relates to the words 'tending to show'. There are two cases which you need to know on this: *Jones* v *DPP* [1962] AC 635 and *R* v *Anderson* [1988] 2 WLR 1017. In *Jones*, 'tending to show' was interpreted as meaning anything which tends to reveal for the first time to the jury that the accused is of bad character. Thus, if the jury already know that the accused is of bad character then the prohibition does not bite. In *Jones* the accused in his evidence in chief had already revealed to the jury that he 'had been in trouble with the police before'. This meant that the cross-examination by the prosecution did not reveal to the jury anything they did not already know. You should also note that, as Lord Reid stated, the word 'show' can include a veiled suggestion as well as a definite statement. By putting this interpretation on the words 'tending to show', the House of Lords went a long way towards resolving the problematic question of the relationship between s. 1(e) and s. 1(f). The major observation we can make on the decision is that it can work very harshly against the accused. As Lord Denning said, dissenting on this point: 'It is one thing to confess to having been in trouble before. It is quite another to have it emphasised against you with devastating detail'. We are sure that Lord Denning would have had even more difficulty with *R* v *Anderson*. Some commentators have interpreted this decision as simply following the principles laid down in *Jones* v *DPP*, but a particularly useful (and somewhat critical) analysis of the approach of the Court of Appeal is provided by the commentary in [1988] Crim LR 298.

The word 'charged' in the section refers to a formal charge. Following *Stirland* v *DPP* [1944] AC 315 it is quite clear that mere suspicion of involvement in criminal activity, or even an accusation of such involvement, does not fall within the definition. Although this is a small and straightforward issue, it is one of the points which often features in an examination question and it is worth looking at *Stirland* for that reason alone.

THE EXCEPTIONS TO THE PROHIBITION

These exceptions must be learnt and understood. Examination questions on character invariably require you to be completely familiar with them.

Under s. 1(f)(i) (which is the least likely of the exceptions contained in the section to appear in an examination) the accused can be cross-examined on his character where the proof that he has committed or been convicted of some other offence is admissible evidence in chief against him. What this means is that if similar fact evidence is admissible then the accused can be cross-examined on it. The wording of s. 1(f)(i) is tighter than that of the actual prohibition in the section, and thus only relates to the occasions where the similar fact evidence shows the commission or conviction of an offence — it does not cover, for example, previous charges not resulting in convictions, or bad character which does not amount to a criminal offence. Normally the prosecution will not be allowed to introduce such issues through cross-examination of the accused unless a proper foundation for the cross-examination has been laid by its evidence in chief (see Lord Morris of Borth-y-Gest in *Jones* v *DPP* [1962] AC 635), in which case the cross-examination will not 'tend to show' any offence of which the jury were previously unaware. However, occasionally situations may arise where cross-examination raising similar fact evidence for the first time may occur — e.g., where a defence not anticipated by the prosecution was raised for the first time by the accused in his evidence in chief.

The section also applies to allow cross-examination of the accused about previous convictions in those exceptional cases where they can be proved as part of the facts in issue for example, proof of disqualification from driving on a charge of driving while disqualified.

Where cross-examination is allowed under s. 1(f)(i) it goes not only to his credibility as a witness but also to the issue of his guilt.

Section 1(f)(ii) is the most commonly examined of the exceptions, as well as being the most topical and interesting. In reality the provision contains two exceptions (usually referred to as the two 'limbs' of the section). The accused can be cross-examined on his character first, where he asks questions of prosecution witnesses, or leads evidence himself, designed to show that he is of good character, and secondly, where the conduct of the defence is such as to involve imputations on the prosecutor or his witness or the deceased victim of the alleged crime.

Before any examination is made of s. 1(f)(ii) it is important to appreciate that, even though the operation of the section may technically have come into play, it does not automatically follow that the accused can be cross-examined on his character. The trial judge has a discretion whether or not to allow such cross-examination. We discuss the issue of discretion later in the chapter.

Under the second limb (and indeed, throughout the whole of s. 1(f)) it is clear that 'character' is wide enough to cover both reputation and disposition. A useful case which illustrates this point is *R* v *Samuel* (1956) 40 Cr App R 8. Cross-examination of Samuel was permitted, even though the only evidence of his own character which he had given related to specific good acts he said he had done. You should remember that blackening someone else's character does not amount to saying that your own character is good, although, as we shall see, if the persons attacked are prosecution witnesses or the prosecutor, then the second limb of s. 1(f)(ii) comes into operation (but only, of course, where the accused gives evidence — see the interesting consequences, where he does not, in *R* v *Butterwasser* [1948] 1 KB 4).

It is also important to realise that the character of the accused is said to be indivisible. By this it is understood that the accused is not entitled to put in evidence a particular aspect of his character (which happens to suit his case) without running the risk of the rest of his character being brought out in cross-examination. You should look at the important case of *R* v *Winfield* [1939] 4 All ER 164. The accused was charged with indecent assault upon a woman. He called a witness and asked her questions to establish his good character for sexual morality. The witness and/or the accused (there is a conflict between the two reports of the case — see also in 27 Cr App R 139) were cross-examined on the accused's previous convictions for dishonesty. On appeal it was held that the cross-examination was perfectly proper as 'there is no such thing known to our procedure as putting half your character in issue and leaving out the other half' (per Humphreys J). This decision was heavily criticised by Gooderson in 'Is the prisoner's character indivisible?' (1953) 11 CLJ 377, where it was argued that the decision was bad in law and bad in principle. It is difficult to counter the telling observation that: 'If a man is charged with forgery, cross-examination as to his convictions for cruelty can have no purpose but prejudice'.

You need also to consider the purpose of the cross-examination under the first limb. It is clear that such cross-examination goes to the credibility of the accused as a witness. The difficult question is whether it goes to his guilt. The conventional view is that where cross-examination is permitted under the first limb it can go to guilt. The authority commonly cited is the judgment of Lord Sankey LC in *Maxwell* v *DPP* [1935] AC 309:

> [I]f the prisoner by himself or his witnesses seeks to give evidence of his own good character, for the purpose of showing that it is unlikely that he committed the offence charged, he raises by way of defence an issue as to his good character, so that he may fairly be cross-examined on that issue, just as any witness called by him to prove his good character may be cross-examined to show the contrary.

This statement is not altogether clear and you will find other judicial comment on the same point is equally obscure (see, for example, Lord Goddard CJ in *R* v *Samuel* (1956) 40 Cr App R 8). However, you will find a first-class statement of the issues of principle in the Australian case of *Donnini* v *R* (1972) 128 CLR 114 where Barwick CJ said:

It is the settled policy of the law that, in general, evidence of a propensity to commit a crime or of a propensity to commit a particular type of crime is not admitted for the consideration of a jury. But evidence of bad character, particularly where it serves no other purpose in a case than the exposure of that character where the accused's credit is involved, is susceptible of use by a jury as indicating a propensity for criminal behaviour. ... [T]here is a high degree of possibility that a juryman will be prone to reason towards guilt by the use of the fact of prior conviction as indicative of a disposition to crime on the part of the accused. To so use the fact of prior conviction is to cut across a deeply entrenched policy of the law. Therefore, the not unnatural tendency of the juryman and the importance of that policy seem to me to require that the trial judge, when evidence of prior conviction is properly before the jury for the sole purpose of combating a suggestion of good character or to weaken or destroy an accused's credibility, must assist the jury by expressly and with emphasis telling them that they may not use the fact of prior conviction as tending to the guilt of the accused. In my opinion, in such a case, he should tell them quite clearly that the fact of prior conviction can only be used as a means of discrediting the accused.

The most detailed academic discussion of the problems of the purpose of the cross-examination under s. 1(f) is that of Pattenden, 'The purpose of cross-examination under s. 1(f) of the Criminal Evidence Act 1898' [1982] Crim LR 707.

The second limb of s. 1(f)(ii) is equally problematic, although in a different way. Under the second limb the accused is exposed to cross-examination on his character where imputations are cast on the character of the prosecutor or his witnesses (and, since the enactment of s. 31 of the Criminal Justice and Public Order Act 1994, an imputation against the deceased victim of the alleged crime). At first sight one might suppose that even a plea of 'not guilty' could amount to an imputation that the prosecution witnesses are lying. The courts have had to avoid such a conclusion, otherwise an accused with anything in the nature of a criminal record would have powerful reasons not to go into the witness-box — and that cannot have been what the draftsman of the 1898 Act intended. But the problem is, where does an assertion alleging innocence stop and an imputation begin?

The first occasion on which the courts examined in detail the construction of the second limb was in R v Hudson [1912] 2 KB 464, where Lord Alverstone CJ, delivering the judgment of the Court of Criminal Appeal, said:

We think that the words ... must receive their ordinary and natural interpretation, and that it is not legitimate to qualify them by adding or inserting the words 'unnecessarily', or 'unjustifiably', or 'for purposes other than that of developing the defence', or other similar words.

However, in some circumstances the severity of the rule in *Hudson* is mitigated. Thus in *R v Turner* [1944] KB 463 it was held that where an accused in a rape case alleged that the complainant had consented to intercourse, that did not involve casting an imputation on her character. Further, in *R v Rouse* [1904] 1 KB 184 it was accepted that the accused is able to deny his guilt of the offence charged in language characterised by its robustness, without triggering the section. A line is drawn between what amounts to no more than an emphatic denial of the crime charged and words which constitute an attack on the character of the witness. This is a difficult line to draw and the cases referred to in the textbooks can really only be regarded as illustrations.

In recent years the resolution of this question has focused on the difficult situation generated where the accused states that a confession, which the prosecution alleges he has made to the police, is in fact untrue. The difficulty for the accused is that this may be a perfectly proper defence for him to run, but in doing so he will almost inevitably have to make some allegation of police impropriety. In the past defence counsel sought to get around this problem by the use of delicate forensic language. Rather than suggesting that a police witness was lying, it may have been suggested to him that he 'misunderstood' or 'misheard' what the accused had said. In ordinary language a suggestion that someone has misunderstood something is not an imputation on his character.

The courts have struggled with this problem, but some decisions have served to clarify the law. In *R v Tanner* (1977) 66 Cr App R 56 the accused was charged with theft. Police officers testified that when he was being questioned about the thefts he had made certain admissions. At the trial the accused denied this. The defence did not cross-examine the officers on the basis that they were lying but simply on the basis that they were wrong in saying that the admissions had been made. However, during his cross-examination, in answer to a question by the trial judge, the accused said that the police evidence on that matter was a complete invention. The trial judge allowed the prosecution to cross-examine the accused about his previous convictions. The correctness of the decision was confirmed on appeal, and the importance of the case rests on the fact that it is now clear that the second limb of s. 1(f)(ii) is activated by implied as well as express imputations. In other words, it is no longer possible to shroud the cross-examination of the prosecution witnesses in forensic niceties in order to side-step the section. We are still faced with the problem of drawing the line between the emphatic denial, which does not bring the section into play, and the implied imputation, which does. The matter is put very clearly by Cohen, 'Challenging police evidence of interviews and the second limb of section 1(f)(ii) — another view' [1981] Crim LR 523:

> It would seem that the more detailed the police evidence is of the alleged interview, the less chance D has of retaining his shield if he wishes to

challenge the police evidence. If the police say that D said, simply, 'I am guilty', then clearly D must be allowed to deny that without losing his shield, for such a denial goes no further than a plea of not guilty. But the more statements the police seek to attribute to D, which D denies having made, the closer he comes to inevitably implying fabrication, rather than mistake, misunderstanding or forgetfulness.

Any police officer who has taken evidence as part of his law degree, and who is prone to a little corruption, can obviously turn the decision in *Tanner* to his advantage!

The *Tanner* approach has been confirmed by the decision in *R v Britzmann and Hall* (1983) 76 Cr App R 134, and we discuss this further below. As part of your study of this aspect of s. 1(f) you should look at the article by Cohen, mentioned above, and also that by Wolchover, 'Cross-examination of the accused on his record when a confession is denied or retracted' [1981] Crim LR 312.

The confession cases are only one example of the wider principle that the accused will lose his shield whenever casting imputations on the prosecution witnesses is a necessary part of his defence. The classic case which confirms this is *Selvey v DPP* [1970] AC 304. In that case the accused was charged with buggery. There was medical evidence that the complainant had been sexually interfered with by someone on the day in question, and also indecent photographs were found in the accused's rooms. The defence was that the complainant had told the accused that he had already 'been on the bed' with a man for £1 and that he would do the same for the accused for £1. The accused denied knowledge of the photographs and suggested that they had been planted on him by the complainant in annoyance at the rejection of his offer. The trial judge allowed the prosecution to cross-examine the accused on his previous convictions for homosexual offences. The House of Lords held that the cross-examination was permissible. However essential it was for the proper presentation of the defence to cast imputations, the shield was lost as a matter of law.

Another useful case (the facts of which frequently appear in some form or other in examinations) is *R v Bishop* [1975] QB 274. Selvey was applied.

The final important question you need to consider on the second limb is the evidential purpose of the cross-examination. The short answer to the question is that such cross-examination goes to credit. The jury must be told that they must not treat the facts about the accused's previous record as evidence of his guilt (see *R v Watts* (1983) 77 Cr App R 126 and *R v Powell* [1985] 1 WLR 1364). A good discussion of the background to the present law can be found in the article by Pattenden previously referred to. As always it is difficult to be convinced that the jury will fully appreciate the subtleties of the distinction between cross-examination as to guilt and cross-examination as to credit (although evidence examiners expect students to have grasped the point).

Section 1(f)(iii) raises fewer problems than s. 1(f)(ii). The paragraph is brought into operation where the accused gives evidence against someone else charged in the same proceedings. This is relatively straightforward. The accused need not say anything about the character of the co-accused. All that must be shown is that he gave evidence against him. The classic definition of this is contained in *Murdoch v Taylor* [1965] AC 574 where the House of Lords made it clear that the key is whether the evidence supports the prosecution case against the co-accused in a material respect or undermines his defence. The test here is an objective one and does not depend on any particular animus on the part of the accused. The issue is simply one of the effect of the evidence.

A denial of having committed the offence by one co-accused will not generally amount to giving 'evidence against' his co-accused, because a denial by A does not usually indicate the guilt of B. But in certain situations it may be clear that the offence was committed either by A or by B. Of necessity, a denial here by A brings the paragraph into operation — see *R v Varley* (1982) 75 Cr App R 242.

As far as the evidential purpose of cross-examination under this part of the section is concerned it can be said with confidence that it goes to the credibility of the accused. None of the standard texts gives a very full account of this issue. This is probably because there is very little to say about it.

One of the important aspects of s. 1(f)(iii) is that both the prosecution and the co-accused may seek to rely on its provisions in wishing to cross-examine the accused. The co-accused is allowed to use the section as of right, but in the case of the prosecution the trial judge has a discretion whether or not to allow such cross-examination. This issue is discussed under the next heading.

JUDICIAL DISCRETION

The existence of a discretion on the part of a trial judge to refuse to permit cross-examination of the accused as to his character, even where it is permissible under the second limb of s. 1(f)(ii), is now well-established. It is recognised in several House of Lords' judgments, most notably in *Selvey v DPP* [1970] AC 304. It is based on the overriding duty of the judge to ensure that a trial is fair. Relevant factors would be, for example, the weakness of the prosecution case or the fact that there were several counts in the indictment and an imputation was cast on a witness to one only of these. The discretion might also be exercised where the accused's record was a bad one, but the attack on the prosecution witnesses, although an imputation, was relatively trivial. In *Selvey* itself the House of Lords said that the fact that the imputation was a necessary part of the defence was only one factor in the exercise of the discretion and not an overriding one. There is also no absolute rule that the discretion should be exercised in favour of the accused where his previous convictions are of a similar kind to the offence charged (see *R* v *Powell* [1985] 1 WLR 1364), although there is a clear risk here that the jury will wrongly treat them as evidence of guilt.

There have been a number of cases in the past few years in which attempts have been made to clarify the guidelines which judges should follow in considering whether or not to exercise a discretion. Most notable among these are *R* v *Watts* (1983) 77 Cr App R 126; *R* v *Burke* (1985) 82 Cr App R 156; *R* v *Powell* [1985] 1 WLR 1364 and *R* v *Owen* (1986) 83 Cr App R 100. It is worth reading all of these cases, but you will find very useful summaries of the present position in the judgment of Ackner LJ in *R* v *Burke* and in that of Neill LJ in *R* v *Owen*. In *R* v *Britzmann and Hall* (1983) 76 Cr App R 134, the Court of Appeal set out some guidelines for the exercise of discretion in those cases where the conduct of the defence necessarily involves an allegation that witnesses for the prosecution have deliberately made up false evidence. Lawton LJ, reading the judgment of the court, said:

> Defendants sometimes make wild allegations when giving evidence. Allowance should be made for the strain of being in the witness-box and the exaggerated use of language which sometimes results from such strain or lack of education or mental instability. Particular care should be used when a defendant is led into making allegations during cross-examination. The defendant who, during cross-examination, is driven to explaining away the evidence by saying that it has been made up or planted on him usually convicts himself without having his previous convictions brought out. Finally, there is no need for the prosecution to rely upon section 1(f)(ii) if the evidence against a defendant is over-whelming.

Other passages in this judgment, however, are less helpful. The court stated that the discretion should be exercised in the accused's favour if there might be mistake, misunderstanding or confusion, rather than an allegation of fabrication of evidence. Also, it should be exercised 'if there is nothing more than a denial, however emphatic or offensively made, of an act or even a short series of acts amounting to one incident or in what was said to have been a short interview'. Yet, have we not seen already that emphatic denials, and evidence of mistake, misunderstanding or confusion might not by themselves amount to an imputation in the first place? If that is correct, then the issue is not really one of discretion at all.

The use of discretion under the second limb of s. 1(f)(ii) is, then, another means of mitigating the possible harshness of the approach to the paragraph taken in *R* v *Hudson* [1912] 2 KB 464. The problem with discretion, however, is that it leads to uncertainty as individual judges differ from each other in their attitude to its use. The defence is therefore put into a quandary as to how far it may safely go. It is submitted, however, that the use of discretion involves a lesser risk of injustice than would 'attempting to shackle the judge's power within a strait-jacket', to use the words of Lord Guest in *Selvey*.

Where cross-examination of the accused is permitted under s. 1(f)(ii) it will in practice almost always be conducted only by counsel for the prosecution. However, counsel for a co-accused may, at the discretion of the judge, also cross-examine the accused if his evidence was prejudicial to his co-accused.

Turning to s. 1(f)(iii), it was held in *Murdoch* v *Taylor* [1965] AC 574 that the judge has no discretion to disallow cross-examination on behalf of a co-accused under that subsection. As far as the co-accused is concerned, the accused is in the same position as if he were a prosecution witness, and so like such a witness he is liable to cross-examination to credit in the normal way. There is also nothing in s. 1(f)(iii) to prevent cross-examination under that subsection on behalf of the prosecution. This was expressly recognised in *Murdoch* v *Taylor* and in *R* v *Lovett* [1973] 1 WLR 241, but stated to be subject to the judge's discretion. Leave to cross-examine would only rarely be granted, perhaps most obviously in a case where two persons charged in the same proceedings both gave evidence against each other but neither cross-examined the other because they both had previous convictions.

PLANNING YOUR REVISION

You will know from your studies of this topic that it is not an easy one to master. We have suggested in the first part of this chapter that the best way to come to terms with character is to approach it in a logical and ordered manner and to break the topic down into a number of constituent parts. As we have indicated above, there are a number of crucial questions which you need to consider, and central among these are the key issues of the meaning of character, the relationship between s. 1(e) and s. 1(f), the prohibition and the exceptions contained in s. 1(f) and the evidential purposes which may be served by cross-examination under s. 1(f). You also need to understand the principles underlying the exercise of judicial discretion.

One of the major problems you will find in dealing with the substantial quantity of case law under the 1898 Act is that the issues which are being addressed in these cases are often not very clear on a first reading. Accordingly, this is one area where you might make fuller use of case books than may usually be the case, because you will find that they are more than usually helpful in directing you to the relevant issues issues you might miss if you read the case in the reports. You will also need to rely heavily on your textbook. Although the textbook treatments of the subject vary somewhat the danger is that those accounts which at first sight look clearer and more straightforward do not necessarily touch on all the difficult issues which undoubtedly persist.

We have indicated in our account of the law where we think the most important issues lie. In examinations the issues which tend regularly to come up centre on the effect of s. 1(f)(ii) and s. 1(f)(iii) of the 1898 Act. Occasionally you may have the opportunity to discuss s. 1(f)(i), but there is less to say about this part of the section and there is not a great deal of authority where it has been discussed. As between s. 1(f)(ii) and s. 1(f)(iii), there is much more to say on the former, and this is the part of the provision you should know well. We have indicated some of the issues which have been the subject of recent judicial activity, particularly in relation to the awkward question of disputed confessions, and this is one aspect of the topic where you can really contribute some thoughts of your own. You should be in a position to review the different approaches taken by such writers as Wolchover and Cohen and you can consider whether the present position is altogether happy. You may feel that it is very hard on the accused, where his defence may be the perfectly proper one of denying the fact or content of a confession he is alleged to have made, that he thus exposes his previous character to the penetrating gaze of the jury. You may be able to suggest some kind of suitable theoretical framework under which the accused will be allowed to make an imputation on the character of the prosecution witnesses without exposing his own character where such imputation is necessary for the conduct of his defence.

You should also consider, and be able to say something about, the way in which the exercise of judicial discretion may mitigate some of the harsher consequences of the present law. Are the guidelines set out in the recent cases right? Or is judicial discretion never a truly satisfactory way of resolving the law?

You will find it helpful to be able to say something about the relationship between s. 1(e) and s. 1(f). Examination questions are rarely directed at this specific issue, but any question which involves a consideration of the position of the accused in relation to character evidence will provide a legitimate vehicle for the discussion of this relationship. We cannot pretend that the matter is an easy one, and you may find that the textbook treatments of the issue are less than illuminating. We think that the reason for the lack of clear exposition in the basic texts rests on the fact that the judges themselves have not been very clear or consistent in the way in which they have handled the question (of these texts, however, we would recommend the discussion by Zuckerman in *The Principles of Criminal Evidence* as worthy of particular study). Accordingly, you will have to pick your way through the relationship as best as you can, remembering always that the most important (and perhaps difficult) case is that of *Jones* v *DPP* [1962] AC 635. If you want to make yourself unpopular with your tutor (or perhaps settle an old score against him!) press him on this point, because apart from anything else, you need all the help you can get. Any student who can say something intelligent about this problematic relationship will get credit for it in an examination, so it is worth grappling with it rather than pushing it to one side.

The final point we would make about revision of this topic relates to the academic literature on the subject. We have made mention of some of the important contributions as we have gone through this chapter and we think it is important that you should make some effort to familiarise yourself with it. We suggest this for several reasons. First, as with any aspect of the subject as a whole, you can only add to the credit you will get in an examination by displaying your familiarity with such material. Secondly, this is an area of law where the rules are less clear-cut than some other parts of the subject. Some textbooks, out of necessity, make the rules seem simpler and clearer than they perhaps are, and it is worth knowing just where the important points of controversy lie. Thirdly, some of the recent literature deals with issues of current topicality and importance. It is such issues which are likely to be ventilated in an examination and any comment you can make on such matters will only improve your examination performance. Finally, you may well find that the more detailed treatment of relatively narrow issues which you tend to find in articles will help you considerably in understanding this difficult topic.

EXAMINATION QUESTIONS

The typical examination question on this topic is a problem question. This is because such a question is a suitable vehicle for raising many of the detailed issues which conventionally arise. We have already made the point earlier in the chapter that the best way of coming to terms with character is to break the topic down into a number of constituent parts, and this is often reflected in the way the subject is examined. However, the good candidate will be able to see the topic as an integrated whole, and this is often the distinguishing feature between an average and a good answer.

Essay questions are not unheard of, but they tend to be general and cover standard ground, in that they require a treatment of the 1898 Act and the problem of the permissible scope of cross-examination of the accused on his previous bad character where he gives evidence.

The following question is perhaps rather longer, and more wide-ranging, than most questions you will see on this topic, but it raises many of the issues which frequently come up. One point to notice about the question is that it requires you to write, albeit briefly, about matters other than character. This, of course, is not unusual in an evidence question and you should always be alert to the prospect that a question which appears at first sight to be centred on one particular area may in fact trespass into other issues.

(a)   'When Parliament by the Act of 1898 effected a change in the general law and made the prisoner in every case a competent witness, it was in evident difficulty and it pursued the familiar English system of compromise.' (per Lord Sankey LC in *Maxwell* v *DPP* (1935)) What were the 'difficulties'? What were the 'compromises'?

(b)   Don and Ed were jointly charged with theft from Frank's house. Don has two previous convictions for indecent assault. Ed has recently been dismissed from his job because he had been suspected of tinkering with the clocking-in machine. Can counsel for the prosecution cross-examine on these matters if:

(i)   Don admits that he had been in Frank's house on the day in question, but it was because they were having a homosexual relationship.

(ii)   The police allege that Don made a confession after protracted questioning. Don denies this, saying that the police must be mistaken. In his evidence in chief, Ed says that he has never previously been charged with an offence.

As far as the first part of the question is concerned, what you must do initially is determine precisely what issues are being raised and what the limits of your treatment will be. Although the bulk of the question is concerned with various issues of character, it is important to pick up the point that the essay ranges more widely than this, and directs you to a consideration of the 1898 Act and not just s. 1(e) and s. 1(f).

You should not begin your answer by discussing general issues of the competence of the accused. The question is not looking for that, and in any event you do not have the time to deal with this matter. You have to assume the competence of the accused, and look at the problems this caused the draftsman of the Act in developing some kind of code to control the reception of his evidence and cross-examination thereon.

The first point to deal with in your answer is the question of the so-called right to silence enjoyed by the accused.

This is a topic which has moved on and off the political agenda, depending on the views of the government of the day. Following the passing of ss. 34–38 of the Criminal Justice and Public Order Act 1994 (CJPOA 1994) it is most certainly on the agenda. It is important to note the two aspects of the right to silence, namely (a) out of court silence and (b) silence at the trial. Here, we are concerned with the latter. The former will be discussed in chapter 9 in connection with the topic of confessions.

Although the 1898 Act made the accused competent, it did not make him compellable. Accordingly, provision had to be made for the accused who declines to avail himself of the opportunity to testify. Was the right not to testify unfettered? Was it permissible for the judge (or the prosecution) to comment on the failure of the accused to give evidence? The answer was that the prosecution was not allowed to comment, but the judge was. However, the line between permissible and impermissible comment was difficult to draw. There was much difference in the approach of individual judges.

There has been a long-running and interesting debate as to whether the right to silence ought to be preserved. Bentham was moved to say: 'If all criminals of every class had assembled, and framed a system after their own wishes, is not this rule the very first which they would have established for their security?' (*Treatise on Evidence*, p. 241).

The opposite extreme was reflected by Devlin J in his summing up to the jury in the famous trial of Dr John Bodkin Adams:

> I hope that the day will never come when [the right to silence] is denied to any Englishman. It is not a refuge of technicality: the law on this matter reflects the natural thought of England. So great is our horror at the idea that a man might be questioned, forced to speak and perhaps to condemn himself out of his own mouth, that we afford to everyone suspected or accused of a crime, at every stage, and to the very end, the right to say: 'Ask me no questions, I shall answer none. Prove your case.'

The range of possible arguments is well rehearsed by Professors Cross and Field in two articles in (1970) 11 JSPTL 66 and 76.

Section 35 of the CJPOA 1994 makes important changes to the law. The section specifically preserves the rule that the accused is competent but not compellable. However, if at the conclusion of the prosecution case, the accused does not propose to give evidence, the court must satisfy itself that he is aware of his right to give evidence and that 'if he chooses not to give evidence, or having been sworn, without good cause refuses to answer any question, it will be permissible for the court or jury to draw such inferences as appear proper from his failure to give evidence of his refusal, without good cause, to answer any question'.

It is early days to give any definitive views on the ambit of s. 35, but guidance has been given to the courts in general terms on how the jury should be directed (see *R v Cowan, Gayle and Riccardi* [1995] 4 All ER 939). The prosecution as well as the judge is free to comment. Clearly, it would be unwise for a legal representative to advise an accused in the position of John Bodkin Adams not to testify.

The rest of your essay will need to cover the problems associated with the code of cross-examination of the accused imposed by s. 1(e) and s. 1(f). A candidate can really shine on this aspect of the question if he is aware of the historical background to the Act. We have already covered, earlier in the chapter, the essential choices open to the draftsman and we do not propose to repeat them here. However, specific mention of the points made by Tapper in his coverage of this issue will elevate the quality of your answer. Three specific points are worth mentioning:

(a)   Do not be tempted to write out the exact words of the statutory provisions. It will not impress an examiner, because it will look like mindless regurgitation and it will waste valuable time.

(b) Tell the examiner what the relationship between s. 1(e) and s. 1(f) is. A reference to *Jones* v *DPP* [1962] AC 635 is essential and a knowledge of the differing approaches taken by the Law Lords in that case is indicative of an ability out of the ordinary.

(c) Make some effort to evaluate the practical consequences of the ways in which these provisions have been interpreted. Note the way in which the wide approach to the relationship perhaps renders s. 1(f)(i) redundant (see, for example, the decision of the High Court of Australia in *Attwood* v *R* (1960) 102 CLR 353). However, a vigorous and persuasive defence of the minority approach in *Jones* v *DPP* is mounted by Zuckerman, *Principles of Criminal Evidence*, pp. 247-57.

Now to part (b). Unlike many problem questions in evidence this problem is already divided into a number of separate issues. Accordingly, there is not the same need as in some questions to begin your answer by spelling out all the issues which are raised. This is already done for you to a considerable extent. We deal with each part of the problem in turn.

On the question of Don's admission of his presence in Frank's house, this raises the primary issue of whether this is an imputation on the character of Frank and thus whether the second limb of s. 1(f)(ii) comes into play. If the section does apply, the second main issue is whether Don can be cross-examined on previous offences unrelated in any way to the present charge, and the purpose of such cross-examination.

Is Don's statement an imputation? If he was accusing Frank of some criminal offence there is little doubt that it would be. Does the fact that the conduct alleged against Frank may be non-criminal change the situation? If Don had said that the reason he had been at Frank's house was because Frank had invited him to a party there, there is no question of any imputation. In the case of *R* v *Bishop* [1975] QB 274, on facts similar to this problem, the Court of Appeal ruled that an allegation such as Don's was an imputation. The court rejected the argument that no reasonable person would think the worse of a man who committed homosexual acts. Accordingly, an imputation on character can cover behaviour which, although not criminal, might be thought of as morally discreditable.

Furthermore, the fact that making such a statement may have been necessary to Don's defence is of no avail on the issue of whether it was an imputation. This has been absolutely clear since *Selvey* v *DPP* [1970] AC 304.

Consequently, Don has lost his shield and s. 1(f)(ii) is triggered. But can he be cross-examined on previous convictions for sexual offences? It is clear from the much criticised decision in *R* v *Winfield* [1939] 4 All ER 164 that the character of the accused is indivisible, but given that the purpose of cross-examination under the second limb goes to credit, how can it be said that convictions for sexual offences make Don any less credible a witness on a charge of theft? The principal consideration here is whether the harshness of that rule can be mitigated by the exercise of judicial discretion. The important practical point is that *all* cases turn on their own particular facts. The most you can do in the examination is to review the applicable authorities, pointing out the inevitable uncertainties which will arise in this area. You must demonstrate that you are familiar with the attempts of the courts to establish a proper framework for the exercise of discretion and make some effort to apply those guidelines to the facts of the problem.

The second part of the problem is concerned with two main matters. First, there is the topical issue, which applies in relation to Don, of whether disputing a confession which the police allege has been made by him is an imputation under the second limb of s. 1(f)(ii). Secondly, there is the question of whether Ed has sought to establish his own good character and so whether the first limb of the subsection is applicable.

Dealing first with Don. We have reviewed the major developments in this area earlier in the chapter and we have little to add to that here. You have a good opportunity in dealing with this issue of showing the examiner that you have mastered the academic contributions to the debate following the decision in *R* v *Tanner* (1977) 66 Cr App R 56 and, once again, you should try to make some pertinent points about the possible availability of judicial discretion. The facts of the problem are not explicit on the nature of the police evidence and so it is probably unwise to be too dogmatic on the question of whether Don has thrown away his shield.

With regard to the evidence of Ed, the only issue here is whether the evidence of his good character which he has given renders him liable to cross-examination under the first limb. He clearly loses his shield. Can he be cross-examined as to the incident at his previous workplace? The answer is no. In the case of *Stirland* v *DPP* [1944] AC 315 it was said:

> It is no disproof of good character that a man has been suspected or accused of a previous crime. Such questions as 'Were you suspected?' or 'Were you accused?' are inadmissible because they are irrelevant to the issue of character, and can only be asked if the accused has sworn expressly to the contrary.

Stirland made it quite clear that where the accused denied that he had ever been 'charged' with an offence, he might be fairly understood to mean that he had never previously been brought before a criminal court.

CONCLUSION

If you survive evidence of character then you will never know fear again. The rigours of a Himalayan winter are as a warm summer's afternoon by comparison. Such is the stuff expected of an evidence student. But unlike the Everest mountaineer, you cannot remain at base camp and merely admire the scenery. Participation in the character expedition is strictly compulsory.

FURTHER READING

Cohen, 'Challenging police evidence of interviews and the second limb of section 1(f)(ii) another view' [1981] Crim LR 523.

Cross, 'The right to silence and the presumption of innocence: sacred cows or safeguards of liberty?' (1970) 11 JSPTL 66.

Field, 'The right to silence: a rejoinder to Professor Cross' (1970) 11 JSPTL 76.

Gooderson, 'Is the prisoner's character indivisible?' [1953] 11 CLJ 377.

Munday, 'Reflections on the Criminal Evidence Act 1898' [1985] CLJ 62.

Munday, 'Stepping beyond the bounds of credibility: the application of section 1(f)(ii) of the Criminal Evidence Act 1898' [1986] Crim LR 511.

Pattenden, 'The purpose of cross-examination under section 1(f) of the Criminal Evidence Act 1898' [1982] Crim LR 707.

Seabrooke, 'Closing the credibility gap: a new approach to section 1(f)(ii) of the Criminal Evidence Act 1898' [1987] Crim LR 231.

Tapper, 'The meaning of section 1(f)(i) of the Criminal Evidence Act 1898', in Crime, Proof and Punishment: Essays in Memory of Sir Rupert Cross (London: Butterworths, 1981), p. 296.

Wolchover, 'Cross-examination of the accused on his record when a confession is denied or retracted' [1981] Crim LR 312.

8   HEARSAY EVIDENCE

INTRODUCTION: THE RULE

If one had to choose a topic which could be regarded as a banker on an evidence paper then hearsay is that topic, although this knowledge may not be particularly helpful when you consider the vast range of material which can be covered in even a straightforward treatment of hearsay. However, there is no need to panic, because it is quite possible to pick a sensible route through the subject, which will limit considerably the amount of information you need to master. You will find that some of the major textbooks deal in exhaustive detail with many issues which, although of some academic interest, are very unlikely to find their way on to a sensible examination paper.

In our experience the basic problem which many students have in dealing with hearsay is in actually recognising hearsay when they meet it. This can lead to a state verging on paranoia. Paranoia, we might add, which is not confined to law students. Murphy and Barnard put it this way in *Evidence and Advocacy*:

> There should probably be an organisation called 'Hearsay Anonymous'. Membership would be open to those judges, practitioners and students (not to mention occasional law teachers) to whom the rule against hearsay has always been an awesome and terrifying mystery. Like its partner in terror, the rule against perpetuities, the rule against hearsay ranks as one of the law's most celebrated nightmares. To many practitioners, it is a dimly remembered vision, which conjures up confused images of complex exceptions and incomprehensible and antiquated cases.

You will find standard definitions of hearsay in the textbooks (all based on what was said in *Subramaniam* v *Public Prosecutor* [1956] 1 WLR 965). For practical purposes we think that you can identify hearsay by applying the following rules:

(a)   hearsay is anything said or written outside the courtroom, if
(b)   it is being used to prove the truth of what is contained in those words or writing.

For example, Alf says outside the courtroom, 'Bill has raped Celia'. Whether or not Alf subsequently gives evidence in court, his statement out of court is hearsay if it is being introduced to prove the rape. On the other hand it is not hearsay if it is used to show that Alf has a high-pitched voice. In other words, the real key to understanding whether or not an out-of-court statement is hearsay is to ask for what purpose the statement is sought to be used. If you understand this you are halfway there. If you understand that it does not make a blind bit of difference that the statement is contained in a document then you are all the way there. The best way to achieve this state of happy bliss is to be familiar with a stock of cases illustrating these essentials. We have set out in the next few paragraphs some of the most useful cases to know and have indicated other cases which it would be helpful to look at.

A simple and valuable case is *R* v *McLean* (1967) 52 Cr App R 80. G was the victim of a robbery. A few minutes later he dictated something, which he could not afterwards remember, to C. C wrote down on a card a car registration number. At the trial of McLean for the robbery it was alleged that this was the registration number of the car used in the robbery and that McLean had hired a car with that registration number. G did not see what C had written down. The issue was whether C could testify as to the car registration mark. (Note: G could not refresh his memory from the card as he had not read it over.) The Court of Appeal (with considerable reluctance) found that C's testimony was inadmissible hearsay. The simple solution to this case rests in what we have said above, that the out-of-court statement of G was being introduced as evidence of the truth of what he said, namely the car registration number. Other useful cases establishing similar points are *Jones* v *Metcalfe* [1967] 3 All ER 205 and *Cattermole* v *Millar* [1978] RTR 258.

A relatively straightforward example of a case where the out-of-court statement was admissible (on the basis that it was not hearsay) is *Subramaniam* v *Public Prosecutor* [1956] 1 WLR 965. S was charged with unlawful possession of ammunition under emergency regulations. It was a defence to have a lawful excuse for possession and the accused sought to give evidence that he had been captured by terrorists and was acting under duress. The trial judge ruled that he could not state in evidence what the terrorists had said to him, on the basis that it was hearsay. However, the Privy Council quashed the conviction on the following basis:

Evidence of a statement made to a witness by a person who is not himself called as a witness may or may not be hearsay. It is hearsay and inadmissible when the object of the evidence is to establish the truth of what is contained in the statement. It is not hearsay and is admissible when it is proposed to establish by the evidence, not the truth of the statement, but the fact that it was made.

What this means in the present case is this: the accused was seeking to introduce the statements of the terrorists, not to show the truth of what the terrorists had said to him (that they would shoot him if he did not join them), but to establish the state of his own mind as a result of what they had said. He was seeking to lay the foundation of his defence of duress. The defence of duress is available whether or not the threat would in fact have been carried out, provided that the accused reasonably believed that it would have been. The truth or falsity of the terrorists' statement was immaterial. It was what the accused thought was going to happen that mattered.

The point at issue can also be illustrated by reference to the offence of handling stolen goods. Suppose a person is charged with this offence. He admits receiving the goods but claims (a) that the goods were not in fact stolen and (b) that even if they were he neither knew nor believed them to be stolen at the time when he received them. Can the accused give evidence that the person from whom he received the goods had told him that they were not stolen? The answer to this question depends once more on the purpose for which he sought to narrate the statement. There are two possible purposes for which this out-of-court statement might be introduced. The first possibility is that the statement could be used to show that the goods were not stolen this would clearly involve a use of the statement as evidence of its truth. This is, of course, the very thing that the hearsay rule prohibits. The second possibility is to use the statement as evidence of the accused's state of mind, namely, that he did not know or believe that the goods were stolen. As far as that question is concerned there is no doubt that the statement is not being used in a hearsay sense and is accordingly admissible. The only issue here is whether or not the statement was in fact made. These principles were applied in the cases of *R* v *Willis* [1960] 1 WLR 55 and *R* v *Marshall* [1977] Crim LR 106.

Other useful decisions which you should examine are *R* v *Chapman* [1969] 2 QB 436; *Woodhouse* v *Hall* (1980) 72 Cr App R 39 and *R* v *Blastland* [1986] AC 41. The last of these embarks on a wide-ranging examination of the authorities and is the subject of an excellent article by Diane Birch in *Criminal Law: Essays in Honour of J. C. Smith*.

We are now halfway towards understanding hearsay. Now the documentary fallacy.

Many of the cases on hearsay involve statements that have been written down in a document, on microfilm or even in some other form. The possibilities are endless. The name and address of a seed merchant stamped upon a potato sack, an airline ticket bearing the name of a passenger or a handkerchief bearing the initials of the owner are all examples. Students often display a marked psychological hang-up when confronted with such exotic examples. This condition, if suitably treated, is not terminal. All you have to do is pretend that the written words are the equivalent of somebody actually saying them. We can illustrate this from the case of *Patel v Comptroller of Customs* [1966] AC 356. The appellant imported a quantity of seed from Singapore to Fiji. For the purposes of import the country of origin was stated to be India, but some of the bags were marked 'Produce of Morocco'. The appellant was charged with making a false customs declaration, and the issue on appeal was whether the statement on the bags was admissible against him. The Privy Council ruled that from an evidentiary point of view the words were hearsay. We would only add that the fact that the words were written (rather than spoken) was neither here nor there. It was as if the person who had stamped the words 'Produce of Morocco' on the bags had simply said 'The contents of this bag are the produce of Morocco'. Another very useful decision (and one you really must read, even though it has subsequently been superseded by statute) is *Myers v DPP* [1965] AC 1001. In this case the House of Lords (admittedly by a bare majority) treated a microfilm record compiled by a car manufacturer in exactly the same way as the seed bag was treated in *Patel*. You might also care to consider the case of *R v Rice* [1963] 1 QB 857 at this point, but this is a very difficult case and we shall be returning to it later.

There are three final points which need to be made:

(a)   For some purposes it is necessary to make a distinction between what is known as 'firsthand hearsay' and 'secondhand hearsay' (or 'hearsay upon hearsay'). For example, if it is alleged that A assaulted B, then evidence by C that D, an eyewitness, told him that A assaulted B is firsthand hearsay. However, evidence by E that C told him of being told by D that A assaulted B is secondhand hearsay.

(b)   It should be remembered that an out-of-court statement of the witness himself is just as much hearsay as the out-of-court statement of a person who is not called as a witness. From an examination perspective, such statements (of the witness) need to be considered not just as straightforward hearsay statements *per se*, but also as 'previous consistent statements'. In an examination this issue is likely to arise in the context of a criminal case, and you will need to be able to show that you know the situations where such statements are admissible. These are discussed in chapter 11.

(c)   The hearsay rule applies just as much to evidence adduced on behalf of the defence as it does to the evidence of any other party. The decision of the Privy Council in *Sparks v R* [1964] AC 964 illustrates this well.

(d)   Statements which fall within the ambit of the hearsay rule, whether they be oral or written, assert particular facts *expressly*. However, an assertion of one fact might enable an inference to be drawn concerning the existence of another fact. The situation is generally referred to as an *implied* assertion. As Zuckerman explains, '[A]ll the dangers involved in relying on the express assertion "The bank was open on Monday" are equally present when we are asked to infer the same fact from the assertion "I paid some money into my bank account on Monday"'. This question as to whether implied assertions are admissible or not is one which has received much examination from academic writers. With regard to implied assertions made orally or in writing (or by a combination of an oral or written statement together with conduct) the cases suggest that the hearsay rule applies, the leading authority being *R v Kearley* [1992] 2 AC 228. The question is, however, still uncertain regarding implied assertions by conduct alone.

EXCEPTIONS TO THE RULE

It is one thing knowing what the hearsay rule is. It is quite another mastering the myriad exceptions to the rule. Examiners, being by nature perverse, are always much more interested in the exceptions than the rule itself.

At common law the exceptions to the rule in both criminal and civil cases become horribly tangled. To a considerable extent, particularly in civil cases, these problems have been resolved by statutory intervention. Nevertheless, a complex web of exceptions still remains and one of the most important tasks you must undertake is to sort out which of the exceptions must be given priority in your study of the topic. Later in this chapter we will explain in the context of an examination question how some of the exceptions operate, but we have set out below those we consider to be the most important. You will find a full (and even exhaustive) treatment of all such cases in the standard texts, but our overriding advice is that under no circumstances should you try to master *all* the exceptions to the same extent. Some are very much more important (in the context of an examinable academic course) than others.

Civil Cases

As we go to press the law is about to be changed in this area. The Civil Evidence Act 1995 is not yet in force, but is likely to be in the near future. The Act abolishes the hearsay rule in civil cases. We set out the present law below and then look at the main facets of the 1995 Act.

The essential orientation which you need to have when thinking about hearsay in civil cases at the moment is that, under the Civil Evidence Act 1968, hearsay is generally admissible as long as it comes within the scope of the Act. The basic issue is generally not so much whether the hearsay is in fact admissible (it usually is in civil cases) but rather how it is admitted. In effect, as far as civil cases are concerned at present, you can forget any route of admissibility other than the 1968 Act. We do not set out here the detailed provisions in the Act you can find those in your standard text but we have outlined a checklist of the relevant factors which you need to understand. The overriding principle to remember is that once you have identified a statement as hearsay, then in order for it to be admissible in a civil case it must comply with one of the following sections of the Act: ss. 2, 4, 5, 9. You should also note that, following the enactment of the Civil Evidence Act 1972, the application of the 1968 Act has been extended to hearsay statements of opinion, as well as hearsay statements of fact.

Section 2
This is one of the more important sections of the Act. It provides for the admissibility of first-hand hearsay. Under the section, if a party wishes to prove a fact by a hearsay statement rather than by calling as a witness the maker of the statement then he must serve a notice on the opposing party. The other side may then serve a counter-notice and if this is done then, generally, the maker of the statement must be called at the trial. However, the court does have a discretion to admit the statement even though a counter-notice has been served, though this would be done only if there were some cogent reason. Therefore if the evidence in question is likely to be disputed the witness will have to be called. There is one class of case where a party can put in a hearsay statement under s. 2 as of right and where no counter-notice may compel the calling of the maker of the statement. This is where one of the five reasons created by s. 8 for not calling the maker exists. The reasons are that the maker is dead, overseas, unfit through bodily or mental condition, cannot with reasonable diligence be identified or found, or cannot reasonably be expected to remember the contents of the statement.

If a s. 8 notice is served, no counter-notice requiring the maker of the statement to be called can be served. A counter-notice can be served alleging that the s. 8 reason relied upon does not apply. If this is done, there is a preliminary hearing to decide this question.

We have not set out the detailed regulations about what must be contained in notices and counter-notices and the time-limits that apply to them. You will find the best treatment of such matters in *Murphy on Evidence*, pp. 277–283. For most degree examinations you will not need a detailed knowledge of these provisions.

Of course, it may be that the person who made the statement out of court is called as a witness in the proceedings. Normally there will be no need to resort to the previous statement of the witness he will simply give his evidence in the normal way. However, it may occasionally be necessary to introduce his previous statement (which is hearsay) as evidence in the proceedings. Realistically, this is only likely to happen where the witness has made a written statement sometime after the events to which it relates and has subsequently forgotten the detail of that statement (see *Morris* v *Stratford-on-Avon Rural District Council* [1973] 1 WLR 1059). For the previous statement to be admissible the party calling the witness must give notice to all other parties of his wish to use the statement (although the court does have a discretion to waive this requirement if good reason is shown). In addition, the leave of the court is required before the statement can be admitted. Previous statements of witnesses as opposed to non-witnesses are less likely to feature in an examination, if only because there is less to say about them and little case law on them.

Even if the procedural requirements for admissibility under s. 2 are not satisfied, the court still has an inclusionary discretion to admit the evidence on grounds of justice (see s. 8(3)(a)).

Section 4
This section deals exclusively with hearsay evidence contained in a document. As with s. 2, we need to consider the question of admissibility both in the case where the document has been compiled from information supplied by a person who is called as a witness and where the person who supplied the information is not called as a witness.

In the case where the supplier is not called as a witness:

(a)   The document must be, or form part of, a record.

(b)   The document must have been compiled by a person acting under a duty.

(c)   The document must have been compiled from information which was supplied by a person (whether acting under a duty or not) who had, or may reasonably be supposed to have had, personal knowledge of the matters dealt with in that information and which, if not supplied by that person to the compiler of the record directly, was supplied by him to the compiler of the record indirectly through one or more intermediaries each acting under a duty.

A party wishing to put in evidence a documentary statement under s. 4 must follow a notice and counter-notice procedure which is very similar to that under s. 2. As with s. 2, if one of the s. 8 reasons for not calling a witness exists and is claimed in the notice then no counter-notice is possible except one disputing the s. 8 reason relied on.

Apart from the above points, there are a number of matters which you should think about when considering the operation of s. 4. Of particular significance to an examinee (although of perhaps less significance in practice) is the question of potential overlap between s. 2 and s. 4. Both sections provide a route for the reception of firsthand hearsay, and the fact that it is contained in a document is not a bar to admissibility under s. 2. Secondhand hearsay, however, can only be admitted under s. 4. The reason why secondhand hearsay is admissible under one section, but not the other, is nothing to do with the fact that it is in writing. The justification for its reception under s. 4 is found in the 'duty' requirement on the part of the compiler of the record, which provides some guarantee of reliability.

A reference to a person 'acting under a duty' is defined as including:

a reference to a person acting in the course of any trade, business, profession or other occupation in which he is engaged or employed or for the purposes of any paid or unpaid office held by him.

The only significant case law on the section has been on the meaning of the 'personal knowledge' requirement. If the 'record' which is being considered by the court is one of some antiquity, the evidence showing that the supplier had such knowledge may be very sparse. In such circumstances the requirement is satisfied relatively easily, particularly where the record is one of a public nature. Thus in *Knight v David* [1971] 1 WLR 1671 a claim by the plaintiffs to certain land depended upon events which occurred in 1886 and for the purpose of establishing that claim, the plaintiffs sought to put in evidence a tithe map and tithe apportionment survey, made under the provisions of the Tithe Act 1836. The court was prepared to infer that the supplier of the information might be reasonably supposed to have personal knowledge.

The Civil Evidence Act 1968 does not define the meaning of 'record' but in *H v Schering Chemicals Ltd* [1983] 1 WLR 143, Bingham J said:

The intention of that section was, I believe, to admit in evidence records which a historian would regard as original or primary sources, that is, documents which either give effect to a transaction itself or which contain a contemporaneous register of information supplied by those with direct knowledge of the facts.

Again, it may be that the person who supplied the information may be called as a witness in the proceedings. Usually there will be no need to rely on the documentary record. He will testify in the normal way, but if it becomes apparent that he cannot remember the information resort may be had to the documentary record, subject to the leave of the court. As with s. 2, the court has an inclusionary discretion even if the procedural conditions are not satisfied.

Section 5

This section deals with the admissibility of computerised records. If this provision comes up in an examination it is very likely that you will need to consider its operation in conjunction with the equivalent provisions (Police and Criminal Evidence Act 1984 (the 1984 Act), s. 69 and sch.3) for criminal proceedings. Section 5 of the Civil Evidence Act 1968 is slightly different from the equivalent provisions in the 1984 Act and we shall deal with it very briefly.

Under s. 5 a statement contained in a document produced by a computer is admissible provided:

(a)   No other exclusionary rule operates.

(b)   The document was produced by the computer, while operating on a regular basis.

(c)   The information contained in the document was the kind of information supplied regularly to the computer over the relevant period.

(d)   The information contained in the document reproduces or is derived from information supplied to the computer in the course of the relevant activities.

(e)   The computer was operating properly during the relevant period.

Detailed examination questions are not often set on the operation of this provision, both because of its complexity in operation and also because of its relatively limited academic interest. This position may change, following the enactment of the 1984 Act, and you may be required in the future to make a comparative assessment of the two sets of provisions. However, unless you have done a special study of this aspect of hearsay as part of your course, such a question would be unfair, and would deprive you of the opportunity in an examination to demonstrate your knowledge of more important aspects of hearsay. Accordingly, you should not get bogged down in this narrow aspect of the topic.

Section 9

This section preserves a number of common law exceptions. If your course has dealt with them in detail then you will need to learn them properly, but otherwise an outline treatment will be sufficient. The most important of the exceptions relate to admissions and to certain public documents.

CIVIL EVIDENCE ACT 1995

As stated above, this piece of legislation has been passed, but is not yet in force. It provides that in civil proceedings evidence shall not be excluded on the ground that it is hearsay.

A party proposing to adduce hearsay evidence in civil proceedings, must give to the other party such notice and, on request, particulars, as is reasonable and practicable in order to allow him to deal with any matters arising from the evidence being hearsay.

The Act provides that in assessing the weight to be given to hearsay evidence in civil proceedings, the court shall have regard to any circumstances from which any inference can reasonably be drawn as to the reliability or otherwise of the evidence.

In relation to computerised evidence, s. 5 of the Civil Evidence Act 1968 has been repealed and a much simpler approach to such evidence is contained in the 1995 Act.

Altogether the new legislation simply recognises developments in practice which have taken place in modern times. In *Ventouris* v *Mountain (No. 2)* [1992] 1 WLR 887, Balcombe LJ puts it very well:

> The modern tendency in civil proceedings is to admit all relevant evidence and the judge should be trusted to give proper weight to evidence which is not the best evidence.

Criminal Cases

We can set out, in the form of a simple list, those exceptions which are going to be most useful to an examinee. These are:

(a) *Confessions.* In practice these are a crucially important exception but on most evidence courses 'confessions' are dealt with as a discrete topic. We consider confessions in chapter 9.

(b) *Firsthand documentary hearsay under the Criminal Justice Act 1988, s. 23.* This provision extends the admissibility of hearsay statements in criminal cases. It permits the introduction of a statement made by a person in a document as evidence of any fact of which direct oral evidence by him would be admissible, subject to certain conditions. The conditions are:

(i) the person is dead or unfit to attend as a witness by reason of bodily or mental condition; or

(ii) the person is outside the UK and it is not reasonably practicable to secure his attendance; or

(iii) the person cannot be found despite all reasonable steps having been taken to find him; or

(iv) the person made the statement to a police officer (or other person charged with the duty of investigating offences or charging offenders) *and* does not give oral evidence through fear or because he is kept out of the way.

The effect of s. 23 is to admit in evidence all firsthand hearsay statements made in documents. Thus, it does not apply to oral hearsay.

Under s. 25 the court of trial may in its discretion direct that a statement admissible under s. 23 shall nevertheless be excluded in the interests of justice. Further, under s. 26 a statement shall not be admitted under s. 23 without leave of the court if it was prepared for the purposes of pending or contemplated criminal proceedings or of a criminal investigation. Leave may be given only if the court is of the opinion that the statement should be admitted in the interests of justice. The primary intention of ss. 25 and 26 is to limit the use by the prosecution of, for example, depositions, witness statements and police officers' notebooks, which would reduce the trial to a paper exercise. In the case of evidence adduced by the prosecution, the court has a general discretion under the 1984 Act, s. 78, to exclude evidence whose admission would have such an adverse effect on the fairness of the proceedings that the court ought not to admit it. This is not affected by the Criminal Justice Act 1988.

Most of the caselaw under s. 23 has concerned the application of the second and fourth of the above exceptions. In particular, the interpretation of 'fear' or being 'kept out of the way' has given rise to some difficulties, which you should note.

(c) *Multiple hearsay under the Criminal Justice Act 1988, s. 24.* This provision, which replaces s. 68 of the Police and Criminal Evidence Act 1984, permits the introduction of a statement in a document as evidence of any fact of which direct oral evidence would be admissible, provided that the following conditions are satisfied:

(i)   the document was created or received by a person in the course of a trade, business, profession or other occupation, or as the holder of a paid or unpaid office; and

(ii)   the information contained in the document was supplied by a person (whether or not the maker of the statement) who had, or may reasonably be supposed to have had, personal knowledge of the matters dealt with; and

(iii)   if the information was supplied indirectly, each person through whom it was supplied received it in the course of a trade, business, profession or other occupation, or as the holder of a paid or unpaid office.

If the statement was prepared for the purposes of pending or contemplated criminal proceedings, or of a criminal investigation, then there is a further condition of admissibility under s. 24, namely that one of the four alternative conditions stated in s. 23 is satisfied (see above) or the person who made the statement cannot reasonably be expected (having regard to the time which has elapsed since he made the statement and to all the circumstances) to have any recollection of the matters dealt with in the statement.

The provisions of ss. 25 and 26 concerning the judge's discretion apply also to statements under s. 24.

You must understand the relationship of s. 23 to s. 24. Under s. 23 a statement in a document is admissible to prove any fact of which direct oral evidence *by the maker* ('by him' as the section says) would be admissible. However, in s. 24 there is no equivalent to those words. What this means is that under s. 23 the admissible statement must relate to matters within the maker's personal knowledge, i.e., firsthand hearsay, whereas under s. 24 there is no such restriction and so multiple hearsay is admissible.

Since multiple hearsay is potentially more unreliable, the law seeks to increase reliability by requiring the document to have been created or received in the course of business or a profession etc., as it is assumed that in such a situation a person is more likely to take care that what is written or passed on is accurate.

There are problems with the interpretation of s. 24, which probably arise out of a drafting error. We are not able to give space to this here, but it may be raised in your course and should be examined. A simple introduction to the issue is contained in Smith, *Criminal Evidence*, pp. 86–88.

(d) *Statements in documents produced by computer.* Section 69 of, and sch. 3 to, the Police and Criminal Evidence Act 1984 provide a comprehensive statutory code for the admissibility of documents produced by computer. These provisions were a welcome development in the law on this matter and resolved a number of problems caused by the inability of the common law rules to deal with this issue. Further conditions of admissibility can be laid down in rules of court made under s. 69(2), which allows for the law to respond quickly in an area of rapid technological change.

In respect of such documents the first question to be asked is whether the document would be admissible if it were not produced by a computer. If the answer is that it would not, then it is excluded and s. 69 is not applicable. If, however, the answer is that it would be admissible, then it is necessary to consider whether s. 69 applies. Space precludes a detailed treatment of this provision, but essentially three possible situations may arise. Again, Professor Smith gives the clearest explanation of these (see *Criminal Evidence*, pp. 91–93). The first situation is where the statement produced by the computer is being offered as evidence of any fact stated therein *by any person*. Here, the statement will be hearsay, and so both an exception to the hearsay rule (generally s. 23 or s. 24 above), *plus* s. 69 will have to be satisfied. The second is where the computer printout is adduced as evidence of a fact 'observed' by the computer and recorded therein (rather than referring to a statement by a person). This would not involve hearsay, but would attract s. 69 since the printout is still offered, in the words of the section, 'as evidence of a fact stated therein'. The third situation is where the computer printout itself is the fact sought to be proved. An example would be a printout adduced to prove that a sum of money was credited to a bank account. Here, no hearsay is involved and s. 69 does not apply, since the document is not offered 'as evidence of any fact stated therein'.

The only other issue which you may have to address in particular concerning s. 69 is when exactly a document is 'produced by a computer'. In deciding this the avowed purpose of s. 69, which is to safeguard against errors produced by the working operation of the computer, should be kept in mind by the courts and by yourself in assessing a particular fact situation.

(e) Res gestae *statements*. As an exception to the hearsay rule the exceptions embraced under this broad umbrella have attracted some critical comment. As one Canadian writer has put it:

This collection of fact situations is so confusing in its scope as almost to demand that a reader cease thinking before he go mad.

Another eminent authority has stated that:

The problem of *res gestae* is intractable. A surfeit of this damnable doctrine may lead to sterility or blindness if not something much worse.

These sentiments are not unfair!

The doctrine is difficult. The basic problem is that the case law on it is impenetrable. You will find, if you look at this topic in detail, that much of the case law is not particularly lively and that the issues it is concerned with do not have much academic, practical or topical significance. The best account of the law on this topic is the comprehensive treatment in *Cross and Tapper on Evidence*, in which the classic categories under which the doctrine is conventionally discussed are analysed in detail.

In our experience the only aspect of *res gestae* which makes a regular appearance on an examination paper relates to those cases dealing with the excited utterances of participants in, or witnesses to, events.

The essential reason why such statements are admitted as an exception to the general rule rests on the belief that their reliability is enhanced because of the circumstances in which they were uttered. The problem for the law of evidence has been to determine the criteria of admissibility. The courts have not been consistent on this question. A former view, exemplified by *R v Bedingfield* (1879) 14 Cox CC 341 insisted that the statement be contemporaneous with the events to which it related, and in this context 'contemporaneity' was given an extremely restricted meaning. *Bedingfield* is worth reading out of pure interest, quite apart from its relevance on this issue. A more modern view, ironically one which mirrors the earliest common law attitude to this question, was adopted in *Ratten v R* [1972] AC 378, where Lord Wilberforce said:

[T]he test should be not the uncertain one whether the making of the statement was in some sense part of the event or transaction. This may often be difficult to establish: such external matters as the time which elapses between the events and the speaking of the words (or vice versa), and differences in location being relevant factors but not, taken by themselves, decisive criteria. As regards statements made after the event it must be for the judge, by preliminary ruling, to satisfy himself that the statement was so clearly made in circumstances of spontaneity or involvement in the event that the possibility of concoction can be disregarded. Conversely, if he considers that the statement was made by way of narrative of a detached prior event so that the speaker was so disengaged from it as to be able to construct or adapt his account, he should exclude it. And the same must in principle be true of statements made before the event.

The Court of Appeal appeared to add a gloss to this test in *R v Nye and Loan* (1977) 66 Cr App R 252 by referring, in addition, to the possibility of mistake on the part of the declarant, but in a later authority, *R v Turnbull* (1985) 80 Cr App R 104, the court applied the *Ratten* test without referring to such a gloss. An opportunity to re-examine the whole basis of the *res gestae* doctrine was afforded to the House of Lords in the case of *R v Andrews* [1987] AC 281. In the case, two men entered the victim's flat and attacked him with knives. Shortly afterwards the victim, seriously wounded, made his way to the flat below his own to obtain help. Two police officers arrived within minutes and the victim informed them that the defendant and another had been the assailants. Two months later the victim died as a result of his injuries. On charges of murder and aggravated burglary, the victim's statement was admitted under the doctrine of *res gestae*. Upholding the decision of the trial judge, the House of Lords summarised the position of a judge when faced with an application to admit such evidence in a criminal trial. Their Lordships set out the law under five heads:

    (i)   The primary question is: Can the possibility of concoction or distortion be disregarded?

    (ii)   To answer the question the judge must first consider the circumstances in which the particular statement was made, in order to satisfy himself that the event was so unusual or startling or dramatic as to dominate the thoughts of the victim, so that his utterance was an instinctive reaction to that event, thus giving no real opportunity for reasoned reflection. In such a situation the judge would be entitled to conclude that the involvement or the pressure of the event would exclude the possibility of concoction or distortion, providing that the statement was made in conditions of approximate but not exact contemporaneity.

(iii)   In order for the statement to be sufficiently 'spontaneous' it must be so closely associated with the event which has excited the statement, that it can be fairly stated that the mind of the declarant was still dominated by the event. Thus the judge must be satisfied that the event, which provided the trigger mechanism for the statement, was still operative. The fact that the statement was made in answer to a question is but one factor to consider under this heading.

(iv)   Quite apart from the time factor, there may be special features in the case, which relate to the possibility of concoction or distortion. This could be, for example, where the victim had a motive of his own to fabricate or concoct in the form of malice or ill-will. If this were the case, then the judge must be satisfied that the circumstances were such that having regard to the special feature of malice, there was no possibility of any concoction or distortion to the advantage of the maker or the disadvantage of the accused.

(v)   As to the possibility of error in the facts narrated in the statement, if only the ordinary fallibility of human recollection is relied upon, this goes to the weight to be attached to and not to the admissibility of the statement and is therefore a matter for the jury. However, here again there may be special features that may give rise to the possibility of error. In the instant case there was evidence that the deceased had drunk to excess, well over double the permitted limit for driving a motor car. Another example would be where the identification was made in circumstances of particular difficulty or where the declarant suffered from defective eyesight. In such circumstances the trial judge must consider whether he can exclude the possibility of error.

R v *Andrews* represents a clear endorsement of the *Ratten* approach. It follows, as the court itself acknowledged, that the *Bedingfield* approach no longer represents the law.

(f)   There are a number of miscellaneous exceptions to the hearsay rule. Although some of these are of considerable practical importance the overwhelming majority of them can justifiably be regarded as meriting no more than a footnote treatment. However, some of these many exceptions do appear in examinations occasionally. Where this happens it is very unlikely that they will form anything other than a very small part of a question. There is no satisfactory way of classifying these exceptions, but the most significant are:

(i)   statements of persons now deceased — against interest; in the course of duty; as to public or general rights; as to pedigree;

(ii)   dying declarations in homicide cases;

(iii)   statements in public documents.

You will find a good short treatment of these exceptions in Heydon, *Evidence: Cases and Materials*, pp. 339-42.

PLANNING YOUR REVISION

The key to successful revision of hearsay is to approach it in a structured, logical and ordered fashion. You have seen from the treatment above that we are dealing with a difficult rule with a complex web of exceptions and your job in revising hearsay is to pick your way through.

There is much dissatisfaction with the hearsay rule today. As we have seen, the Civil Evidence Act 1995, soon to be in force, abolishes the rule in civil cases. For criminal cases, the Law Commission has issued a Consultation Paper (No. 138) which gives a comprehensive account of the rule and exceptions to it. The Paper proposes to retain the rule in an amended form and to create new exceptions to it. Examination of the paper will give you a rounded view of the subject, both in its present state and in relation to ideas of reform.

The Rule

As we have said above, the basic difficulty for many students is that of identifying hearsay when they come across it. Part of your task in revising this subject is to become familiar with those situations which give rise to a hearsay problem. We have already made the point that characterisation of evidence as hearsay does not depend on whether the statement in question is oral or written; it depends on the use to which the statement is put. Such characterisation is not always easy — even the judiciary has problems from time to time, as the useful case of *R* v *Rice* [1963] 1 QB 857 illustrates. We have more to say on this case later in the chapter.

Examiners often set questions requiring discussion of whether names on airline tickets, monograms on old school ties and initials on handkerchiefs are admissible to prove the presence of a person at a particular place and time. Case law on such issues is sparse, but you will find that the writers of the standard texts provide an abundance of useful illustrations. We would suggest that you analyse such examples in the same way as you would decided cases. Incidentally, if you are the sort of person who finds diagrams useful in understanding the law, there are several articles in which the authors attempt to unravel the mysteries of the subject in this way. Notable examples are Tribe, 'Triangulating hearsay' (1974) 87 Harvard LR and the wonderfully named 'Stickperson hearsay: a simplified approach to understanding the rule against hearsay' by Graham in (1982) University of Illinois LR 887.

One aspect of the rule which it may be useful to consider relates to the hearsay status (or otherwise) of implied assertions. If you spend a little time penetrating the secrets of this aspect of hearsay, this will give you a deeper understanding of the basic structure of the doctrine. Certain texts give only a cursory treatment of this matter. *Cross and Tapper on Evidence* gives the most detailed analysis. A sound knowledge of the leading authority of *R* v *Kearley* [1992] 2 AC 228 is essential. What is still an extremely useful discussion of the theoretical basis of implied assertions can be found in Finman, 'Implied assertions as hearsay' (1962) 14 Stan L Rev 682.

The Exceptions

A full practical understanding of the operation of the hearsay rule involves a complete familiarity with the large number of exceptions to the rule. However, the needs of an evidence student on an academic course are more restricted. The first thing you must do is work out just which exceptions are important in the context of your particular course. Inevitably this will require you to be familiar with the relevant provisions of the Civil Evidence Act 1968 (shortly to be replaced by the Civil Evidence Act 1995), the Police and Criminal Evidence Act 1984 and the Criminal Justice Act 1988. In the context of the 1968 Act you will have discovered that a number of the old common law exceptions are now contained in s. 9. The 1995 Act does not replace the common law and expressly provides that where a statement is admissible under a common law exception to the rule against hearsay in a civil case, there is no need for the party seeking to adduce the statement to follow the procedures and safeguards laid down in the 1995 Act. We would suggest that it is generally unnecessary to worry about these exceptions, except perhaps in a very general sense, unless they have had specific coverage in your course.

In the context of all the relevant legislation on hearsay since 1968 you should consider, as part of your revision, what guarantees of reliability are provided by these statutes. If you understand the rationale for the exception, that will give you an insight into the rule itself. The fundamental reason why hearsay is the subject of an exclusionary rule in the first place is because of the inherent untrustworthiness of such evidence. Any statutory exception (or common law exception for that matter) must have some strong rationale, based either on reliability or necessity (such as in the case of dying declarations in homicide cases) to overcome such untrustworthiness. The way these statutes meet this issue in the context of documentary hearsay is by requiring, *inter alia*, that the compiler of the document act, in civil cases, under some kind of duty and, in criminal cases, in the course of business etc.

In dealing with the common law exceptions to the rule (which, as we have pointed out earlier in the chapter, are now only applicable in criminal cases), be guided by your teachers as to the depth of treatment which is necessary. All else being equal, an outline knowledge of statements of deceased persons, dying declarations and statements in public documents will be ample. *Res gestae* statements are more problematic and the soundest advice we can offer here is not to become bogged down with historical detail. Both *Ratten* v *R*

[1972] AC 378 and *R* v *Andrews* [1987] AC 281 are extremely useful here and will repay detailed consideration. Confessions, in practice by far the most important exception, are dealt with separately in the next chapter.

EXAMINATION QUESTIONS

Both problem and essay questions are regularly set on hearsay. Such questions can spread over the whole field of hearsay, and may well involve a detailed knowledge of both (or either) the rule in civil and in criminal cases. Some examiners, probably those of independent means, have even been known to cross the wires between hearsay and, say, competence. One point worth mentioning is that problem questions on hearsay are often subdivided into a number of separate parts, each involving some slightly different aspect of the rule. In your answer to such a question it is quite permissible to cross-reference any authorities you use you should not write out the same information twice. We should perhaps emphasise that this observation is of general application.

The following is a typical problem question:

Jim, a cyclist, was knocked down by an open-top sports car on his way to work and was seriously injured. The car did not stop. The police have now charged Keith with reckless driving and wish to adduce the following items of evidence:

(a)   The registration number of a car written on the back of a cigarette packet. This was dictated by Jim to Len, an off-duty police officer who arrived on the scene a few minutes after the accident. Len wrote the number down, but did not read it back to Jim. Jim cannot now remember what he dictated to Len.

(b)   The statement of Margaret, a pedestrian, that she heard an unknown passenger in the car shout to the driver just before the accident, 'Slow down Keith, or I will get out of the car'.

(c)   Ownership of the car is traced to Keith. He claims that he sold the car to Neville six months before. The police have found wedged at the back of the driver's seat a letter addressed to Keith dated the day before the accident.

Advise the police on admissibility.

Issue 1: The dictated registration mark

There are two main issues subsumed under this head. First, there is the possibility that it might be open to Jim to refresh his memory from the written note made by Len. Secondly, there is the question of whether Len, who did not witness the accident with his own unaided sense, can testify on the basis of what Jim said as to the registration number.

The refreshment issue can be dealt with shortly. It does not seem to be a major aspect of the question and you should not spend too much time on it. 'Refreshment of memory' is dealt with in chapter 11, and the basic rules are straightforward. Essentially, Jim will not be able to refresh his memory from a document which he neither prepared nor verified. The case of R v *Kelsey* (1982) 74 Cr App R 213 suggests that it may be sufficient verification if the person making the note from which the witness's memory is refreshed simply reads it back to the witness, who hears rather than sees what has been noted. It is certainly arguable that this case serves to undercut the full rigour of R v *McLean* (1967) 52 Cr App R 80, which is discussed above.

The narrow hearsay point raised by this aspect of the question is particularly interesting in the light of the Criminal Justice Act 1988. At common law there would have been no doubt that any testimony given by the police officer about the car number would have been inadmissible hearsay. Despite the fact that Jim would swear that he dictated to Len exactly what he saw, and that Len wrote down what was dictated, the effect of the reluctant decision of the Court of Appeal in *McLean* is that such evidence is clearly hearsay and not admissible, at common law, under any exception. However, in order to deal with this issue in an examination you will need to examine carefully the effect and consequences of the statutory changes made by the 1988 Act. Initially it may appear that either or both ss. 23 and 24 could be applicable. Ultimately, however, s. 23 can be discounted on the basis that it applies only where the conditions of admissibility established in that section are met, and on the facts of the problem it is clear that the requirements of s. 23(2) have not been satisfied. Under s. 24, statements contained in documents may be admissible in criminal proceedings where, *inter alia*, the document was created or received by a person in the course of his occupation, and the person who made the statement recorded in the document cannot reasonably be expected to have any recollection of the matters dealt with in the statement (s. 24(4)(b)). There are other conditions of admissibility in s. 24, but the two we have identified above are the crucial ones in the context of the problem.

As far as the second condition ('cannot reasonably be expected to have any recollection') is concerned, you can make useful reference to the literature on refreshment of memory, which demonstrates how quickly observers of mundane information, such as a car registration number, can forget the detail of their observation. The first condition is more problematic. Is Len acting in the course of his occupation in recording Jim's dictated statement?

Presumably the justification for the precise terminology of s. 24(1)(c)(i) rests in the argument that the primary guarantee of reliability of the hearsay statement was that it was recorded by a person who had no motive to record the statement incorrectly and in fact had every incentive to record it accurately. Do such considerations apply in law and in fact to the problem? The position *in fact* must surely be that Len will record the statement in exactly the same way, and for the same motives and purposes, as if he were on duty. The position *in law* is a very open question. Undoubtedly if the words 'in the course of [an] occupation' were given their literal construction they would appear to bar the possibility of Len giving evidence on the issue of the registration number.

Issue 2: Margaret's evidence

There is no doubt that the statement of the unknown passenger, when related by Margaret, is hearsay. If it is to be admitted it will have to be under the *res gestae* doctrine. The key issue, as stated earlier in the chapter, is whether the general requirements of the test in *Ratten* v *R* [1972] AC 378 as approved in *R* v *Andrews* [1987] AC 281 are satisfied. As we have noted above, the key to whether the excited utterance of a bystander or a participant in an event was admissible as an exception to the hearsay rule used to depend upon whether the utterance was contemporaneous with the event. Tortuous case law on the meaning of contemporaneity evolved, and achieved its high-water mark, in the dreadful case of *R* v *Bedingfield* (1879) 14 Cox CC 341. The more modern authorities have restored a degree of sanity to the law, by providing that evidence was admissible under the *res gestae* doctrine where the statement was so clearly made in circumstances of spontaneity or involvement in the event that the possibility of concoction can be disregarded. It is interesting that in the more recent cases the *res gestae* doctrine has been argued rather than basing admissibility on the dying declaration exception, where very difficult problems of proof arise.

Issue 3: Admissibility of the letter

The question of the admissibility of the letter raises some potentially difficult issues, not least of which is a consideration of whether or not the letter is in fact hearsay at all. In the case of *R* v *Rice* [1963] 1 QB 857 the Court of Criminal Appeal treated a used airline ticket bearing the name of the accused as admissible evidence that a person by that name had travelled on the flight to which the ticket related. The court treated the ticket, not as hearsay, but as a piece of real evidence, on the basis that the ticket did not 'speak as to its contents'. The reasoning of the court is unconvincing and Cross makes the point that the ticket was valueless as a piece of evidence unless regard was had to the actual inscription on the ticket. The ticket was the equivalent of an airline official saying, 'A man named Rice travelled on this aeroplane', which appears to be classic hearsay. *Rice* is probably not very strong authority and it was treated roughly by the House of Lords in *Myers* and was not mentioned by the Privy Council in *Patel* v *Comptroller of Customs* [1966] AC 356. See also the comments in *R* v *Lydon* (1986) 85 Cr App R 221.

The letter referred to in the problem is rather different in nature from the airline ticket in *Rice*, which was being used to prove passage of a person on an aircraft, but we would suggest that the essential issues are the same. The letter is worthless unless regard is had to its actual contents namely that it was addressed to Keith and bore a particular date. Accordingly, we would suggest that the letter is created as straightforward hearsay, and should be excluded. It is probably worth noting that if the facts of *Rice* were to recur, a straightforward solution is provided by s. 24 of the Criminal Justice Act 1988.

As a practical matter, you may find that instead of a letter you may be faced with other, more obscure, articles. Suppose that the issue is whether a woman was present at a particular time and place, and an item of female apparel bearing a label carrying the name of the owner is found there. In so far as it was sought to use the name tag as evidence of the presence of a particular woman then this would be caught by the rule. However, the item of clothing would undoubtedly be admissible as circumstantial evidence of the presence of a woman.

ESSAY QUESTIONS

Hearsay lends itself equally to problem and essay questions, and there is a wide range of legitimate possible essay titles which can be set. Essays on hearsay can be very specific in what they require. For example, you may see something along the following lines:

'Implied assertions ought not to be classified as hearsay.' Discuss.

Such a title as this is very specific and ought not to be attempted unless you have made a particular study of this rather esoteric (although very interesting) part of the subject. The decision in *R* v *Kearley* [1992] 2 AC 228, however, has given an added dimension of topicality to this issue. The difficulty of the subject may appeal to an examiner as one likely to sort out the good students from their less able colleagues.

Much more common are general essay titles, which frequently require a comparison and appraisal of the rules in civil and criminal cases. The following are typical:

'Following the passing of the Civil Evidence Act 1968 the rule against hearsay does not exist in any important sense in civil proceedings. It is about time that the rule in criminal cases is put on the same footing.' Discuss.

'The sooner the rules on hearsay in criminal cases are assimilated to those in civil cases, the better. ' Discuss.

The very real difficulty which a student may have in coming to terms with titles as widely drawn as these is that in the short time at his disposal in an examination he may not do anything more than provide the examiner with a descriptive and fairly low-grade treatment of the relevant issues. The reason will be obvious — such an essay is not one which can be tackled with any originality or authority unless you have prepared your ground well and in advance. There is simply too much material, and too many issues for you to consider, to come to the question with a fresh mind in the examination room.

However, such a question as those outlined above is perhaps not going to appear so frequently given the large-scale legislative changes of recent years. More likely, perhaps, would be one of the following titles:

'The Criminal Justice Act 1988 has gone some way towards resolving the problems caused by the hearsay rule in criminal cases. The job ought to be finished by the complete abolition of this troublesome rule.' Discuss.

'There are several broad possibilities for reforming the rule against hearsay. One is ... to enact statutes on a piecemeal basis to destroy particular anomalies forced on the courts by the common law rules. ... Another is to enact a hearsay code containing a broad hearsay rule with numerous clearly stated exceptions. A third is to abolish the ban on hearsay completely; the judge would exclude evidence of too little weight to go to the jury, but apart from that the weight of hearsay evidence would be left to the jury in the same way as direct evidence is now.' (Heydon) Discuss.

Both these titles invite a wide discussion of broad issues of policy relating to the operation of the rule and whether the exceptions thereto work satisfactorily in practice. To tackle them properly you will need to have some appreciation of the theoretical justification for the exclusion of hearsay and an understanding of the ways in which the various statutory derogations from the rule meet the theoretical objections. A very good examination of the rationale of the hearsay rule, together with an analysis of the ways in which the courts have attempted to evade the application of the rule, can be found in Zuckerman, *Criminal Evidence*, pp. 187–201.

Wherever you are dealing with a title as general as those indicated above you must be careful not to let your treatment of the issues slide into a simple catalogue of half-remembered statutory provisions. Time is limited, so you must put down your information in a concise and punchy way.

FURTHER READING

Birch, 'Hearsay-logic and hearsay-fiddles: *Blastland* revisited', in P. Smith (ed.), *Criminal Law: Essays in Honour of J. C. Smith* (London: Butterworths, 1987), pp. 24-39.

Carter, 'Hearsay: whether and whither' (1993) 109 LQR 573.

Finman, 'Implied assertions as hearsay' (1962) 14 Stan L Rev 682.

Graham, 'Stick person hearsay: a simplified approach to understanding the rule against hearsay' (1982) University of Illinois LR 887.

Pattenden, 'Conceptual versus pragmatic approaches to hearsay' (1993) 56 MLR 138.

Rein, 'The scope of hearsay' (1994) 110 LQR 431.

Smith, 'The admissibility of statements by computer' [1981] Crim LR 387.

Tribe, 'Triangulating hearsay' (1974) 87 Harvard LR.

9   CONFESSIONS AND IMPROPERLY OBTAINED EVIDENCE

INTRODUCTION

It is inconceivable that the evidence course you are studying will not deal with the law relating to confessions, with perhaps some coverage of related issues such as the confirmation of a confession by the discovery of subsequent facts and the question of the admissibility of improperly obtained evidence. In recent times a number of well-publicised miscarriages of justice involving confession evidence has focused attention on this subject. This whole area of law is still in a state of radical transition and as a result provides a very interesting point of focus for the discussion of a number of fundamental issues about the role of the law of evidence.

Conceptually the law relating to confessions forms the major exception in criminal cases to the rule against hearsay. However, it is quite normal for confessions to be dealt with as a separate and free-standing aspect of an evidence course. 'Confirmation by subsequent facts' and 'improperly obtained evidence' are topics which are sometimes taught as being parasitic on confessions. All three areas were the subject of considerable statutory reform by virtue of the Police and Criminal Evidence Act 1984 (the 1984 Act). Two simple consequences flow from this:

(a)   The topicality of these areas will make them high on any examiner's list of priorities.

(b)   A detailed and easy familiarity with the relevant provisions of the 1984 Act is vital for a successful examination performance in the topic.

In the following pages we have dealt separately with these three issues. However, from an examination point of view you must be prepared to amalgamate your learning on them, as they are frequently combined in an examination paper.

One of the important things to bear in mind when considering these topics is that the rules which originally applied to the admissibility of these categories of evidence were the exclusive creatures of the common law. The 1984 Act changed all that, although many of the common law principles find expression therein. From a practical point of view we think that you should devote your efforts to understanding these rules in the context of the Act, although you will need some background understanding of the way the law stood before its date of commencement.

In addition to these three topics we have also dealt with the related issue of the so-called right to silence, in particular in relation to the topic of confessions, which is now back in the spotlight as a result of the Criminal Justice and Public Order Act 1994.

CONFESSIONS

Before the passing of the 1984 Act the rules which governed the admissibility of confessions were easy to state but difficult to apply. The basic rule was that in order for a confession (which had been made to a 'person in authority') to be admissible, the confession had to be voluntary. The leading authority was the old case of *Ibrahim* v *R* [1914] AC 599 where Lord Sumner said:

> It has long been established as a positive rule of English criminal law, that no statement by an accused is admissible in evidence against him unless it is shown by the prosecution to have been a voluntary statement, in the sense that it has not been obtained from him either by fear of prejudice or hope of advantage exercised or held out by a person in authority.

Under the original *Ibrahim* formulation there was no mention of 'oppression' as a distinct ground for excluding a confession, but from the mid-1960s onwards there was an increasing number of cases where oppression was mentioned by judges as a reason for exclusion. In *Callis* v *Gunn* [1964] 1 QB 495 Lord Parker CJ said:

> There is a fundamental principle of law that no answer to a question and no statement is admissible unless it is shown by the prosecution not to have been obtained in an oppressive manner.

A revised version of the Judges' Rules appeared in 1964 (now, of course, replaced by the Codes of Practice under the 1984 Act) in which 'oppression' was given specific mention as a circumstance where a judge could, in his discretion, exclude a statement made to the police. Further decisions in the 1960s and 1970s entrenched the notion of oppression as a basis for exclusion and if there were any lingering doubts over the matter the decision of the House of Lords in *DPP* v *Ping Lin* [1976] AC 574 went some way towards removing them.

The 1984 Act has now recast the law on confessions. Under s. 82(1) of the Act a confession includes any statement wholly or partly adverse to the person who made it. It is no longer necessary for a confession to have been made to a 'person in authority', although in practice it is usually made to just such a person, namely a police officer.

The modern law on the admissibility of confessions now centres on s. 76 of the 1984 Act. Because it is so important we have set out the relevant parts of the section in full:

(1)   In any proceedings a confession made by an accused person may be given in evidence against him in so far as it is relevant to any matter in issue in the proceedings and is not excluded by the court in pursuance of this section.

(2)   If, in any proceedings where the prosecution proposes to give in evidence a confession made by an accused person, it is represented to the court that the confession was or may have been obtained:

(a)   by oppression of the person who made it; or

(b)   in consequence of anything said or done which was likely, in the circumstances existing at the time, to render unreliable any confession which might be made by him in consequence thereof, the court shall not allow the confession to be given in evidence against him except in so far as the prosecution proves to the court beyond reasonable doubt that the confession (notwithstanding that it may be true) was not obtained as aforesaid. . . .

(8)   In this section 'oppression' includes torture, inhuman or degrading treatment, and the use or threat of violence (whether or not amounting to torture).

It is immediately obvious that the whole basis of exclusion was recast by this provision. The wording of the section makes it clear that there are two separate (although not mutually exclusive) grounds on which a confession can be excluded:

(a)   oppression;

(b)   where circumstances exist which are likely to render any confession unreliable.

The notion of 'oppression' was given some definition by s. 76(8) of the section, but it can hardly be supposed that the statutory description embraces the whole of the meaning of oppression. The terminology used to describe oppression in the Act is borrowed from Article 3 of the European Convention on Human Rights, but the case law on Article 3 shows a wide gulf between the kind of activity prohibited under the Convention and the notion as it has been commonly understood in the context of the law on confessions in UK domestic law. The leading authority on the interpretation of oppression under the Act is *R v Fulling* [1987] QB 426, in which the Court of Appeal held that oppression should be given its ordinary dictionary meaning. This was said to be 'an exercise of authority or power in a burdensome, harsh or wrongful manner; unjust or cruel treatment of subjects, inferiors etc.; the imposition of unreasonable or unjust burdens'. This definition is not, however, consistent with the later reference by the court in the same case to oppression as being 'detestable wickedness'. Further, the court went on to say that it was hard to envisage there being oppression without impropriety on the part of the police. This last point was taken up in a later Court of Appeal decision, *R v Hughes* [1988] Crim LR 519, in which it was made clear that there can be no oppression without misconduct. However, you should remember that it does not follow from this that all impropriety ipso facto amounts to oppression, although, of course, where there is some impropriety this may assist an argument that the confession may yet be excluded under the reliability ground (s. 76(2)(b)). The rationale behind the oppression ground of exclusion seems to be that there are certain minimum standards of decent behaviour to be expected from interrogators and that failure to meet these standards should result in the automatic exclusion of any resulting confession, irrespective of any question of unreliability. Caselaw on the question of 'oppression' is starting to build up (see, in particular, *R v Beales* [1991] Crim LR 118; *R v Paris* (1993) 97 Cr App R 104; and *R v Heaton* [1993] Crim LR 593).

As far as the question of unreliability is concerned, the first thing to note is that there is no statutory definition of this term. This is perhaps understand-able as its meaning is relatively clear in the ordinary case. What you must understand is that the question under the 1984 Act is a hypothetical one in the sense that the court must consider whether *any* confession which *might be made* by the accused would be unreliable. The section specifically states that the truth of the actual confession is to be excluded from consideration by the court: see *R v Cox* [1991] Crim LR 276 and *R v Crampton* (1991) 92 Cr App R 372, both of which illustrate this point.

The court is required to consider 'anything said or done' which was likely in the circumstances to affect reliability. Thus, there is no need for any threat or inducement, as there was under the common law. However, in *R v Goldenberg* (1988) 88 Cr App R 285, the Court of Appeal held that the section does not cover anything said or done by the person making the confession. One may wish to question whether this decision marks a definitive interpretation of the statutory words or, indeed, is consistent with the philosophy appearing to underpin those words. However, it is noteworthy that the decision in *R v Goldenberg* has been followed in *R v Crampton*.

It is clear that the accused's own physical and mental condition may be part of the 'circumstances' under s. 76(2)(b), as illustrated by the decisions in *R v Everett* [1988] Crim LR 826 and *R v McGovern* (1991) 92 Cr App R 228.

Unlike the oppression head of exclusion, it is not necessary to prove that anything improper was done to the suspect by the person questioning him. This was confirmed in *R v Fulling*. In connection with this, it is true that a breach of other provisions of the Act (for example, the right of access to a solicitor under s. 58) or of the Codes of Practice does not necessarily rule out a confession. However, such breaches can be considered in deciding whether a confession is unreliable (just as they may also bear on the question of oppression). A useful case in this context is *R v Delaney* (1988) 88 Cr App R 338.

Be sure not to miss the point that the words 'in consequence of' in s. 76(2)(b) mean that there must be a causal link between what is said or done and the risk of unreliability. It is interesting to note that this point seems to have been missed by the Court of Appeal in *R v Doolan* [1988] Crim LR 747, in which the court took account of breaches of one of the Codes of Practice which occurred *after* the confession was made.

Even if a confession satisfies s. 76 and is therefore admissible in law, that is not the end of the story. A confession may also be challenged under s. 78(1), which gives to the judge a statutory discretion to exclude prosecution evidence, or under s. 82(3), which preserves the common law. At common law the discretion could be exercised where the prejudicial effect of the evidence outweighed its probative value; where the confession was obtained by unfair means; and where the confession was obtained in breach of the old Judges' Rules.

Although there are some unsettled aspects of this area, one point which is quite clear is that confessions can be excluded under s. 78(1). It was argued in *R v Mason* [1988] 1 WLR 139 that s. 78(1) did not apply to confessions since they are dealt with in s. 76. The Court of Appeal rejected this argument and held that the word 'evidence' in s. 78(1) includes all the evidence which might be introduced into the trial by the prosecution, including evidence of confessions.

What is much less certain is the relationship between the common law and s. 78(1), which states:

> In any proceedings the court may refuse to allow evidence on which the prosecution proposes to rely to be given if it appears to the court that, having regard to all the circumstances, including the circumstances in which the evidence was obtained, the admission of the evidence would have such an adverse effect on the fairness of the proceedings that the court ought not to admit it.

Does this merely restate the common law or does it widen the discretion afforded to judges? Thus far the courts have not spoken with one voice on this point. In *R* v *Mason*, the Court of Appeal said that s. 78 did no more than restate the power which judges had at common law. However, in *R* v *Fulling*, Lord Lane CJ said that the Act was a codifying statute, which should be looked at on its own wording and not simply be taken as enacting common law. In a later case, *R* v *O'Leary* [1988] Crim LR 827, it was said that the common law authorities do not fetter the construction of s. 78, which is a separate entity. When one looks at the day-to-day decisions of the criminal courts it is clear that, whereas judges are quite prepared to exclude evidence under s. 78, in a way in which they were not at common law. There is very little consideration today of the common law.

Little exists in the way of authority on the fundamental principles to be applied in exercising the discretion under s. 78 and in fact in *R* v *Samuel* [1988] QB 615, the Court of Appeal stated that it was undesirable to give any such general guidance since the circumstances of each case varied enormously. However, the authorities recognise that certain considerations are of importance in the application of the section. The first of these relates to the seriousness of the breach of the provisions of the Act or the Codes of Practice. In the context of the important provision of the right of access to a solicitor under s. 58, the Court of Appeal in *R* v *Walsh* (1989) 91 Cr App R 161 put the matter in this way:

> ... if there are significant and substantial breaches of s. 58 or the provisions of the Code, then prima facie at least, the standards of fairness set by Parliament have not been met. So far as a defendant is concerned, it seems to us also to follow that to admit evidence against him which has been obtained in circumstances where the standards have not been met, cannot but have an adverse effect on the fairness of the proceedings.

A similar approach was taken in *R* v *Keenan* [1990] 2 QB 54, where the court was concerned with those provisions of the code concerning the conduct of interviews.

A second important consideration is the question of bad faith on the part of the police. Despite the fact that the courts have said that it is not their function to discipline the police (see, for example, *R v Mason*) the presence of bad faith on the part of the police, where there has been a breach of the Act or code, is more likely to lead to the evidence being excluded under s. 78. In *R v Alladice* (1988) 87 Cr App R 380 the Court of Appeal stated that in the case of bad faith a court would have 'little difficulty' in excluding any confession under the section. It should be remembered, however, that where there is a breach of the code, albeit in good faith, this does not mean that of necessity a confession *will* be admitted in evidence. The question then would depend on whether or not that would have an adverse effect on the fairness of the proceedings. The point is summed up in *R v Walsh*:

> ... although bad faith may make substantial or significant that which might not otherwise be so, the contrary does not follow. Breaches which are in themselves significant and substantial are not rendered otherwise by the good faith of the officers concerned.

In view of the courts' willingness to exclude confession evidence under s. 78, the common law discretion to exclude such evidence would seem to have little practical significance today.

SILENCE

Before we leave the issue of confessions it is important that we say something about a related topic. A person may respond to a statement (usually a question) made in his presence by remaining silent. In everyday life the silence of someone who is, say, accused of doing something disreputable (for example, committing a crime) may be thought, in some circumstances, to connote an acknowledgment of guilt, something tantamount to a confession. What does the law say about this?

This brings us back to something which we touched upon earlier (in chapter 7), namely the so-called 'right to silence' and specifically the issue of out-of-court silence. The whole question is now affected by the Criminal Justice and Public Order Act 1994 (CJPOA 1994), but since the Act provides that any inferences which could be drawn at common law may still be drawn, we must first say something about the common law position.

At common law it was clear that where an accusation was made in the presence of a person in circumstances which are such that it would be reasonable to expect a denial and he remains silent, his silence may be evidence from which the jury may infer that he admitted that the accusation was true (see *R v Christie* [1914] AC 545). However, the person's silence was *not* evidence against him if: (a) he had been cautioned (using the old, traditional form of caution: 'You do not have to say anything unless you wish to do so, but what you say may be given in evidence'); or (b) the accusation was made by the police or other persons with whom the suspect was not 'on even terms' (see *Hall* v *R* [1971] 1 WLR 298 and *Parkes* v *R* [1976] 1 WLR 1251). In either of these two situations, so the reasoning went, it would no longer be reasonable to expect the suspect to make some reply.

The question of drawing inferences from a suspect's silence is now affected by the CJPOA 1994, most notably by s. 34. This section applies to a failure by the accused to mention a fact relied on in his defence in those proceedings (being a fact which he could reasonably have been expected to mention). The occasions on which a failure to mention any such fact may apply are (a) at any time before the accused was charged with the offence, when he was being questioned under caution by an officer trying to discover whether, or by whom, the offence has been committed; and (b) on being charged with the offence or officially informed that he might be prosecuted for it. Remember that, as we have seen, the Act preserves the admissibility in evidence of silence of the accused *before caution*, including the drawing of appropriate inferences, at common law. Section 34 goes on to provide that a court in determining whether there is a case to answer, or a court or jury in determining whether the accused is guilty of the offence, may draw such inferences from the failure as appears proper. The purpose behind this provision can be seen by looking at the new form of caution. This is: 'You do not have to say anything. But it may harm your defence if you do not mention when questioned something which you later rely on in court. Anything you do say may be given in evidence'.

You should also make yourself familiar with ss. 36 and 37 of the CJPOA 1994, which make similar provisions. These sections apply to the accused's failure or refusal on arrest to account for the presence on his person, clothing, footwear, or in his possession, or in the place of arrest, of any object, substance or mark (s. 36); or the accused's own presence at the place at or about the time, of the alleged commission of the offence (s. 37). Under either section if the accused is requested to account by a constable who reasonably believes, and so informs the accused, that the presence of the thing, or the accused's own presence, may be attributable to his participating in the commission of the offence specified by the constable, the court or jury may draw such inferences from the failure or refusal as appear proper.

The question of silence out of court and the appropriate inferences, if any, to be drawn from it is a controversial matter. The whole issue has been debated on a number of occasions and there has been much disagreement. The new statutory provisions are based on the recommendations made over 20 years ago by the Criminal Law Revision Committee in its notorious 11th Report in 1972. Since then the Royal Commissions on Criminal Procedure and Criminal Justice, which reported in 1981 and 1993 respectively, have come down against changing the law. One can expect there to be considerable case law on the new provisions as their limits come to be tested in the courts.

IMPROPERLY OBTAINED EVIDENCE

From a historical perspective it was always known that the fact that evidence was tainted in some way by illegality in the manner in which it was obtained was not a bar to the subsequent admissibility of that evidence in criminal proceedings. In the old case of *R* v *Leatham* (1861) 3 E & E 658 Crompton J said: 'It matters not how you get it; if you steal it even, it would be admissible in evidence.'

Further support for such an approach can be found in a number of other cases. Thus, in *Elias* v *Pasmore* [1934] 2 KB 164 Horridge J was able to say:

[T]he interests of the State must excuse the seizure of documents, which seizure would otherwise be unlawful, if it appears in fact that such documents were evidence of a crime committed by anyone.

However, the important decision in *Kuruma* v *R* [1955] AC 197 seemed to establish that there was, in fact, a general discretion on the part of the court to exclude improperly obtained evidence, although it was technically admissible, if the strict rules of admissibility would operate unfairly against an accused.

However, in order to understand this issue it is essential to distinguish between two kinds of unfairness. The first relates to the use of the evidence at the trial. The second relates to the method of obtaining the evidence.

As to the first kind, it has long been recognised that the trial judge may exclude evidence which, although technically admissible, is likely to have a prejudicial effect on the jury out of all proportion to its probative value.

In *Kuruma* v *R* and in several subsequent authorities the discretion recognised by the court seemed to extend to the second kind as well as the first. For example, in *Callis* v *Gunn* [1964] 1 QB 495, Lord Parker CJ gave examples of where such discretion would operate and said that evidence would be excluded: 'if there was any suggestion of it having been obtained oppressively, by false representations, by a trick, by threats, by bribes, anything of that sort'.

However, the real problem with the authorities before *R* v *Sang* [1980] AC 402 is that although the courts said that a discretion existed, there is little evidence that the courts ever acknowledged its reality in practice. There are very few reported decisions where evidence was excluded in the exercise of such a discretion. Therefore it was hardly surprising that when the House of Lords confronted the issue in *Sang*, the conclusion reached was that no discretion of the kind referred to in such cases as *Kuruma* and *Callis* v *Gunn* in fact existed. The House summarised the position as follows (per Lord Diplock):

(1)   A trial judge in a criminal trial has always a discretion to refuse to admit evidence if in his opinion its prejudicial effect outweighs its probative value.
(2)   Save with regard to admissions and confessions and generally with regard to evidence obtained from the accused after commission of the offence, he has no discretion to refuse to admit relevant admissible evidence on the ground that it was obtained by improper or unfair means. The court is not concerned with how it was obtained.

Except, then, in the residual categories of case where the prejudicial effect of the evidence obtained outweighed its probative value or where the improperly obtained evidence was 'tantamount to a confession' (and where, presumably, the policy considerations underpinning the exclusion of confessions obtained by improper means overrode the policy considerations relating to the admissibility of illegally obtained evidence in general) no discretion relating to the method by which the evidence was obtained exists.

However, although the Law Lords in *Sang* seemed unanimous in their answer to the certified question, there are disagreements in the separate judgments.

The inclusion of s. 78 into the Police and Criminal Evidence Act 1984 threw the topic open once again.

We have already examined some of the issues which have arisen under this section as one of the principal applications of the section has been in the context of confessions. The section also applies, of course, to non-confession cases.

There are two further broad issues which you may need to consider. The first relates to the interpretation of the words 'fairness of the proceedings' in s. 78. It is idle to pretend that these words can be easily defined. Does 'proceedings' refer simply to what happens in court or to everything that happens following the arrest of the accused? Ordinary linguistic conventions would point to the former but the practical effect of such decisions as there are appears to point to the latter. This issue awaits authoritative determination. The second issue to note is that cases vary infinitely and in the final analysis everything depends upon the facts of the case.

Later in this chapter we discuss further some of the issues you should consider when preparing this topic for examination.

CONFIRMATION BY SUBSEQUENT FACTS

We are here concerned with the general question of the evidential status of facts which are discovered as a result of a confession which ultimately turns out to be wholly or partly inadmissible. The theoretical issue is straightforward: is evidence discovered as a result of a confession which is 'tainted' to be regarded as also tainted and therefore inadmissible, or are we to regard facts as facts and admissible in evidence irrespective of the fashion in which the facts came to be discovered? As with improperly obtained evidence, the matter is governed by the Police and Criminal Evidence Act 1984. Section 76(4) provides:

> The fact that a confession is wholly or partly excluded in pursuance of this section shall not affect the admissibility in evidence:

> (a)   of any facts discovered as a result of the confession.

It is probable that the provision does little more than reflect the position at common law, although one can point to the decision in *R v Barker* [1941] 2 KB 381 where not only was the confession excluded, but also everything found as a consequence of that confession. *Barker* can, in fact, be explained on the basis that the subsequently found evidence was closely related to the tainted confession, and was accordingly to be regarded as tainted in the same way. There appears to be no other common law decision which goes as far as *Barker*.

The problem with s. 76(4)(a) is that it is all very well introducing evidence discovered as a result of an inadmissible confession, but that evidence of itself is not a great deal of use to the prosecution unless it can link the finding of that evidence to something the accused has said. A simple example illustrates the point. Suppose Jack makes a confession to the police in which he admits to a theft and indicates where the proceeds of the theft have been hidden. The confession is subsequently ruled out as having been obtained as a result of oppressive behaviour on the part of the police. Even if the police go and recover the stolen items, unless they are found with Jack's fingerprints on them or with other evidence which links them with Jack, that evidence is of little use to the prosecution in trying to get a conviction. Accordingly, it is vital for the prosecution to know whether it can indicate to the jury in some way that the evidence discovered as a result of the inadmissible confession was in fact found as a result of something the accused had said, in order to link the finding with the accused. The few reported common law decisions on this issue provided a diversity of possible answers, ranging from the solution that if any part of the accused's inadmissible confession was subsequently confirmed then the whole of his confession became admissible, to the rule that no part of his confession, including that part subsequently confirmed, could be admitted. The matter is now clarified by s. 76(5) and (6) of the 1984 Act:

(5)   Evidence that a fact to which this subsection applies was discovered as a result of a statement made by an accused person shall not be admissible unless evidence of how it was discovered is given by him or on his behalf.
(6)   Subsection (5) above applies:

   (a)   to any fact discovered as a result of a confession which is wholly excluded in pursuance of this section; and
   (b)   to any fact discovered as a result of a confession which is partly so excluded, if the fact is discovered as a result of the excluded part of the confession.

The position is now that, unless the accused who has made an inadmissible confession which leads the investigator on to other evidence gives evidence himself as to how that material was discovered, the prosecution will not be able to prove that the evidence was discovered as a result of something that the accused said by linking the finding with the confession.

   Given the statutory footing on which this issue is now based, and given that the law is now very much clearer than had previously been the case, the question of the admission of subsequent fact evidence is now a relatively straightforward issue. It is likely to come up in an examination, if at all, only as a minor part of a problem question.

PLANNING YOUR REVISION

The amount of material contained in the three topics in this chapter is vast. We have given a very simple outline above of the main issues which are of concern across these topics. The impact of the Police and Criminal Evidence Act 1984 is obviously fundamental. The sea change in the law which the Act represents does, of course, give an enormous amount of scope for generalised essay-type questions which require an analysis of the impact of the new provisions or seek a comparison between the new and the old regimes. Equally, these are topics on which detailed problem questions can be set. Your revision of these areas should prepare you for either kind of question. In addition, the issue of silence on the part of the accused in response to an accusation put to him, and of the inferences which may be drawn from such silence, is another area which is topical and certain to be the subject of examination quetions.

Improperly Obtained Evidence

We would suggest the following strategy when grappling with this topic.

(a)   You need some idea of the history of the whole question of the admissibility of such evidence. The law has always been, as it remains today following the 1984 Act, that the fact that evidence (in general, not confessions) has been obtained improperly does not affect the admissibility of that evidence in court. See, for example, *R v Leatham* (1861) 8 Cox CC 498.

(b)   You will find it helpful (and interesting) to be able to contrast the position in this country with the stance which is taken elsewhere. In this country the courts tend to reason along the lines that 'facts are facts', irrespective of how those facts are come by. In the United States, for example, where evidence has been obtained improperly, this may involve a breach of fundamental constitutional guarantees, with the consequence that a completely different set of policy factors become relevant. The classic discussion of this whole issue is to be found in two articles by Heydon in [1973] Crim LR at pp. 603 and 690. The amount of comparative material which is discussed is large and you should be careful not to be overwhelmed by the detail, but you will find the comparisons between the position in the UK and elsewhere in the world of interest.

(c)   You will find that some acquaintance with the following cases is helpful. First, the case of *Kuruma v R* [1955] AC 197 should be learnt, if only to illustrate the extreme narrowness of the discretion which the judges seemed to permit themselves at common law. You also need to spend some time assessing the impact of the decision in *R v Sang* [1980] AC 402 because within the judgment in that case is a consideration of the various alternative approaches to the exercise of discretion. Finally, and crucially, you must be able to assess the impact and effect of s. 78 of the 1984 Act.

Confirmation by Subsequent Facts

Unlike with improperly obtained evidence, such vitality as this topic might have retained for the purposes of an examination has been largely lost as a result of the passing of the 1984 Act. This topic is one which has always been a little unclear, mainly because of the dearth of reported cases, but whatever scope for discussion which existed before 1984 has now gone. A knowledge of the ebb and flow of the authorities from the decision in *R v Warickshall* (1783) 1 Leach 263 onwards has little more than straightforward historical value now, although you will find a helpful review of the arguments surrounding the admissibility/inadmissibility in an admirable article by Andrews, 'Involuntary confessions and illegally obtained evidence in criminal cases' [1963] Crim LR 15, 77.

The essential material you need to know and understand is that contained in s. 76(4), (5) and (6) of the 1984 Act. To focus your thoughts in relation to these provisions you should extract the following points from them:

(a)   The fact that a confession is inadmissible does not affect the admissibility of anything found as a consequence thereof (s. 76(4)(a)).

(b)   However, the prosecution is not allowed to lead evidence to the effect that this consequent evidence was found as a consequence of anything that the accused had said, unless the accused himself (or one of his witnesses) gives evidence of how it was discovered.

The practical effect of the above is to rob the evidential status of that which is found of much of its potential value (s. 76(5) and (6)).

Confessions

We have set out below, in the form of a checklist, those key issues which we think are important for examinations. Space precludes a detailed treatment of each of these issues, but we have indicated those matters which we think will repay sustained study.

(a)   Any truly comprehensive treatment of the law on confessions needs to display some knowledge of the seminal influence of Lord Sumner's crucial dictum in *Ibrahim* v *R* [1914] AC 599.

(b)   You must have some thoughts on the 'oppression' doctrine. The outline treatment of 'oppression' contained earlier in the chapter can help you to focus on the kind of behaviour which may be regarded as oppressive because, under the 1984 Act, you will need to be aware of the type of misconduct on the part of the police which amounts to oppression.

(c)   You need a thorough understanding of the way in which s. 76(2)(b) may operate to exclude a confession on grounds of unreliability. The relationship between this ground of exclusion and exclusion on the ground of oppression needs to be appreciated and understood. *R* v *Fulling* [1987] QB 426 is particularly useful here.

(d)   Where does the burden of proof lie in relation to all those matters surrounding the question of the admissibility of a confession? The answer is to be found in s. 76(2) of the 1984 Act:

> [T]he court shall not allow the confession to be given in evidence against him except in so far as the prosecution proves to the court beyond reasonable doubt that the confession (notwithstanding that it may be true) was not obtained as aforesaid.

(e)   What are the respective functions of the judge and jury in a case where it is alleged that a confession ought to be excluded? Before the passing of the 1984 Act it was easy, in a conceptual sense at any rate, to draw a clear distinction between the respective functions of the judge and the jury. The job of the judge was to decide whether the confession was voluntary within the principles of *Ibrahim*. The job of the jury was to assess the evidential weight of the confession, once it had been admitted. Superficially, under the 1984 Act, the procedure is very similar. The job of the trial judge will be to examine the circumstances of the confession (on a voir dire) and rule on whether or not the confession was obtained as a consequence of oppression or 'in consequence of anything said or done which was likely, in the circumstances existing at the time, to render unreliable any confession which might be made by him in consequence thereof' (s. 76(2)(b)).

It is this latter part of the judge's duty which will in fact cause his function to overlap with the jury. The job of the jury is to decide on the reliability of the confession. The job of the judge is slightly different, in that he has to rule on the issue of whether the confession was tainted by anything which might make it unreliable. The two jobs are not very far apart.

(f)   Suppose on the voir dire the accused admits that his confession is true. What evidential issues does that raise?

The essential question which used to be asked before the 1984 Act was passed was whether or not the admission of the accused on the voir dire that his confession was in fact true (although, on his evidence, involuntary) was in some way relevant to the question of whether or not the confession was made voluntarily or not. In the old case of *R v Hammond* (1941) 28 Cr App R 84 the Court of Criminal Appeal held that the accused could be asked on the voir dire about the truth or otherwise of his confession, on the basis that it was relevant to the issue of his credibility. The difficulty with such a conclusion is that if the accused admits on the voir dire that his confession was true, then this tends to show that he does not tell lies. Accordingly, when he testifies that the confession was involuntary because of some impropriety on the part of the police, the court ought to believe him and accordingly rule out the confession as being involuntary (although true). The whole matter was exhaustively reconsidered by the Privy Council in *Wong Kam-Ming* v *R* [1980] AC 247 where it was decided (with Lord Hailsham of St Marylebone LC dissenting in part) that questions as to the truth or the falsity of the confession were never permissible on the voir dire, and that the decision in *Hammond* was wrong. Lord Hailsham thought that it was not possible to say that the question of the truth or otherwise of the confession was never relevant to the question of its voluntariness. The decision of the House of Lords in *R v Brophy* [1982] AC 476 confirms the approach taken in *Wong Kam-Ming*, and both cases give credence to the following comment made in *Phipson on Evidence*, 14th ed. (1990):

These two cases strengthen the criticism levelled at the English rules of evidence in criminal cases that they are more suited to a game than to an enquiry designed to arrive at the truth. It is difficult to see why on any ethical principle a jury should be precluded from knowing that a defendant has freely and on oath confessed his guilt, or a judge without a jury should be prohibited from acting on such a confession made before him. Law should be the handmaid of justice, not its mistress.

The position with regard to such questions remains unaffected (directly at any rate) by the 1984 Act.

(g)   Following the passing of the 1984 Act what discretion do the courts have to exclude a confession which is admissible in law?

It will be apparent from the many issues that we have raised in the context of confessions that the topic is a massive one. In order to tackle your revision of this area in a logical and reasonably comprehensive way, you must make a good attempt to break the subject down into manageable proportions. We have indicated above what we perceive to be some of the topically important issues, but it may be that the bias of your own course has taken you down different pathways. In such a case you will have to be guided by the specific programme that you have followed, always ensuring, of course, that you do not lose sight of the overall structure of the topic.

Silence

We have looked earlier at the way in which out-of-court silence is now back on the agenda as an issue of evidential importance as a result of the CJPOA 1994. The inevitable flow of case law on the new provisions is yet to come, so that in the short term it may well be that essay-type questions exploring the arguments for and against the new law may be more common. Much assistance in your revision may be gained by examining the relevant parts of the 11th Report of the Criminal Law Revision Committee (1972) and the Royal Commission on Criminal Procedure (1981). Depending upon the amount of emphasis given to this topic on your course, it may be wise to look at some of the specialist guides to the CJPOA 1994.

EXAMINATION QUESTIONS

Problem questions on confessions have always been favourites with examiners, both because it is easy to set suitably testing questions on the topic and because it is a topic which lends itself well to the format of a problem question. The difficulty which any examiner is going to have over the next few years is that the scope of operation of the Police and Criminal Evidence Act 1984 takes time to be worked out by the courts and for a clearly defined body of case law and principle to emerge. On the other hand, there is enormous scope for essay questions in this area. These can range from the broadly descriptive, requiring a generalised treatment of perhaps the whole of the confession provisions of the Act together with the Codes of Practice. There is also scope for the more 'comparative' type of question, where the examinee is asked to consider the merits (or demerits) of the scheme contained in the 1984 Act as against the previously existing law. The third type of essay which may be set is one which is very precise in the kind of material which is being sought. For example, an examiner might ask you to discuss in some form or another the operation of the doctrine of oppression in the context of confessions, or ask you to examine the notion of unreliability as the basis for exclusion as contained in s. 76(2)(b). Since the passing of the CJPOA 1994, the related issue of silence on the part of the accused in the face of police questioning is likely to be examined increasingly in evidence papers. You might also need to be prepared for the very wide-ranging type of question covering the whole issue of the acquisition of evidence by means which can be considered improper. This may require you to pull in threads from illegally obtained evidence, confirmation by subsequent facts and confessions and given that these three areas are now all contained within the ambit of one statute, such a question may not be unlikely.

The following question is fairly typical of the kind of problem which covers these topics:

The police raided Albert's house, during the course of which they carried out a search without having any legal right to do so. Subsequently Albert was arrested and charged with the unlawful possession and supply of a controlled drug. The police also seized, during the course of the search, a notebook in which Albert kept a daily record of his transactions in the drug market.

After his arrest Albert was taken to a police station. He immediately asked that he be allowed to contact his solicitor, but the request was refused. He made a number of similar requests over the next three days, but all of these requests were refused.

After three days of sustained questioning, during which Albert was allowed very little sleep or refreshments, he made a confession to the police. As a result of this confession the police searched a lock-up garage rented by Albert, where they discovered further quantities of drugs.

At Albert's trial his counsel argues that the confession, and everything found as a consequence of the confession, should be excluded from evidence. On the voir dire Albert was asked in cross-examination whether or not the confession he had made to the police was in fact true. Albert's counsel objects to the question.

Discuss the issues raised above.

This is fairly typical of the kind of problem asked on this area. The first thing you must appreciate is that, assuming you have done your work throughout the year thoroughly and that you have revised these topics properly, you will in all probability have far too much material at your fingertips to put down in the space of 40 or so minutes. Accordingly, you are going to have to be very selective in your use of material, and in being selective you will want to ensure two things:

(a)   that you cover the issues in the problem and answer the question which has been asked, and

(b)   that you display to the full the essential theoretical knowledge which you may have and show to the examiner the depth of your reading.

The first thing you should do in answering this question is to determine for your own benefit the precise issues being raised in the question. As we have indicated in other chapters, it is often sensible to begin your answer by identifying in the first paragraph those issues which you have isolated. We would repeat the point that we have made in other chapters that you do not need to worry too much if you do not spot every tiny side-issue which the question might raise. The examiner is trying to find out whether you have grasped the basic issues, not whether you have managed to acquire a footnote knowledge of the subject.

The following are the main issues raised in the question:

(a)   The major issue, and the one to which the majority of your discussion should be devoted, is the question of the admissibility of Albert's confession. *Inter alia*, this will need some discussion of the concept of oppression and will require an examination of the 'reliability' concept contained in s. 76(2)(b) of the 1984 Act.

(b)   What is the evidential status of the notebook which the police discovered as a result of their unlawful search?

(c)   What is the evidential value of the finding of the concealed store of drugs in the lock-up garage?

(d)   What significance, if any, has the fact that Albert was not allowed to see his solicitor?

(e)   You will also need to be prepared to discuss the question of whether breach of these provisions provides an opportunity for the exercise of judicial discretion, enabling the court, if it is so minded, to exclude evidence which is technically admissible.

(f)   What significance does the questioning on the voir dire have? For this you will need to look to the common law decisions.

One thing which you should try to avoid when dealing with the large number of issues raised in the problem is trying to cover in exhaustive detail every little piece of information which you know on that topic. Inevitably, in a question as broad-ranging as this one, you will (if you have done your revision properly) have far too much information to be able to deploy all of it. You should try to be sophisticated in presenting your material in order to display to the full your knowledge of the topic. Above all, you must apportion your time between the issues in the question in a way which reflects the respective importance of those issues. For example, although it would be possible to cover exhaustively the question of the confirmation of the confession by subsequent facts, the 1984 Act provides a substantial resolution of practically all of the outstanding issues in this area. All you need to do is display evidence that you are familiar with the old doctrines and understand the backdrop that they provide for the modern law. What really matters is your recollection and appreciation of the position after 1984. In any event, interesting though the issue of confirmation by subsequent facts may be, in the context of this particular question it is nowhere near as important as, say, the general question of the admissibility of the confession of the accused.

The Admissibility of Albert's Confession; the Burden of Proof; Relevance of Admission on the Voir Dire

You must deal with this part of the question firmly in the context of the substantive provisions of the 1984 Act and the accompanying code of practice. As outlined above, the essential provisions in the Act dealing with this issue are ss. 76 and 78.

In your consideration of the grounds of exclusion you should also be prepared to explain briefly where the burden of proving the various issues lies and to explore any possible differences in the discretions which the court may have available to itself in examining the two possible grounds of exclusion.

On the general question of the burden of proof, the principle is, where the admissibility of a confession is challenged, the prosecution must prove beyond reasonable doubt that the confession was not obtained as a result of oppression or that it was not obtained as a result of anything said or done which would, in the circumstances, render the confession unreliable. These issues are dealt with on a voir dire (trial within a trial) in the absence of a jury. The judge will decide on the question of admissibility, although it is, of course, open to the defence to repeat its allegations of oppression or whatever before the jury if the judge decides to admit the confession. You should note that there is no burden at all on the defence with regard to any allegations of oppression which it may make — all that the defence needs to do to activate the burden on the prosecution is to represent 'that the confession was or may have been obtained' as a result of oppression (s. 76).

It is convenient in this part of your answer to deal with the significance of the question asked of the accused on the voir dire as to whether or not his confession was in fact true. You should make the following points in your discussion of this issue:

(a)   There is no provision in the Act dealing directly with this question, and accordingly one must resort to the common law to provide the solution.

(b)   The decisions at common law have not been entirely consistent in the approach that has been taken. In the case of *R* v *Hammond* [1941] 3 All ER 318 the Court of Criminal Appeal thought that the question put to the accused on the voir dire as to whether or not his confession was true was a perfectly natural one to put and that the answer 'went to the credit of the person who was giving evidence'. This was a strange approach for the court to take, given that if the man admitted on the voir dire that his confession to the police was in fact true (although, as he was alleging, made involuntarily) one would accordingly assume that the accused was an honest witness, and thus worthy of belief when he alleged that the confession had been made involuntarily. It is submitted that the approach taken by the majority in the decision of the Privy Council in *Wong Kam-Ming* v *R* [1980] AC 247 is to be preferred, where it was held that *Hammond* was wrong and that it is impermissible to ask on the voir dire whether the confession is true. The correctness of the decision in *Wong Kam-Ming* for English law was established by the House of Lords in *R* v *Brophy* [1982] AC 476. In terms of the narrow issue raised by the examination question we are dealing with, it is unlikely that Albert will be compelled to answer the specific question put to him on the voir dire. In *R* v *Davis* [1990] Crim LR 860, the Court of Appeal referred to *Wong Kam-Ming* as 'strong persuasive authority' for the view that an accused could not be cross-examined as to the truth of his confession when giving evidence on the voir dire, but the point was not essential to the court's decision.

Moving now to the major issue of whether Albert's confession should be excluded, it is necessary to examine the possible ambit of ss. 76 and 78. When the 1984 Act was passed, most commentators envisaged that if a confession were to be excluded then, generally, this would be done by the application of s. 76. Section 78 was seen as a kind of long-stop which could be used to cover deserving cases which might slip through the net of s. 76. Things have not, however, worked out in this way. Section 78 has been used by the courts increasingly as a first step to exclusion and quite often s. 76 has not been referred to, even in cases where there was considerable doubt as to the reliability of a confession.

However, in the context of an examination question you must show that you have the required knowledge of both of these sections. Logically, it is sensible to look at questions of admissibility first (i.e., s. 76) and then questions of discretion (s. 78). First of all, then, we are concerned with whether anything which has happened to Albert amounts to oppression and whether any confession which he has made will be excluded on that ground. We have indicated elsewhere within this chapter some of the present difficulties that exist in trying to work out exactly what oppression does mean in the context of the present law, given that a new statutory foundation has been provided where none existed before and that the decision in *R v Fulling* [1987] QB 426 is not without its difficulties. We would identify the following areas of possible oppression in the way that Albert was treated by the police:

(a) The fact that Albert made a number of requests to see his solicitor, which were refused.
(b) Sustained questioning over a period of three days.
(c) Few breaks for refreshments or sleep.

The aspects of Albert's treatment which may amount to oppression need to be tested against the *Fulling* guidelines, remembering that they are somewhat ambiguous.

As far as the first of the three grounds is concerned, under s. 58 of the 1984 Act a person arrested and held in custody in a police station or other premises is entitled, if he so requests, to consult a solicitor privately at any time. Where (as in the present problem) a person makes a request to consult a solicitor, he must be permitted to do this as soon as practicable unless delay is permitted — under s. 58 delay is permitted where the police have reasonable grounds to believe that the exercise of this right will lead to interference with evidence connected with a serious arrestable offence, or to physical injury to other persons, or will alert other suspects who have not yet been arrested, or will hinder the recovery of any property obtained as a result of the offence. Under the Code of Practice on Detention, Treatment and Questioning further details as to how this right can be exercised are set out. Accordingly, the refusal to allow Albert to speak to a solicitor is a breach of both the Act and the accompanying code of practice. It is clear that neither a breach of the Act nor a breach of the code *per se* renders evidence inadmissible. There has to be oppression or potential unreliability before the confession will be excluded and, although evidence of breach may give rise to such an inference, breach alone does not necessarily rule out a confession.

The second and third aspects of oppressive conduct identified above as inadequate refreshment and rest facilities are matters which can quite clearly amount to oppressive conduct. Under the provisions of the Code of Practice, such matters as the length of periods of questioning and the kind of refreshment break which should be allowed are dealt with in some detail. It is provided in the Code that in any period of 24 hours a detained person must be allowed a continuous period of at least eight hours for rest, free from questioning or interruption. This period should normally be at night. Breaks from interviewing should be made at recognised mealtimes and short breaks for refreshment should be provided at intervals of approximately two hours.

Pre-1984 decisions such as that in *R v Hudson* (1980) 72 Crim App R 163 show that the questioning was oppressive where the accused was held by the police for more than two days without a charge being brought and during the course of which some 700 questions were asked. Similarly, in *R v Allerton* [1979] Crim LR 725, where the accused was left in a cold cell without heating for four-and-a-half hours, during which there were two periods of rigorous questioning (but no refreshments), it was held that the questioning was oppressive.

As far as the possible grounds of oppression are concerned, our view, on the basis of the authorities, is that denial of access to a solicitor, *simpliciter*, is unlikely to lead to exclusion on the basis of oppression. However, when taken in conjunction with the other aspects of Albert's treatment, there seems little doubt that a court would conclude that his confession was obtained in circumstances of oppression.

Turning now for completeness to the second possible ground of exclusion — that of the circumstances in which the confession was obtained being such as to render it likely that it was unreliable there is nothing yet in terms of case law that provides a hard-and-fast answer as to whether such circumstances prevailed. We have set out some of the relevant considerations earlier.

You should also mention the possible role of s. 78 in relation to confessions, if only because the courts have frequently sidestepped s. 76 and moved directly to a discretionary exclusion of the confession under s. 78. As we stated earlier, each case turns to a great extent on its own facts, although some considerations, such as bad faith on the part of the police or the seriousness of any breach of the Act or codes, are of importance in deciding whether or not the discretion will be exercised.

Evidential Status of Discovered Notebook

The search of Albert's house is an unlawful one. As a result, any evidence which the police have seized has been seized unlawfully. This presents the clear issue for discussion of the admissibility, or otherwise, of the notebook. The following points should be made in your answer:

(a) The law of evidence has always taken the view that the fact that evidence is in some way tainted, for example, by illegality in the way that it was obtained, does not necessarily affect its admissibility (see, for example *R v Leatham* (1861) 3 E & E 658).

(b) Although any common law discretion to exclude improperly obtained evidence which might have existed prior to the 1984 Act is preserved by s. 82(3) of the Act, the essential question now will be whether s. 78 operates in this situation.

How the court will utilise s. 78 in the future is still a somewhat open question. The section indicates that the key to the operation of the discretion under the section is whether the admission of the evidence would operate unfairly on the accused. No statutory definition of the concept of unfairness is provided and we have already referred to difficulties of interpretation of the word 'proceedings'.

(c)   In order to provide your answer with a measure of polish you may feel that it is useful to display any knowledge which you may have of the differing attitudes which the courts of different jurisdictions have towards the whole question of improperly obtained evidence. You will find that Heydon, *Evidence: Cases and Materials* has a particularly useful survey of a number of United States, Commonwealth and Scottish authorities. We are not suggesting that you throw the cases mentioned in such a treatment into your answer in an indiscriminate fashion, but if you are able to pull together some of the more significant overseas contributions to the topic it will undoubtedly improve the look of your answer.

Evidential Status of the Discovery of Drugs

Unlike the situation discussed above, which related very clearly to the unlawful acquisition of evidence by the police, we are here dealing with the more straightforward issue of the admissibility of something which has been discovered as the result of a confession which the suspect has made to the police. If the confession is ultimately found to be admissible in evidence then there is no doubt as to the admissibility of anything found as a consequence of that confession. Where the confession is ruled to be inadmissible the whole matter is now governed by s. 76(4)(a) of the 1984 Act discussed earlier in this chapter.

In our view there is not a great deal of point, in a question of this kind, in spending very much time on an issue which is now as straightforward as this. The statutory provisions in the 1984 Act provide a clear statement of the applicable rules and in order to answer the question it is really not necessary to go beyond the statutory provisions. However, it is probably worth making the point that the introduction of such evidence may often not be of much assistance to the prosecution unless it is possible to link it in some way with something that the accused has said and this is, of course, generally prohibited under the provisions of the Act.

CONCLUSION

The most difficult thing about answering a question on this topic is the range and diversity of the material you may be called upon to deploy in your answer. Both at the stage of revising the material and at the stage when you answer examination questions you will need to be very careful to delineate clearly, both in your mind and on paper, the boundaries of the particular rules which you are considering. It is very easy to become bogged down in the wealth of case law and other material which is relevant to this issue and the matter is not made any easier by the fact that the law is in a state of rapid evolution following the passing of the Police and Criminal Evidence Act 1984 and the Criminal Justice and Public Order Act 1994.

FURTHER READING

Birch, 'The pace hots up: confusions under the 1984 Act' [1989] Crim LR 95.
Heydon, 'Illegally obtained evidence' [1973] Crim LR 603, 690.
May, 'Admissibility of confessions: recent developments' (1991) 55 JCL 366.
Mirfield, 'The future of the law of confessions' [1984] Crim LR 63.
Robertson, 'The looking-glass world of section 78' (1989) 139 NLJ 1223.

10   OPINION EVIDENCE

INTRODUCTION

When you come to revising you will find that opinion is one of the most straightforward of the topics you will have covered. This is because the rules can be stated fairly clearly (although they are frequently departed from in practice) and because the range of cases and statutes you will need to be familiar with is reasonably confined. Opinion is not one of the areas of the subject which has generated a great deal of academic heat and the only major tactical decision you may need to make is to work out where the boundaries of your coverage of the subject lie, for example, should you include some coverage of such issues as the admissibility of evidence obtained by hypnosis, by the use of polygraph machines or following the administration of a truth drug, all of which impinge on opinion.

You will find that most of the standard texts give adequate accounts of the law. The most succinct is that of Heydon, *Evidence: Cases and Materials*, pp. 385-400, but you will find that the treatment in *Cross and Tapper on Evidence* is particularly good. In addition, although the relevant journal literature is not extensive, the following articles are helpful Pattenden, 'Expert opinion evidence based on hearsay' [1982] Crim LR 85; Jackson, 'The ultimate issue rule: one too many' [1984] Crim LR 75; Munday, 'Excluding the expert witness' [1981] Crim LR 688 and Samuels, 'Psychiatric evidence' [1981] Crim LR 762.

The basic rule when one considers the admissibility of opinion evidence is that witnesses are not allowed to testify to anything but facts. It is the function of the jury to draw such inferences from these facts as may be necessary; it is not for the witness to treat the jury to his view and opinions on the matter.

To this rule there are two main exceptions:

(a)   the opinions of experts are admissible on matters calling for special knowledge and expertise;
(b)   the opinions of non-experts may be admissible where such an opinion is necessary for the witness to convey his evidence to the jury.

There is one other important rule which you need to be familiar with, the rule against reception of evidence on the ultimate issue. Ultimate issues can be regarded as the very issues which the court has to decide. The courts have leaned against the reception of opinion evidence on such an issue on the basis that it is up to the jury, and not the expert witness, to draw inferences on such matters. The scope of the ultimate issue rule is one of the more interesting, and more difficult, aspects of opinion evidence and as such is likely to make an appearance in any question on the topic.

EXPERT WITNESSES

Some matters may be so specialised or technical that if the court is to be able to reach sensible conclusions on such matters it will inevitably need to hear the evidence of experts. Such evidence has for long been received by the courts — see, for example, the judgment of Lord Mansfield in *Folkes* v *Chadd* (1782) 3 Doug KB 17, where it was held that the opinions of men of science on matters within their own science is admissible.

It is not possible to draw up a closed list of those matters on which expert opinion evidence is admissible — indeed the list seems to be expanding all the time — but the following are the most common matters: science (including, most importantly in practice, medical reports), technical terms, matters of trade, handwriting, foreign law and obscenity. From your point of view the most common issues which tend to come up in examinations relate to the proof of handwriting and evidence on the question of obscenity. These are dealt with more fully below.

A preliminary issue, which sometimes needs to be discussed in an examination, is the question of just who is an expert? Murphy, *A Practical Approach to Evidence*, explains the matter as follows:

Qualification to give expert evidence is technically a matter of competence, and the court should investigate the credentials of a proposed witness before permitting him to give expert evidence. No doubt a witness who lacks any apparent qualification should not be heard, but if the witness has some claim to expertise, the modern practice is to receive his evidence, though its weight may be open to serious adverse comment if the apparent expertise is not translated into reality. (p. 305)

A particularly useful case which illustrates that expertise does not have to be gained by any formal training is *R v Silverlock* [1894] 2 QB 766 where a solicitor, who had made a study of handwriting but who had no formal qualifications on the matter, was allowed to testify as an expert. *Silverlock* was relied on in the Canadian decision of *R v Bunniss* (1964) 50 WWR 422, where the question was whether the opinion of a police officer, who had made a special study of a device called a 'Borkenstein Breathalyser' and had also researched into the physiological effects of alcohol in the human bloodstream, was admissible on the physiological effects of alcohol on the body. The general argument against the admissibility of such evidence was that such testimony should only be given by a duly qualified medical practitioner, but Tyrwhitt-Drake CCJ said:

[S]o long as a witness satisfies the court that he is skilled, the way in which he acquired his skill is immaterial. The test of expertness, so far as the law of evidence is concerned, is skill, and skill alone, in the field in which it is sought to have the witness's opinion. . . .

I adopt, as a working definition of the term 'skilled person' one who has, by dint of training and practice, acquired a good knowledge of the science or art concerning which his opinion is sought. . . .

It is not necessary, for a person to give opinion evidence on a question of human physiology, that he be a doctor of medicine.

As a point of examination technique, remember that the above case is not from the UK courts and is therefore not binding. If you cite the case as though it were binding in the English courts your examiner would be justified in pulling his hair out, on the basis that you have got to the final stages of your course without mastering *stare decisis*! If you cite it simply as 'a useful Canadian decision' you are likely to impress your examiner by the width of your comparative knowledge!

You should note two further points. First, an expert witness can be cross-examined just like any other witness. This may just be to show that he is incompetent, or it may go further and seek to show that he is actually biased in favour of the party calling him. One of the problems with the evidence of an expert is that it may be altogether too partisan in favour of the party calling him. Thus Heydon says (p. 385):

There is a general feeling ... that expert witnesses are selected to prove a case and are often close to being professional liars.

The courts have also said that an expert witness should be objective and should not attempt to be an advocate for the party calling him (see, for example, *National Justice Compania Naviera SA* v *Prudential Assurance Co. Ltd* [1993] 2 Lloyd's Rep 68).

In view of the risk of bias here, it has been suggested that there should be 'neutral' court experts. The arguments for and against are well put by Howard and Spencer in [1991] Crim LR 98 and 106.

Secondly, an expert witness is compellable just like any other witness — see *Harmony Shipping Co. SA* v *Saudi Europe Line Ltd* [1979] 1 WLR 1380 — although generally such witnesses will not be required to give evidence in a case with which they are not connected.

NON-EXPERTS GIVING OPINION EVIDENCE

The theoretical position from which the reception of all opinion evidence is judged is that witnesses can only testify to facts, not to inferences drawn from them. The category of 'experts' discussed above provides an important exception to this general principle, but it is also possible for a non-expert to pass opinions in certain circumstances where the opinion is a compendious method of stating his evidence. Landon, (1944) 60 LQR 201, puts the matter in this way:

> [W]e have never felt any hesitation, on this side of the Atlantic, in admitting statements by witnesses which are a compendious mode of summarising a sequence of inferences, based upon perceived facts. We should be surprised here if objection was raised to such remarks as 'He was an old man'; 'He could not lift his arm above his shoulder'; 'The defendant agreed to repair the premises'. These are inferential statements, and they can, of course, be broken down by cross-examination; but the evidence itself would never be excluded on the ground that it was evidence of opinion and not of fact.

In a Northern Ireland decision Lord MacDermott stated in *Sherrard* v *Jacob* [1965] NI 151 that the following (non-exhaustive) categories constitute the subjects on which non-expert inferential evidence can be received:

(a) identification of handwriting, persons and things;
(b) apparent age;
(c) bodily plight (e.g., illness);
(d) emotional state;
(e) the condition of things (e.g., whether new, old etc.);

(f)   questions of value;

(g)   estimates of speed or distance.

You will find an adequate exposition of the appropriate principles in the main textbooks, but it is useful to know examples of some of the more important of the categories listed above. In particular, the issues of handwriting and drunkenness make quite frequent appearances on examination papers. A useful case to know is *R v Davies* [1961] 1 WLR 1111 where the Courts-Martial Appeal Court allowed a witness to state that in his opinion the accused had been drinking, with the proviso that the facts on which that opinion was based had to be stated. However, the witness was not allowed to go on to say that in his opinion the accused was unfit to drive through drink — that is a matter for the opinion of an expert.

On the question of proof of handwriting, this is a matter where you need to consider both expert and non-expert opinion evidence. For the sake of convenience we have dealt with them both under this heading. A starting-point for consideration of the matter is s. 8 of the Criminal Procedure Act 1865 (which applies equally to civil proceedings):

> Comparison of a disputed writing with any writing proved to the satisfaction of the judge to be genuine shall be permitted to be made by witnesses; and such writings, and the evidence of witnesses respecting the same, may be submitted to the court and jury as evidence of the genuineness or otherwise of the writing in dispute.

The comparison referred to in the section can be made by experts or non-experts, but, as a general principle (despite what is said in s. 8), it should not be left to the jury to make such a comparison without the assistance of an expert. In *R v Harvey* (1869) 11 Cox CC 546 Blackburn J ruled: 'I do not think it would be right to let the jury compare the handwriting without some such assistance [of an expert]'.

Similarly in *R v Rickard* (1918) 13 Cr App R 140, Salter J said: 'It is clear from the nature of things that to leave a question of handwriting to a jury without assistance is a somewhat dangerous course'.

There are some instances where disputed handwriting has gone to the jury without the benefit of assistance. This can happen where documents, perhaps containing disputed signatures, have to go to the jury as part of the other evidence in the case. In this situation the trial judge must be particularly careful to give a stringent warning to the jury to take care in assessing such evidence. The difficulty which the court has to face in such a situation is that the jury may, nevertheless, make such prohibited comparisons. There is no doubt that such a danger is very real, but as a matter of practical reality all that can be done is to remind them that such comparisons should not be made and that they are not qualified to make them: see *R* v *O'Sullivan* (1969) 53 Cr App R 274.

THE ULTIMATE ISSUE

At common law a rule existed under which a witness could not give his opinion on any issue of law or of fact which the court had to determine. This was the rule against evidence on the ultimate issue, and it applied to both expert and non-expert witnesses. The reason for the existence of the rule was the readily comprehensible one of the reluctance of the courts to allow the witness to become involved in the decision-making process (but see Jackson, 'The ultimate issue rule: one rule too many' [1984] Crim LR 75, for the most recent analysis of the rule).

With the disappearance of the jury trial the ultimate issue rule has also disappeared for civil cases. Section 3 of the Civil Evidence Act 1972 provides:

> (1)   Subject to any rules of court, . . . where a person is called as a witness in any civil proceedings, his opinion on any relevant matter on which he is qualified to give expert evidence shall be admissible in evidence. . . .
> (3)   In this section 'relevant matter' includes an issue in the proceedings in question.

The position is not quite so clear-cut in criminal cases. It might be thought that because the jury method of trial is much more significant the rule would apply in all its rigour, but the decisions are a little uncertain in their direction, although it is certainly fair to say that the strength of the common law rule has been considerably eroded in criminal cases. Jackson defines ultimate issues in criminal trials as:

> [T]he ultimate, sometimes called material, facts which must be proved by the prosecution beyond reasonable doubt before a defendant can be found guilty of a particular offence and those facts, if any, which must be proved by the defendant in order to avoid guilt for that offence. Thus the ultimate facts in the offence of murder are that the accused of sound mind and of the age of discretion did unlawfully kill another with malice aforethought so that the other died within a year and day after the same.

A useful illustration of the difficulties caused by the application of the rule can be seen in the Canadian decision in *R* v *Lupien* (1970) 9 DLR (3d) 1. L had been observed leaving a cabaret with another person who was made up as, and looked like, a woman. L was subsequently found by the police in a hotel bedroom with another man, who was a female impersonator, and the police evidence was that they were in such a position in relation to each other that they were justified in thinking that an act of gross indecency was taking place or had taken place. L's defence was that until just before the police burst into the room he thought the other person was a woman and he sought to introduce the evidence of a psychiatrist to show that he had a certain type of defence mechanism which made him react violently against any homosexual activity and that he would not have knowingly engaged in any homosexual activities. The Canadian Supreme Court had great difficulty with this case. The majority took the view that such evidence should have been admitted, on the basis that the particular issue in this case — whether L had homosexual tendencies — was one to which the evidence of a psychiatrist was particularly suited. The minority would have excluded such evidence and the cogent argument of Martland J is difficult to counter:

> If such evidence is held to be admissible in a case of this kind, then there would seem to be no reason why, on a charge of murder, psychiatric evidence could not be led as to the innate abhorrence of the accused in respect of physical violence, or on a charge of theft, of the innate respect of the accused for private property rights....
> In my opinion evidence of this kind should not be admitted.

More typical of the approach taken in the courts of the United Kingdom is a group of decisions on questions of obscenity. On the question of whether an article is actually obscene, expert evidence is not generally admissible to prove obscenity — see *R v Anderson* [1972] 1 QB 304, *Re Attorney-General's Reference (No. 3 of 1977)* [1978] 3 All ER 1166 and *DPP v Jordan* [1977] AC 699. In *DPP v A & BC Chewing Gum Ltd* [1968] 1 QB 159, where the defendants were charged with offences under the Obscene Publications Acts of 1959 and 1964 by publishing cards (free with packets of gum) it was ruled that the evidence of experts in child psychiatry was admissible on the question of the effect of these cards on the minds of children. In the course of his judgment, Lord Parker CJ made a useful general observation:

> I cannot help feeling that with the advance of science more and more inroads have been made into the old common law principles. Those who practise in the criminal courts see every day cases of experts being called on the question of diminished responsibility, and although technically the final question 'Do you think he was suffering from diminished responsibility?' is strictly inadmissible, it is allowed time and time again without any objection.

You should also look at *R v Skirving* [1985] QB 819.

You should note, if you are considering the issue of obscenity, that s. 4(1) of the 1959 Act (as amended) provides a defence of 'public good' whereby it is a defence, once an article has been found to be obscene, to show that publication was justified as being for the public good in the interests of science, literature, art or learning. Under s. 4(2) expert evidence is admissible to prove or negative this defence. You must remember that such defence only comes into play once an article is ruled obscene, and it must be re-emphasised that on that issue expert evidence is not generally admissible. The decision in the *A & BC Chewing Gum* case must, therefore, be regarded as exceptional, explicable on the grounds that the case involved the particularly difficult issue of the effect of such material on the mind of a child, a matter on which (surely) the jury need all the help they can get.

The examination of the *A & BC Chewing Gum* case leads into a discussion of a more general point that is conventionally considered when looking at the ultimate issue rule, namely that an opinion (whether from an expert or not) is inadmissible on an issue upon which the jury can form their own conclusions without assistance. This is precisely the reason why such evidence is not generally admissible in obscenity cases. The case which is normally used to illustrate this point is that of *R* v *Turner* [1975] QB 834. The defendant, who had been charged with the murder of his girlfriend by hitting her with a hammer, admitted that he had killed her but argued the defence of provocation on the basis that she had told him of her affairs with other men and that the child she was carrying was not his. He sought to introduce the evidence of a psychiatrist to the effect that his personality was such that he would have been provoked by what his girlfriend had told him. The Court of Appeal ruled that the evidence was inadmissible on the basis that jurors do not need psychiatrists to tell them how ordinary people, such as the defendant, who are not suffering from any mental illness, are likely to react to the strains and stresses of life.

Turner is difficult to reconcile with the interesting decision in *Lowery* v *R* [1974] AC 85. In that case a girl had been murdered. At the trial one of the two accused (L) argued that he had not been the dominant partner in the killing, and said that at one point he had tried to restrain his co-accused (K) from killing the girl. To counter this evidence K called a psychologist, whose expert evidence tended to show that L was in fact the more aggressive and dominant personality, whereas K was merely a follower. L appealed against his conviction for murder on the basis that the psychologist's evidence should not have been admitted. The Privy Council ruled the evidence admissible on the basis that not only was it relevant to the case being advanced by K, but that its admissibility was placed beyond doubt by the case advanced by L.

One can try to reconcile the cases of *Turner* and *Lowery* in several ways, and the standard texts deal with this issue, but it was worth pointing out that in *Lowery* the court was dealing with an issue more complex than that of deciding the mental state of an ordinary man. The court had to determine which of two men was the more aggressive and dominant, and in determining that question the evidence of a psychiatrist may be invaluable.

On the whole, more recent authorities have adopted the approach taken in *Turner*. Cases which are of relevance here are *DPP* v *Camplin* [1978] AC 705, *R* v *Weightman* (1991) 92 Cr App R 291 and *R* v *Robinson* (1994) 98 Cr App R 370.

OPINION AND PREVIOUS JUDGMENTS

This is an aspect of opinion which is sometimes covered. Space precludes a detailed coverage of this issue, but the relevant principles can be easily stated.

A judgment is a specialised kind of opinion — that of a court. At common law the weight of authority leaned against the admissibility of a previous judgment as evidence of the facts on which it was based as regards third parties — this is known as the rule in *Hollington* v *F. Hewthorn & Co. Ltd* [1943] KB 587. The common law rule was abrogated in certain civil proceedings by ss. 11–13 of the Civil Evidence Act 1968 and has been modified for criminal proceedings by s. 74 of the Police and Criminal Evidence Act 1984. The standard texts give perfectly adequate accounts of this topic.

PLANNING YOUR REVISION

Revising this topic does not cause very many difficulties. It is probably useful to have a close look at the examination papers which have been set in previous years to see just what kind of questions came up on opinion, because it is one of those areas of evidence where the range of questions set tends to be fairly limited. If you can work out where the boundaries of that range lie then you can concentrate your revision more fully on certain aspects of the topic.

Although it is dangerous to over generalise, opinion questions tend to fall into one of three categories. First, there are questions, which are often very general in nature, which in effect require you to write down everything you know about the topic, or at the very least require a fairly wide treatment of one aspect of the topic. Very general questions on the effect of the exclusionary rule, taken as a whole, or questions directing you to the ultimate issue, are those which would fall within this category. Second, there are traditional problem questions which direct you to the major aspects of opinion, and which may require you to deal with issues such as proof of obscenity, proof of diminished responsibility, proof of provocation, proof of handwriting and so on. Third, there are questions (often of a problem type) which are a little more advantageous in their demands and which require you to deal with matters on the fringe of opinion such as evidence obtained following the administration of a truth drug, following hypnosis or following the use of a lie detector. Such questions are not particularly common, and will depend on the idiosyncracies of your examiner. There is little English authority on such matters, and you will only be able fully to discuss these areas if you have dealt with them specifically as part of your course. However, it may be that you get a question like the one examined later in this chapter, where such an issue is only a small part of the question taken as a whole. In this situation it may be possible to answer the question perfectly adequately from first principles, without a detailed knowledge of the particular case law. We discuss how you can do this in the context of the question.

The first thing to do when revising this topic is to understand the nature of the exclusionary rule and why the exclusionary rule exists. At different times in history different justifications have been put forward for the exclusion of opinion, and it can sometimes be helpful (and impressive) in an examination to understand what these justifications have been. Thus if you look at the judgment of Coke CJ in *Adams v Canon* (1612) 1 Dyer 53bn you will see that he explained the rule as based partly on the fact that the sanction of a prosecution for perjury is not as strong where a witness is talking about his opinion rather than about facts. Landon, on the other hand, (1944) 60 LQR 201, explains that one of the dangers of opinion is that the jury may be too readily influenced by it, whereas other writers, such as Cross, talk of the entitlement of an accused to have his fate decided by a jury rather than by experts.

The second thing to do is understand the nature of the exceptions to the exclusionary rule. You will need to consider here quite separately the positions of the expert witness giving evidence of opinion and the non-expert witness giving such evidence. All the textbooks give the usual illustrations of where expert evidence can be received, but on the particular issues of the admissibility of psychiatric evidence and forensic evidence there are some useful points made in two articles by Samuels, 'Forensic evidence: some recent developments' (1981) 131 NLJ 721 and 'Psychiatric evidence' [1981] Crim LR 762. In the case of the non-expert witness it will be helpful if you can classify the common categories of case where different types of opinion evidence are given. You should also work out exactly why the courts are prepared to receive non-expert opinion. To what extent is it inevitable that such evidence is admitted?

A third matter, and one which can be handled very easily, is to learn the appropriate test for determining who can be classified as an expert. Mention has been made above of the cases of *R v Silverlock* [1894] 2 QB 766 and *R v Bunniss* (1964) 50 WWR 422, but you will find that some of the cases involving expert evidence on the proof of foreign law are the most useful on this issue — see, for example, *Brailey v Rhodesia Consolidated Ltd* [1910] 2 Ch 95. You should also understand the procedure by which such evidence is received and the way in which it may be possible to discredit the alleged abilities of the expert. On some of the procedural aspects of calling expert evidence you will find the article by Munday, mentioned at the start of this chapter, of interest and value.

Next, you must have a clear idea of what the rule is (such as it is) against opinion evidence on the ultimate issue. For civil cases the rule is, of course, a dead letter. However, in criminal cases the rule still retains a certain vitality, although its application is a somewhat erratic one. Knowledge of the arguments employed in the article by Jackson [1984] Crim LR 75 is important, where the unsound theoretical basis for the rule is explored and exploded. You should also be familiar with one or two of the more important Commonwealth authorities and you will find *R v Lupien* (1970) 9 DLR (3d) 1 of particular value. In this context you should also consider the importance of the rule that opinion evidence is not admissible where the jury can form their own conclusion without the assistance of opinion evidence. A consideration of such cases as *DPP v A & BC Chewing Gum Ltd* [1968] 1 QB 159, *R v Turner* [1975] QB 834 and *Lowery v R* [1974] AC 85 is essential. Bear in mind, when you are considering the ultimate issue, that it is one of the possible aspects of opinion to appear in an examination, and it is not unknown for complete questions to be set on this aspect of the rule alone.

Finally, if only to add a little polish in your examination, you may find it possible to introduce some discussion of such matters as the relationship between the rules on opinion and the rules on hearsay (see Pattenden's article) and a treatment of the opinion problems associated with hypnosis, polygraph machines and truth drugs. You should not go overboard on this, but you may find the following articles of help: Mathieson, 'The truth drug: trial by psychiatrist' [1967] Crim LR 645; Haward and Ashworth, 'Some problems of evidence obtained by hypnosis' [1980] Crim LR 469; Munday, 'The admissibility of hypnotically refreshed testimony' (1987) 151 JP 404, 426, 452 and Elliott, 'Lie detector evidence: Lessons from the American experience', in *Well and Truly Tried: Essays on Evidence in Honour of Sir Richard Eggleston* (eds. Campbell and Waller) (1982), p. 100.

EXAMINATION QUESTIONS

Examination questions on opinion in the form of either problems or essays are commonplace and they tend to be relatively straightforward.

We have set out below a two-part question on opinion, the first part is in the form of an essay and the second part is in the form of a problem. Such questions are quite common on evidence papers, although they are very hard to do a really good answer on, simply because of the range of material that such a question requires you to cover. Two-part questions, and, for that matter, any very long problem question raising a large number of issues, can be helpful to the weaker candidate, because the very length and complexity of the question serves to dilute the expectations of the examiner of what can realistically be achieved in the time at the candidates' disposal. However, you ought to be thinking about how you can best use the question to maximise your performance so that you can do as well as possible — you are interested in more than mere survival. This means that you must approach your answer to a question such as that set out below in a fairly robust manner, prepared to deal with the issues at the greatest level of sophistication which you can manage and prepared to avoid the temptation to write down every last little piece of material you may have.

(a)   'It is the desirability of protecting the function of the trier of fact that forms the substantial bedrock of policy underpinning the rule which purports to exclude opinion evidence.... The risk of usurpation by the witness of the function of the trier of fact is often greatest if the witness expresses an opinion on the very question, or "ultimate issue", which the trier of fact has finally to decide.' (Carter) Discuss.

(b)   J, K and L are jointly charged with murdering a prostitute by beating her to death. Consider the admissibility of psychiatric evidence on the following issues:

(i)   J pleads that he was provoked beyond endurance by her taunts about his lack of sexual prowess.

(ii)   K pleads that he was suffering from diminished responsibility.

(iii)   L wishes to lead psychiatric evidence to the effect that the psychiatrist had questioned him while he (L) was under the influence of a truth drug and that the answers tended to exculpate him from involvement in the crime.

At the very most you are likely only to have some 45 minutes available to you to answer this question. Sensibly you should allocate your time, initially at least, evenly between the two parts of the question because unless the rubric of the examination indicates otherwise the available marks for the question will probably be so divided. It may become apparent to you as you plan and write your answer that some of the information you are dealing with in the first part of the answer is relevant to the second part in which case it may be sensible to deal fully with that aspect of the question at that stage and simply make a cross-reference when you come to it again. Of course, what you must not do is write the same material out twice, because you will only get credit for it once.

The width of the quotation set for the first part of the question may cause you some problems. Is the question inviting you to discuss the reasons why there is an exclusionary rule with regard to opinion evidence? Is it asking you to write about the ultimate issue rule? Or is it asking you to do both? Working out just what a general essay of this type is really after is often a problem, and it can arise with regard to any aspect of the subject. Where a question may legitimately be interpreted in one of several ways, it is usually best to begin your answer by explaining how you understand the question and how you propose to deal with it. As long as your interpretation of the issues raised is not a fanciful one then such an approach is a useful start to your answer, because it states very clearly for the examiner where the limits of your answer will lie and what issues you are going to discuss. Many examinees will leap, for the worst possible reasons, at an essay of this type. Using the third-class-mark rule of interpretation (hitherto known as the 'grapeshot rule') they will treat the question as an invitation to write down, in an undetailed and uncritical form, everything they know about opinion. It is obvious, if you think about it, that anyone who throws everything at the examiner, including the kitchen sink, is hardly going to be in a position to say anything interesting or clever about the subject. Examiners are not impressed by an ability on the part of a candidate to reproduce vast amounts of irrelevant information at a generalised and low level of treatment. They are much more impressed by the candidate who can take a confined issue by the neck and make an informed and critical appraisal of it.

Accordingly, how are we to narrow down part (a) of the question? One thing is clear: you are not being invited to throw in all you know. The question is specifically concerned with the relationship between the exclusionary rule and the function of the jury as the trier of fact, and specifically refers to the question of opinion evidence on the ultimate issue. One legitimate interpretation of this essay title would be to place emphasis on the second part of the quotation, and deal exclusively with the law on proof on the ultimate issue. However, such an approach may be regarded as a little narrow, not paying enough weight to the first sentence, and might not appeal to the jaundiced eye of your examiner. Consequently, we think that you could usefully adopt the following structure:

(a)   Make the general point, referred to by most of the writers, that the basic reason why evidence of opinion is excluded is because it is the job of the jury to draw inferences and the job of the witness to testify to facts.

(b)   It has long been recognised, however, that on some matters a jury need the evidence of an expert to assist them in coming to terms with the complexities of some issues. For example, no jury can reach a sensible decision on the long-term medical prognosis of someone severely injured in a car accident without some assistance from a medical practitioner. The interests of justice would hardly be served by a rule which completely excluded such evidence.

(c)   Nevertheless, the courts have been careful to ensure that the permissible scope of the use of opinion evidence does not intrude too far into the function of the jury, even in areas where the evidence of an expert may be of assistance. For example, although case law on these matters is very sparse, it is improbable, at least in the present state of the law, that the evidence of experts would be admitted in relation to examinations of a witness carried out under the influence of hypnosis. Various justifications for excluding such evidence could be given — it might be argued that the reliability of such techinques is unproven and that potentially unreliable evidence of this type should not therefore go to the jury, or it might be argued that such evidence is hearsay (unless the hypnosis were carried out in court under the supervision of the judge). But one justification would surely be that the admission of such evidence would elevate the role of the psychiatrist or psychologist at the expense of the ordinary juror.

(d) Equally, the courts have been careful not to allow the expert to trespass into areas where the court can manage without his assistance. Thus in the case of *R* v *Turner* [1975] QB 834 Lawton LJ said:

> An expert's opinion is admissible to furnish the court with scientific information which is likely to be outside the experience and knowledge of a judge or jury. If on the proven facts a judge or jury can form their own conclusions without help, then the opinion of an expert is unnecessary. In such a case if it is given dressed up in scientific jargon it may make judgment more difficult.

On the same point see also *R* v *Chard* (1971) 56 Cr App R 268, where the Court of Appeal confirmed that the evidence of an expert was not admissible, in the absence of any evidence of insanity or diminished responsibility, on the question of the intention of the accused at the time of a killing. You should make the point that it is not always very easy to say where the line is drawn between those matters which do not require expert evidence and those matters which do — *Lowery* v *R* [1974] AC 85 is a useful case illustrating circumstances at the other side of the line. It is probably worth mentioning the clutch of obscenity cases where it has been established, as a matter of general principle, that expert evidence is not admissible on the issue of whether or not an article is obscene — see *R* v *Stamford* [1972] 2 QB 304; *R* v *Anderson* [1972] 1 QB 304; and *DPP* v *Jordan* [1977] AC 699 although such evidence may be admissible, exceptionally, where the recipients of the material are children: *DPP* v *A & BC Chewing Gum Ltd* [1968] 1 QB 159.

(e)   It is commonly said, and forcefully put by Carter in the quotation on which the question is based, that evidence of opinion is inadmissible on the ultimate issue. We have discussed this point earlier in the chapter and you will know that this rule has already been abandoned in civil cases by virtue of s. 3 of the Civil Evidence Act 1972. It is worth making the point that for most practical purposes there is no jury whose function can be usurped in civil cases, and therefore the demise of the ultimate issue rule should be no surprise, if its rationale is based on the fact of jury trial.

As far as criminal cases are concerned you can review the standard authorities, some of which manifest concern for this rule and some of which do not, and you can spread your discussion into the giving of both expert and non-expert opinion evidence on the ultimate issue. However, you should not let your account degenerate into a descriptive treatment of every known case on the subject. Nevertheless, let the examiner know through the general sophistication of your approach that you have mastered at least as many cases on the topic as he has. You should make the point that the Criminal Law Revision Committee, in its 11th Report, recommended the abolition of the rule for criminal cases. This has not been acted upon, although significant judicial inroads have been made into the rule.

Jackson in [1984] Crim LR 75, argues that the ultimate issue rule has no separate justification apart from the opinion evidence rule and suggests that it is therefore superfluous. All the cases in recent years which have relied on the rule are explained on other grounds. Given that the principal justification for the exclusion of opinion in general rests on a non-usurpation of the function of the jury, Jackson's findings are of particular interest in the context of the specific question we are examining and, arguably, provide strong support for Carter's comment. Of course, familiarity with academic contributions of this kind will not only help to improve the quality and look of your examination answer, you will also find that an article such as Jackson's can help you to focus your thoughts on a particular aspect of the law and can assist you in formulating some ideas of your own about the topic. For example, you may wish to challenge the conclusion that the ultimate issue rule is superfluous in the context of the opinion evidence rule, given that it provides a useful marker for a trial judge to define the limits of admissible opinion evidence. Admittedly, judges often break the ultimate issue rule, but it is at least arguable that it serves some useful function, even if only as a convenient label.

(f) It is probably worth making the point that undue concern for the inviolability of the function of the jury is not always displayed where non-experts are allowed to give opinions in evidence. The basic justification for the admissibility of such evidence is necessity, in that it may be impossible for the witness to confine his narration to evidence of facts, expunging all mention of opinion.

(g) In conclusion you will need to come up with some kind of response to the invitation to discuss Carter's statement. Given the relatively uncontroversial nature of the bulk of the content of the statement, it would be foolhardy to go out on a limb and allege that he is talking through his hat — such a conclusion is simply not justified on the law. You may wish to take issue with some aspect or other of what is said — and your analysis of the ultimate issue may give you an opportunity on which to do this — but make sure that your conclusion bears a close relationship with the reasoning which has gone before.

And so on to part (b) of the question. The fact that there are three subdivisions to this part means that you will only have a few minutes to devote to each element of the question. Accordingly you must not waste any of the time available — do not rewrite the question and do not recite the facts of well-known cases. One general point of technique is to make sure that you separate clearly your treatment of each of the issues. Candidates frequently attribute supernatural powers to examiners and expect them to be able to perceive, without the benefit of any obvious indications, where the answer to one part of a question ends and where another part begins. Number the different parts of your answer clearly so that it is obvious to anyone, including a congenital idiot, which part of which question you are dealing with.

Potentially you can say a great deal about (b)(i), but the way *not* to start your answer is by restating, either in a detailed or even undetailed form, the fact that opinion evidence is excluded, there being an exception in respect of the opinions of experts etc., etc. This is not going to get you any extra marks and will reduce the time you have available to deal with the more direct issues in the question. The fact that you can write sensibly about the particular issues the question raises tells the examiner that you know what is going on in terms of the basic rules without the need for you to spell it out.

This part of the question raises the linked questions of whether the fact that the accused has been provoked is an issue on which the opinion of an expert is receivable, and if so whether the ultimate issue rule is thereby likely to be infringed. Be careful not to rewrite the information contained in your answer to part (a) of the question, but clearly you will have to say something about the decision in *R v Turner* [1975] QB 834 which appears to be directly in point. You will recall that in that case the accused, whose defence to a charge of murder was provocation, sought to introduce the evidence of a psychiatrist for three purposes: first, because it helped to show lack of intent; secondly, because it helped to establish that the accused was likely to be easily provoked; and thirdly, because it helped to show that the accused's account of what happened was likely to be true. The Court of Appeal refused to admit the evidence. While conceding that the opinion of the psychiatrist was *relevant* (on the basis that opinions from a knowledgeable person play a part in many human judgments), the opinion was not *admissible* because jurors do not need psychiatrists to tell them how ordinary people, not suffering from any mental illness, react to the vicissitudes of life. The evidence was accordingly not admissible on the issue of provocation (and, as intent was not in issue, not admissible on that ground, or to prove credibility).

You will need to make some attempt to deal with the problem of reconciling the decision in *Turner* with that in *Lowery v R* [1974] AC 85. You will recall that in the latter case expert evidence was admissible on the issue of which of two people (neither of whom was suffering from any mental illness) had a more aggressive and dominant personality. It can be explained on the basis that the issue with which the jury were concerned was one more complex, and more suited to the expertise of a psychiatrist than the unassisted judgment of a jury, than the issue in *Turner*, and in any event the opinion was made admissible by the manner in which *Lowery* conducted his defence. It is worth making the point that the question of the ultimate issue was not considered by the Privy Council in *Lowery*.

As far as the ultimate issue is concerned it is probably legitimate to include a brief explanation of the uncertain state of the law and reiterate the rule. However, given that your answer to part (a) of the question has included a discussion of this rule there is probably no need to detail the law. An appropriate cross-reference will suffice, backed up with the conclusion that the operation of the ultimate issue rule will exclude the evidence of the psychiatrist. In any event, the second part of this problem raises the question of the ultimate issue quite directly and there is no real need to discuss the point here, as long as you make it plain to the examiner that you have spotted the point.

Accordingly, as far as (b)(i) is concerned, there is little realistic possibility that the expert evidence will be admitted.

On (b)(ii) the question of the ultimate issue is squarely raised. You cannot do better than begin your answer to this part of the question by direct reference to the dictum of Lord Parker CJ in *DPP* v *A & BC Chewing Gum Ltd* [1968] 1 QB 159 quoted earlier in this chapter where he observes the frequency with which expert witnesses are asked the question 'Do you think he was suffering from diminished responsibility?', even though technically such a question is inadmissible. The key point here is that issues of diminished responsibility (and some other matters, such as insanity) are not issues which are within the ordinary and everyday purview of the members of the jury. The matter was well put by Roskill LJ in *R* v *Chard* (1971) 56 Cr App R 268 where he said:

> [O]ne purpose of jury trials is to bring into the jury-box a body of men and women who are able to judge ordinary day-to-day questions by their own standards, that is, the standards in the eyes of the law of theoretically ordinary reasonable men and women. That is something which they are well able by their ordinary experience to judge for themselves. Where the matters in issue go outside that experience and they are invited to deal with someone supposedly abnormal, for example, supposedly suffering from insanity or diminished responsibility, then plainly in such a case they are entitled to the benefit of expert evidence.

Although not directly in point, the case of *R* v *Smith* [1979] 1 WLR 1445, illustrates a similar approach where the defence of the accused was automatism.

There is not a great deal more to say on this issue. However, it is worth trying to make some observation about the state of the law if you can, and in this context it is perhaps worth repeating the view of Samuel, that whenever there is any live issue in a case going to normality or otherwise, the accused should be entitled to adduce such expert evidence on that issue as he wishes, for it should always be open to him to challenge the presumption of normality if he can. However, the other side of this particular coin is that the evidence of an expert has to be treated carefully, because of the danger that what is in reality a situation of normality may be obscured by the scientific evidence, and the impression of abnormality be given.

With regard to the third part of the problem, you should appreciate that the examiner is probably not looking for a treatment of every known case where truth drugs may have been used — there are few in any event. It will make your answer appear impressive if you are able to refer to such authority as there may be, but paradoxically, perhaps, the fact that you may not know of any specific case law need not necessarily deter you from attempting to answer this part of the question. This problem happens to raise the question of truth drugs. It could equally have asked you about hypnosis or polygraphs — the theoretical issues are similar in each case.

The only English authority on the question appears to be the poorly reported case of *R v Barker* [1954] Crim LR 423. Psychiatric evidence was admitted to the effect that following the administration of a drug on the accused, the psychiatrist could not restore the accused's memory of the events surrounding the killing. Accordingly he concluded that the accused was deranged at the time. The report, unfortunately, does not record any arguments on the admissibility of this evidence.

A much fuller treatment of the relevant issues was provided by the New Zealand Court of Appeal in *R v McKay* [1967] NZLR 139, where such evidence was excluded for four principal reasons:

(a)   Evidence of previous consistent statements is inadmissible (see chapter 11).

(b)   Such evidence was hearsay when related by a psychiatrist (see chapter 8).

(c)   Evidence of a psychiatrist on the issue of innocence or guilt infringed the ultimate issue rule.

(d)   The proposed evidence was too unreliable.

Barker was distinguished on the basis that the evidence in that case went to the accused's state of mind (i.e., the question of normality) whereas in the instant case it was being adduced on the question of whether the accused did the relevant acts.

There is really little more to say. Show the examiner that you are aware of some academic literature on the point and if you have time make some conclusion as to the merits or otherwise of the presently rigid attitude of the law to evidence of this genre. The question 'Why should the accused be deprived of the benefits of the latest medical and forensic techniques?' will focus your mind on the kind of conclusion you may reach.

CONCLUSION

We hope we have said enough in this chapter to illustrate the kind of strategy you can adopt in learning this topic. We have not dealt with every aspect of opinion, but from what we have covered you will see that this topic is more straightforward than most. The range of potentially examinable issues is limited and, if your course has covered the topic, you can regard this as a banker.

FURTHER READING

Elliott, 'Lie detector evidence: Lessons from the American experience', in *Well and Truly Tried: Essays on Evidence in Honour of Sir Richard Eggleston* (eds. Campbell and Waller) (1982), p. 100.

Haward and Ashworth, 'Some problems of evidence obtained by hypnosis' [1980] Crim LR 469.

Howard, 'The neutral expert: a plausible threat to justice' [1991] Crim LR 98.

Jackson, 'The ultimate issue rule: one rule too many' [1984] Crim LR 75.

Kenny, 'The expert in court' (1983) 99 LQR 197.

Landon, Review of *Opinion Evidence in Illinois* by Willard L. King and Douglas Pillinger (1944) 60 LQR 201.

Mathieson, 'The truth drug: trial by psychiatrist' [1967] Crim LR 645.

Munday, 'The admissibility of hypnotically refreshed testimony' (1987) 151 JP 404, 426, 452.

Pattenden, 'Conflicting approaches to psychiatric evidence in criminal trials: England, Canada and Australia' [1986] Crim LR 92.

Pattenden, 'Expert opinion evidence based on hearsay' [1982] Crim LR 85.

Samuels, 'Forensic evidence: some recent developments' (1981) 131 NLJ 721.

Samuels, 'Psychiatric evidence' [1981] Crim LR 762.

Spencer, 'The neutral expert: an implausible bogey' [1991] Crim LR 106.

11   THE COURSE OF THE TRIAL

INTRODUCTION

This topic is dealt with under a number of headings in the standard texts on evidence. The terms 'examination of witnesses', 'course of evidence' and 'rules of trial' have all been used. They refer to the rules of law which deal with the actual mechanics of evidence, what questions may be asked of a witness in examination in chief, cross-examination and re-examination and to what effect. The question of the cross-examination of the accused in criminal cases is one which involves difficult and technical questions. We have considered this whole issue separately in chapter 7.

Some areas of the law of evidence are painted in by the courts with broad strokes. In the present context, however, we are concerned with rules of narrow application. This is a topic with which it is essential to be familiar, if only because an examiner can easily set one or two points from this area in order to fill out a problem question. The topic can be combined in a question with virtually any of the others and so it would be very misguided to omit it entirely. This is not to say that a very deep knowledge of it is generally required. You would be better advised to concentrate on the fundamentals of this topic and explore in more detail those areas which will provide you with more of an opportunity to shine in the examination. However, there are perhaps one or two topical and/or controversial matters here, which we shall examine in more detail later in the chapter.

There is a further preliminary point. Many of the standard texts on evidence do include within the present topic some miscellaneous procedural matters in addition to the rules of evidence at the trial itself. For example, in

Cross and Tapper on Evidence there is a brief consideration of the question of evidence given *before* the trial, the right to begin calling evidence, the order of the advocates' speeches, the calling of witnesses and the role of the judge. This is useful background material and sometimes impinges on the main part of this topic, but it very rarely forms even a part of an examination question.

EXAMINATION IN CHIEF

The purpose of questions put to a witness in examination in chief is to obtain evidence supporting the case of the party calling the witness.

There are four matters to consider in relation to evidence in chief:

    (a)   leading questions;
    (b)   refreshing memory;
    (c)   previous consistent statements;
    (d)   unfavourable and hostile witnesses.

Leading Questions

These are questions which either suggest the desired answer or assume the existence of disputed facts. They are generally not permissible in chief. Exceptionally, however, such questions are allowed for introductory, formal or undisputed matters.

Refreshing Memory

On this question, it is first of all clear that *before* he gives evidence in a case a witness is entitled to read the statement which he made at the time of the relevant events or subsequently. However, when he enters the witness-box to give evidence, stricter rules come into play. He may now refresh his memory by referring to a document only if the following conditions have been satisfied:

    (a) The document was made at *substantially* the same time as the occurrence of the events about which the witness is testifying. This will be a question of fact in each case, and the authorities referred to in the textbooks are merely illustrations and not intended to set out strict limits. Generally, however, the longer the gap, the less likelihood that the court will allow the witness to refresh his memory from the document.

    (b) The document must either have been made by the witness or verified by him while the facts were still fresh in his memory.

Note that although we have used the word 'document', any form of document will suffice provided it complies with the conditions above. It may be a copy or even a more informal note, as where a witness to a traffic accident scribbles down a car registration number on a cigarette packet. The archetypal case is of course the police officer's notebook but the possibility of refreshing memory is not open merely to police officers. Cases which illustrate the liberal approach to these questions adopted by the courts are *R v Cheng* (1976) 63 Cr App R 20, *Attorney-General's Reference (No. 3 of 1979)* (1979) 69 Cr App R 411 and *R v Sekhon* (1987) 85 Cr App R 19.

It is quite permissible for two or more witnesses to an event to pool their recollections to produce the best possible note. This was approved by the Court of Criminal Appeal in *R v Bass* [1953] 1 QB 680.

The opposing party is entitled to inspect the document and also to cross-examine with regard to those parts used to refresh the witness's memory, without making the document evidence in the case. The evidence is the witness's testimony, not the document. However, counsel may wish to cross-examine the witness on other parts of the document. He may do so, but if he does then the party calling the witness is entitled to put the document in evidence as part of his case. The cross-examiner must therefore take great care since there may be other items in the document which are unfavourable to his case.

It is very important to appreciate a distinction in this context between criminal and civil cases. If a memory-refreshing document comes to be put in evidence in a criminal case, it goes only to the *credit* of the witness. It is not evidence of the truth of its contents, of course, since it would be hearsay, and it cannot corroborate the witness's testimony (*R v Virgo* (1978) 67 Cr App R 323). It would be a case of self-corroboration anyway. In a civil case, however, such a document, if admitted, is 'evidence of any fact stated therein of which direct oral evidence by [the witness] would be admissible' (Civil Evidence Act 1968, s. 3(2)). In any event, the law relating to refreshing memory in civil cases has been made of much less practical importance by the 1968 Act, because the documents are now admissible in their own right provided they comply with ss. 2 and 4.

Refreshment of memory is a straightforward and uncontroversial area. It will help you flesh out your understanding of the topic if you read Howard, 'Refreshment of memory out of court' [1972] Crim LR 351; and Newark and Samuels, 'Refreshing memory' [1978] Crim LR 408. The wider possibilities of the doctrine in relation to refreshment of memory by hypnosis are explored by Haward and Ashworth, 'Some problems of evidence obtained by hypnosis' [1980] Crim LR 469. A useful review of many of the central issues of the subject is contained in the judgment of the Court of Appeal in *R v Britton* [1987] 1 WLR 539.

Previous Consistent Statements

The general rule is that a witness may not be asked in chief whether he has made a previous statement consistent with his present testimony, nor may other witnesses prove it. This is also referred to as the rule against self-serving statements or the rule against narrative.

Such a rule is logical. The statement is hearsay, as we have seen in chapter 8, and it does not generally add anything to the in-court testimony of the witness who made it.

In civil cases, the rule has very little importance since it has been greatly modified by ss. 2 and 4 of the Civil Evidence Act 1968.

There are, however, certain common law exceptions to the rule which will still be applicable in criminal cases. These are set out below.

(a) Where a witness has identified the accused as having committed the offence charged, the witness may state that he previously made an out-of-court identification of the accused.

(b) Statements made by an accused when questioned which are favourable to himself are often admitted, not as evidence of the facts stated, but as showing his reaction when first taxed with the incriminating fact. Such evidence may be very valuable, if he later testifies to the same effect, as showing his consistency.

(c) Similarly, statements made by the accused on being found in possession of incriminating articles are admissible on the same basis.

(d) In any sexual case (whether heterosexual or homosexual), evidence may be given by the complainant and/or by any person to whom the complaint was made, of a complaint made voluntarily, and at the first opportunity reasonably afforded, of the offence.

The complaint is not evidence of the truth of what is asserted, but of the consistency of the complainant's testimony. Therefore, if the complainant does not testify evidence of the complaint is inadmissible.

(e) At common law, if in cross-examination it is put to a witness that he has recently fabricated his story, he may rebut this suggestion by showing that before that time he had made a statement consistent with his evidence.

A good illustration of this is *R v Oyesiku* (1971) 56 Cr App R 240. The accused was charged with assault upon a police officer. At his trial, his wife gave evidence that the police officer was aggressive. During cross-examination it was put to her that her evidence was a late invention and concocted with a view to helping the accused. The trial judge refused to admit in evidence an earlier statement made by the wife to a solicitor before she had seen her husband after his arrest. This statement was to the same effect as the evidence she gave in court. The Court of Appeal quashed the accused's conviction on the basis that the statement was admissible.

Such a statement is admitted, not as evidence of the truth of what the witness stated, but as evidence of his consistency. In civil cases, however, such a statement is admissible as evidence of any fact stated therein of which direct oral evidence by the witness would be admissible (Civil Evidence Act 1968, s. 3(1)(b)).

(f)   In addition to these exceptions, there may be cases in which the doctrine of *res gestae* will apply and thereby create another exception to the general rule. As we have seen, most applications of this doctrine involve A narrating to the court what B said. However, on occasions A will seek to narrate what he himself said previously. Any mention, however brief, of the term *res gestae*, is liable to bring a rush of blood to the head of most students of evidence. Nevertheless, we append an example of the doctrine operating as an exception to the rule against previous consistent statements. In *R v Fowkes* (1856) The Times, 8 March, the accused, who was commonly known as 'the Butcher', was charged with the murder of A by shooting him through a window. B and C were sitting in the room with A, when a face appeared at the window and the fatal shot was fired. Both B and C were allowed to testify that immediately before the shot was fired, B shouted, 'There's Butcher'.

The most scholarly treatment of the whole issue of previous consistent statements is in Gooderson's article of that name in [1968] CLJ 64.

Unfavourable and Hostile Witnesses

A witness called by one party may 'fail to come up to proof' and thus disappoint the party calling him. What can be done? This depends upon whether the witness falls into one or other of two possible categories: is he merely an *unfavourable* witness or is he a *hostile* witness?

Both give evidence that is less than favourable to the party calling them, but a hostile witness is one who, in addition, has no desire to tell the truth, and is not simply doing his incompetent best.

In the case of an unfavourable witness, the party calling him may simply call other available evidence and hope that the court will give this more weight.

If, however, leave is obtained to treat the witness as hostile, then, in addition to calling other evidence, if there is any available, the witness may be asked leading questions and may be challenged regarding his means of knowledge and powers of observation. In addition, he may be asked whether he has made a previous statement inconsistent with his present testimony and such a statement may be proved against him under the procedure set out in s. 3 of the Criminal Procedure Act 1865.

The student may be tempted at this point to infer that a hostile witness may be treated just like a witness who was called for the opposing party and who is now being cross-examined. This is not so. There is an important limitation in relation to a hostile witness, which is that the party calling him cannot actually attack his character by asking him about earlier bad character or convictions, or calling a witness to say he is a liar.

There are two further questions to consider concerning a hostile witness. First, what if the witness, having been called, simply refuses to say anything? How can it then be said that he has given evidence inconsistent with his previous statement? In *R v Thompson* (1976) 64 Cr App R 96, the Court of Appeal side-stepped that question, contenting itself with saying that the judge retains a residual power at common law to require the witness to answer any question he thinks necessary in the interests of justice.

Secondly, what is the evidential effect of a previous inconsistent statement proved against a hostile witness? Once again, a distinction has to be drawn. At common law and therefore in criminal cases still, the statement goes only to credibility. The purpose of proving it is to discredit the witness. In civil cases, it may be used for that purpose, of course, but it is also admissible as evidence of the fact asserted (Civil Evidence Act 1968, s. 3(1)(a)).

CROSS EXAMINATION

The general nature of cross-examination is expressed succinctly by Heydon, *Evidence: Cases and Materials* (p. 466):

> The purpose of cross-examination is to destroy those parts of the witness's testimony which tell in favour of the party calling him and to obtain testimony favourable to the cross-examiner. Both aims are achieved by cross-examination to the issue; only the first aim is achieved by cross-examination which seeks to destroy the witness's credit. The normal rules of admissibility apply, but the cross-examiner has greater freedom than the examiner-in-chief. He may use leading questions, he may ask about previous inconsistent statements and prove them if they are denied, he may ask questions about bad character, previous convictions, unreliability or bias, and prove the convictions, the physical or mental causes of unreliability, or the bias if they are denied.

There are two specific matters on cross-examination which you must examine in detail:

(a)   previous inconsistent statements;
(b)   collateral questions.

Previous Inconsistent Statements

We have seen how these may be used against a hostile witness. They are also a powerful means of attacking the credit of a witness called by the opposing party. Similar rules apply in such cases, which are contained in the Criminal Procedure Act 1865, ss. 4 and 5, both of which are reproduced below:

4.   If a witness, upon cross-examination as to a former statement made by him relative to the subject matter of the indictment or proceeding, and inconsistent with his present testimony, does not distinctly admit that he has made such statement, proof may be given that he did in fact make it; but before such proof can be given the circumstances of the supposed statement, sufficient to designate the particular occasion, must be mentioned to the witness, and he must be asked whether or not he has made such statement.

5.   A witness may be cross-examined as to previous statements made by him in writing, or reduced into writing, relative to the subject-matter of the indictment or proceeding, without such writing being shown to him; but if it is intended to contradict such witness by the writing, his attention must, before such contradictory proof can be given, be called to those parts of the writing which are to be used for the purpose of so contradicting him: Provided always, that it shall be competent for the judge, at any time during the trial, to require the production of the writing for his inspection, and he may thereupon make such use of it for the purposes of the trial as he may think fit.

With regard to the evidential value of such a statement, it is exactly the same as for a hostile witness. At common law, which is still applicable to criminal cases, the statement goes only to the credit of the witness. In civil cases, it is admissible also as evidence of the facts stated.

It is important to note that, in spite of the title of the Criminal Procedure Act, these sections apply to both civil and criminal cases. Since s. 5 refers to statements made in or reduced into writing, it is generally assumed that s. 4 is intended to refer to previous oral statements, although there is nothing expressly stated in the section itself.

Collateral Questions

We have seen that cross-examination may range widely. It may often be directed to matters going solely to the credit or character of the witness. There is a danger that the time and attention of the court may be taken up unduly with matters which are not directly relevant to the issues before the court. There is, therefore, a sensible rule to the effect that answers given by a witness to questions put to him in cross-examination concerned with what are called 'collateral facts' must be treated as final.

Although *questions* as to credit are not limited to matters relevant to the issues, the bringing of evidence is so limited, and the cross-examining party cannot usually introduce evidence of matters not relevant to the issues merely in order to contradict a witness's answers on credit. The trial would never end if such collateral issues had to be thrashed out and the central issue between the parties would be submerged beneath a mountain of irrelevancies. (Elliott and Phipson, *Manual of the Law of Evidence*, pp. 118–19)

The vital question is how to identify whether or not a matter is collateral. The classic test was laid down by Pollock CB in *Attorney-General* v *Hitchcock* (1847) 1 Exch 91. The essence of this is to ask whether the party cross-examining could have introduced evidence on the matter if the witness had never given evidence at all. If the answer to this question is 'yes' then it is relevant to the issue and may be further pursued. If the answer is 'no' then it is collateral only.

An example of the distinction in operation is *R* v *Burke* (1858) 8 Cox CC 44. An Irish witness, giving evidence through an interpreter, stated that he was unable to speak English. When cross-examined he denied that he had spoken English to two persons while in court. This was a collateral issue and so the cross-examiner was not allowed to call evidence to prove that the witness had spoken English. However, if the witness's command of English had been directly relevant to an issue in the case, for example, his ability to make an alleged confession, then the position would have been different.

The rule of finality is subject to four exceptions, based on both fairness and convenience.

(a) Previous inconsistent statements. These have been dealt with earlier in the chapter.

(b) Previous convictions. If a witness denies having been convicted of a criminal offence, or refuses to answer, the conviction may be proved.

(c) Bias. Any fact tending to prove bias or partiality on the part of a witness may be proved if denied in cross-examination.

(d) Unsoundness of mind or other disability. Medical evidence to the effect that the reliability of the witness is open to doubt may be given to rebut the witness's evidence. This is so whether the unreliability is due to a physical condition (for example shortsightedness) or a mental condition (see *Toohey* v *Commissioner of Police of the Metropolis* [1965] AC 595).

The final point regarding cross-examination as to credit and evidence of collateral matters is that there has been some modification by statute. Section 2 of the Sexual Offences (Amendment) Act 1976 provides that at a trial for rape, attempted rape, aiding and abetting or inciting rape the complainant may not be cross-examined about her sexual experience with anyone other than the accused except by leave of the judge. Such leave is also required before evidence on this matter can be adduced. Leave may only be given in either case if the judge is satisfied that its refusal would be unfair to the accused.

Since the last edition of this book the definition of rape has been amended by the Criminal Justice and Public Order Act 1994, s. 142. This provides that the offence of rape can be committed against either a woman or a man. The authorities on the interpretation of the Sexual Offences (Amendment) Act 1976 must be read in the light of this fact.

It is essential to grasp the point that the effect of s. 2 is not to render any answer to such a question final but to prevent the question being put in the first place. Of course, the section does not prevent questions about the sexual experience of the complainant with the accused, which may go to the issue of consent (and if she denies previous voluntary intercourse with him she may be contradicted by further evidence).

The provision has spawned a considerable amount of literature, which is concerned with whether the section strikes the correct balance between protecting the interests of the accused in securing a fair trial and the interests of the complainant in not having marginally relevant aspects of her private life put before the court. These matters are debated in Adler, 'Rape — the intention of Parliament and the practice of the courts' (1982) 45 MLR 664, and Elliott, 'Rape complainants' sexual experience with third parties' [1984] Crim LR 4. They are also discussed in detail in a series of articles written by Jennifer Temkin and referred to at the end of this chapter. The present legal rules are set out most fully by the Court of Appeal in *R v Viola* [1982] 1 WLR 1138.

One of the major practical consequences of s. 2 is that it has deprived the less reputable members of the tabloid press of a primary source of information. It now looks increasingly to secondary sources.

RE-EXAMINATION

This is a matter which hardly ever comes up in examinations and we can therefore dispose of it very briefly. The only relevant rule you need to remember is that the re-examination of a witness must be confined to matters raised in cross-examination. The leave of the judge is required before any new matter can be introduced.

PLANNING YOUR REVISION

As we stated at the start of this chapter, this is a topic where for the most part you should simply concentrate on the fundamentals. These are the areas upon which you should direct your attention:

(a) refreshing memory;

(b) the rule against previous consistent statements, in particular the exceptions relating to recent complaints;

(c) unfavourable and hostile witnesses;

(d) the distinction between cross-examination to the issue and cross-examination to credit, and in particular its application to the finality rule in relation to collateral questions;

(e) the use of previous inconsistent statements in cross-examination.

The rules of law applicable to this topic lend themselves more to problem questions than to essays. It is relatively easy for an examiner to add a couple of points from this area in order to fill out a problem which is based chiefly on other issues, and for this reason we shall not consider any specific examination questions in this chapter. The rules here are fairly narrow and can be combined with virtually any other topic.

When revising on this topic one very important matter must be constantly borne in mind. Evidence, as we have seen earlier, is a very integrated subject, demanding frequent cross-references between several topics. Examiners are always on the look-out for such areas because of their potential for use in problem questions. The able student should be able to recognise these interrelationships and not just to apply the rules in their most obvious application. We would identify in particular the area of overlap between the rules relating to refreshment of memory and the question of hearsay.

When a witness refers to a document in order to refresh his memory, then there are two distinct situations. First, the witness may find that his present recollection of the events recorded is revived by what he reads. In this case, the position is quite straightforward. The evidence on which the court is invited to act is the witness's testimony, although the document itself must be available for inspection should any question as to the credibility of the witness arise. Secondly, the witness may find that his memory remains a blank or is only partly revived, but he is able to testify that what he recorded at the time, or shortly afterwards, was accurate. The English authorities have proceeded on the basis that even in the second situation the matters contained in the document are proved by the witness's testimony. In reality, however, what the witness is doing here is testifying to matters of which he in fact lacks personal knowledge. He is narrating an out-of-court statement in order to prove the truth of the facts stated. Is this not, then, in truth another exception to the rule against hearsay? As *Cross and Tapper on Evidence* state (p. 291): 'A hearsay statement is nonetheless a hearsay statement because someone who has no recollection of the matters to which it refers swears that it is accurate'.

Of course, in civil cases the point here is somewhat academic, since under the Civil Evidence Act 1968 the previous statement of a witness, whether or not it is to be used to refresh memory, may be admitted as evidence of the facts stated.

Nevertheless, the common law rule still applies in criminal cases and it is noteworthy that recent cases have adopted a very easygoing attitude towards the whole question of refreshment of memory. In *R* v *Kelsey* (1982) 74 Cr App R 213, a witness to an incident concerning a car subsequently traced to the accused, dictated the registration number to a police officer who wrote it down and read it back to the witness. The witness did not *see* the written note, but he was nevertheless allowed to refresh his memory from it. The officer had given evidence to prove that the note he produced was the one the witness saw him making and heard him read back. The Court of Appeal stated: 'In our view there is no magic in verifying by seeing as opposed to verifying by hearing'. After all, as the court also pointed out, what of a case involving an illiterate or (in certain contexts) blind person? It is easy to be sympathetic with such an approach to this question. It does seem somewhat pedantic to insist on actual sight of the document. Yet, in fact, this distinction between sight and hearing is at the heart of the whole question of hearsay evidence. If a witness actually sees a police officer write the number down or reads the number for himself afterwards, then he has personal knowledge of that number. But where he does not see the number, and the officer merely reads it out to him, then he is relying upon the officer for the number itself. He is then repeating a statement made out of court (the police officer's statement) for the purpose of proving the truth of the facts contained within that statement; and that, as we emphasised in chapter 8, is hearsay.

The problem is, of course, that verification by hearing, as in *Kelsey*, may be just as reliable as verification by reading. Things can be misread just as they can be misheard. However, the rule against hearsay is a technical one and unless an item of hearsay can be brought within the exceptions to the rule, then in spite of any reliability it may have, it is inadmissible. *Kelsey*, therefore, is an example (*R* v *Rice* [1963] 1 QB 857, dealt with in chapter 8, being another) of the courts' desire on occasion to break free from the restraints of the hearsay rule. Further evidence of this trend is supplied by Zuckerman, *The Principles of Criminal Evidence* (see pp. 187–201).

Is there any other means by which this may be done? Might it not be argued that if the maker of the original observation is called, then even if he can remember only part of what he told the officer, the officer's evidence of what he wrote down is not hearsay. Is he, then, merely stating that certain words were spoken by a particular person, and not asserting their correctness. The usual dangers associated with hearsay are not so apparent here, since the maker of the original statement is available to be cross-examined on the accuracy or otherwise of his observation. This approach to the matter is suggested by Ashworth in his article 'The manacle of the hearsay rule: 2' (1977) 141 JP 728. It had been previously put forward in relation to the analogous case of evidence of previous identification by Libling ('Evidence of past identification' [1977] Crim LR 276). The balance of authority is against such an approach. However, *R v Osbourne and Virtue* [1973] QB 678 (a case of past identification) is explicable only on such a view. No argument was put there, however, on the question of hearsay.

A stout defence of the traditional analysis can be found in Cross's article, 'The periphery of hearsay' (1969) 7 Melbourne Univ Law Rev 1.

We have insisted in our general treatment of the topic of hearsay on the importance of becoming familiar with common situations involving hearsay issues. The present question is also useful in this context.

We have one parting shot for the astute examinee. Where refreshment of memory comes up in an examination it often involves policemen writing things down in their notebooks. Section 24 of the Criminal Justice Act 1988 provides a possible route of admissibility for such a documentary record. Spot the point and the plaudits will follow.

CONCLUSION

We have made the point earlier that the rules relating to the course of the trial can come up almost anywhere in an evidence examination. Complete questions on these matters are not very common, although sometimes whole or half questions *are* set where specific aspects of these rules have been covered in depth. For example, refreshment of memory lends itself to a range of possible questions, perhaps linked with such matters as hearsay or opinion (in the context of refreshment via hypnosis).

Because the normal context in which these issues are examined is as a part of a larger question we have not dealt with a specific examination question. In any event, we have said enough in earlier chapters to give you an idea of the general strategies you can employ in handling the material.

The main problem you have to resolve is how much of this area you need to learn. We have indicated the major important rules together with some of the relevant literature on the more interesting or controversial aspects. You need to be guided by whatever treatment has been imposed on you by your tutors. It would be foolhardy to omit the topic altogether because it is inevitable that one or more aspects will come up somewhere. The main point of advice we can give is not to become submerged in too much detail. View the topic in a functional manner in order to safeguard your interests in the examination room. One thing is clear: you cannot afford not to revise this area.

FURTHER READING

Adler, 'Rape the intention of Parliament and the practice of the courts' (1982) 45 MLR 664.

Ashworth, 'The manacle of the hearsay rule: 2' (1977) 141 JP 728.

Cross, 'The periphery of hearsay' (1969) 7 MULR 1.

Elliott, 'Rape complainants' sexual experience with third parties' [1984] Crim LR 4.

Gooderson, 'Previous consistent statements' [1968] CLJ 64.

Haward and Ashworth, 'Some problems of evidence obtained by hypnosis' [1980] Crim LR 469.

Howard, 'Refreshment of memory out of court' [1972] Crim LR 351.

Libling, 'Evidence of past identification' [1977] Crim LR 276.

Munday, 'Calling a hostile witness' [1989] Crim LR 866.

Newark and Samuels, 'Refreshing memory' [1978] Crim LR 408.

Temkin, 'Evidence in sexual assault cases' (1984) 47 MLR 625.

Temkin, 'Regulating sexual history evidence: the limits of discretionary legislation' (1984) 33 ICLQ 942.

Temkin, 'Sexual history evidence — the ravishment of section 2' [1993] Crim LR 3.

BIBLIOGRAPHY

P. B. Carter, *Cases and Statutes on Evidence*, 2nd ed. (London: Sweet & Maxwell, 1990).

S. Cooper, P. Murphy, J. Beaumont, *Cases and Materials on Evidence*, 3rd ed. (London: Blackstone Press, 1994).

Criminal Law Revision Committee, *11th Report: Evidence (General)* (Cmnd 4991) (London: HMSO, 1972).

Sir R. Cross and C. Tapper, *Cross and Tapper on Evidence*, 8th ed. by C. Tapper (London: Butterworths, 1995).

Sir R. Eggleston, *Evidence, Proof and Probability*, 2nd ed. (London: Weidenfeld & Nicolson, 1983).

D. W. Elliott and S. L. Phipson, *Manual of the Law of Evidence*, 12th ed. by D. W. Elliott (London: Sweet & Maxwell, 1987).

Evidence of Identification in Criminal Cases: Report of the Departmental Committee [Chairman: Lord Devlin], HC (1975-76) 338.

J. D. Heydon, *Evidence: Cases and Materials*, 3rd ed. (London: Butterworths, 1991).

L. H. Hoffmann, *The South African Law of Evidence*, 3rd ed. by L.H. Hoffmann and D.T. Zeffertt (Durban: Butterworths, 1981).

Keane, A., *The Modern Law of Evidence*, 3rd ed. (London: Butterworths, 1994).

P. Murphy, *Murphy on Evidence*, 5th ed. (London: Blackstone Press, 1995).

S. L. Phipson, *Phipson on Evidence*, 14th ed. by J. H. Buzzard, R. May and M. N. Howard (The Common Law Library, No. 10) (London: Sweet & Maxwell, 1990).

J. C. Smith, *Criminal Evidence* (London: Sweet and Maxwell, 1995).

Sir J. F. Stephen, *A History of the Criminal Law of England* (London: Macmillan, 1883).

G. Williams, *Learning the Law*, 11th ed. (London: Stevens, 1982).

G. Williams, *The Proof of Guilt*, 3rd ed. (Hamlyn Lectures, No. 7) (London: Stevens, 1963).

G. Williams, *Textbook of Criminal Law*, 2nd ed. (London: Stevens, 1983).

A. A. S. Zuckerman, *The Principles of Criminal Evidence* (Oxford: Clarendon Press, 1989).

INDEX

TITLES IN THE SERIES